The Library of World Biography

Cromwell

by Roger Howell, Jr.

THE LIBRARY OF WORLD BIOGRAPHY
J. H. PLUMB, GENERAL EDITOR

Little, Brown and Company — Boston — Toronto

T   05/77

FIRST EDITION

Library of Congress Cataloging in Publication Data

Howell, Roger.
  Cromwell.

  (The Library of world biography)
  Bibliography: p.
  Includes index.
  1. Cromwell, Oliver, 1599–1658. 2. Statesmen—
Great Britain—Biography. 3. Generals—Great Britain—
Biography. 4. Great Britain—Politics and government—
1642–1660.
DA426.H68   942.06′4′0924 [B]   76–52498
ISBN 0–316–37581–0

*Published simultaneously in Canada
by Little, Brown & Company (Canada) Limited*

PRINTED IN THE UNITED STATES OF AMERICA

Contents

Acknowledgments

DR. JOHNSON, having abandoned his scheme to write a biography of Cromwell, declared that "all that can be told of him is already in print." Few of his judgments were so ludicrously far of the mark. The career and personality of Cromwell have attracted vast numbers of historians since Johnson's time; this book is yet another example of the fascination Cromwell exerts on those who have lived after him. In the Epilogue I have attempted to give a very brief view of the widely varying assessments that have been made of Cromwell. It is deliberately no more than a minute selection from a vast literature, and I hope at some later date to return to the theme of Cromwell and the historians in a book-length study. Here, I have sought only to provide a straightforward life of the Lord Protector. I have eschewed footnotes, though the source is usually indicated in the text. With the exception of a few quotations in the Epilogue, all quotations are taken from contemporary sources. The "old style" dating has been used throughout, except that the year has been taken to begin on 1 January.

If I were to attempt to list all those who have helped in

the preparation of this short book, the acknowledgments would reach formidable length and I would be sure to omit someone. But I cannot let the opportunity pass to acknowledge a few particular debts. To Keith Thomas and Hugh Trevor-Roper I owe the greatest debt of all, for they awakened my interest in Cromwell and his times when I was a student at Oxford. With Austin Woolrych, Robin Jeffs, and David Underdown, I have had many useful discussions of the period over the years. Needless to say, none of these scholars is responsible for errors or infelicities that have crept into my account. Indeed, they may on occasion be startled by conclusions I have drawn. In like manner, I owe a great debt to the students in my seminar on Cromwell in 1975; they bore with fortitude the exploration of many of these themes and added their own useful criticism. The staffs of the British Library, the Bodleian Library, and the Bowdoin College Library have all been models of helpfulness over the years. To Drusilla Fielding, Grace Lott, and Joan MacKenzie, who deciphered my handwriting and turned scratched-up pieces of paper into neat typescript, my heartiest thanks. Finally, I want to extend my thanks to the trustees and overseers of Bowdoin College for providing me with leave from my position as president in the summer of 1975. If being president of a college has been one of the factors shaping my view of Cromwell, that leave became the crucial means by which I found time to put my thoughts in writing.

–ROGER HOWELL, JR.

Introduction

WHEN WE LOOK BACK at the past nothing, perhaps, fascinates us so much as the fate of individual men and women. The greatest of these seem to give new direction to history, to mold the social forces of their time and create a new image, or open up vistas that humbler men and women never imagined. An investigation of the interplay of human temperament with social and cultural forces is one of the most complex yet beguiling studies a historian can make; men molded by time, and time molded by men. It would seem that to achieve greatness both the temperament and the moment must fit like a key into a complex lock. Or rather a master key, for the very greatest of men and women resonate in ages distant to their own. Later generations may make new images of them — one has only to think what succeeding generations of Frenchmen have made of Napoleon, or Americans of Benjamin Franklin — but this only happens because some men change the course of history and stain it with their own ambitions, desires, creations or hopes of a magnitude that embraces future generations like a miasma. This is particularly true of the great figures of religion, of politics, of war. The great creative spirits, however, are used by subsequent generations in a reverse manner — men and women go to them to seek hope or solace, or to confirm despair, reinterpreting the works of imagination or wisdom to ease them in their own desperate necessities, to beguile them with a sense of beauty or merely to draw from them strength and understanding. So this series of biographies tries in lucid, vivid and dramatic narratives to explain the greatness of men and women, not only how they managed to secure their niche in the great pantheon of Time, but also why they have continued to fascinate subsequent generations. It may seem, therefore, that it is paradoxical for this series to contain living men and women, as well as the dead, but it is not so. We can recognize, in our own time, particularly in those whose careers are getting close to their final hours, men and women of indisputable greatness, whose position in history is secure, and about whom the legends and myths are beginning to sprout — for all great men and women become legends, all become in history larger than their own lives.

Greatness may come in strange guises and to unlikely human beings, but there are few more remarkable careers than that of Oliver Cromwell. He knew little success in life until middle age. From youth he was consumed with religious doubts about his own worthiness. He was often in conflict with authority because of his instinctive compassion for those browbeaten by men of power. In 1640 he was an indifferently successful country gentleman of modest local standing. Like many perplexed, frightened, God-consumed Englishmen, he seriously considered emigrating to the New Jerusalem in Massachusetts, but he stayed to become one of England's greatest generals, its only republican head of state, and to be revered or execrated by generations of Englishmen. His greatness, except in action, is still enigmatic, still disputable.

He possessed no training as a soldier, no experience of

battle or of generalship until he fought in the English Civil War. In less than three years he had become the most effective organizer of armies on the Parliamentary side and its most brilliant leader in battle. From Marston Moor in 1644 he was the architect of victory after victory — at times, as at Dunbar in 1651, almost of miraculous victories. Cromwell thought that they were all miracles, or rather expressions of God's will. Throughout his life he believed himself to be merely the agent of God's purpose, which was to bring true religion to the English people — and true religion to Cromwell was the individual's search for God and subsequent rebirth, a quest that did not require either a state church or a priest. Hence Cromwell's lifelong belief in the liberty of conscience: conscience, not church institutions, was the way to God. God's purpose was often indefinable, the future obscure, and to his detractors Cromwell appeared to be a Machiavellian opportunist who justified everything, from regicide to the massacre of innocent Irish at Drogheda, as a manifestation of God's will through his humble instrument Oliver Cromwell. Anyone who has read his letters and his soul-searchings knows that Cromwell was not a hypocrite. His beliefs, because he was successful, may seem highly convenient, justifying as they did his actions and decisions, but they were utterly sincere. His belief in religious toleration, in the sharing of political power among men was utterly sincere; sincere too was his hatred of royal absolutism; equally sincere was his supreme confidence that God had reserved for Englishmen a peculiar yet wonderful Destiny. Today that may seem almost insanely chauvinistic, but to men of the time it was as clear and as true as it was to Cromwell. To defeat a king and his army, to bring him to public trial and execute him in the name of the people was so incredible to men of that age that they could not conceive of such achievements without the sustaining knowledge that it was God's purpose as well as their own.

Oliver Cromwell's achievements were very great: he

changed the course of British history; never again were royal absolutism and religious intolerance allowed to flourish unchallenged. That, apart from his brilliance as a general, would make him worthy of inclusion in this Library. He deserves to be here for other reasons. He was one of those very rare men of action with complex and deeply fissured personalities, therefore a fitting subject for the historical and biographical skills of Roger Howell. There is no better short life of one of the greatest men in British history.

J. H. Plumb

20 October 1976

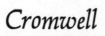

Cromwell

ONE

The Career of Cromwell
to 1640

IN THE EARLY HOURS of the morning of 25 April 1599, Elizabeth Cromwell of Huntingdon bore a son. He was given the name Oliver in honor of his uncle, Sir Oliver, who probably acted as his godfather when the child was baptized four days later. At some subsequent time, the words "England's plague for five years" were penned above the entry of his baptism in the register of the Church of St. John the Baptist, where the ceremony was performed.

Such sentiments would have been far from the mind of anyone present on that spring day. The long and glorious reign of Queen Elizabeth I was still four years from its end. In later days, people would look back to that reign as an age of firm and positive rule at home and honor abroad. In like fashion, they would come to think of the succeeding reigns of the first two Stuart kings, James I and Charles I, as a period of increasing disunity, corruption, and loss of prestige. The first of these conceptions contained substantial elements of myth, while the second involved a considerable amount of truth. For Oliver, both the myth and the reality were to be of enduring significance as he grew to manhood.

The reality he would experience directly and strike out against; the myth provided him with something of a guide and a justification.

Speaking to Parliament in 1654, Cromwell commented, "I was by birth a gentleman, living neither in any considerable height, nor yet in obscurity." The self-assessment was quite accurate. His father, Robert Cromwell, was the second son of Sir Henry Cromwell, the Golden Knight of Hinchinbrooke, while his mother, Elizabeth Steward, came from a respectable Norfolk family and her father farmed the lands of Ely Cathedral. On both sides, the family had risen to its current position of gentility in the wake of the Reformation, the Stewards having risen on the basis of monastic lands around Ramsey and Ely while the Cromwells rose on the basis of patronage in the reign of Henry VIII. The greatest representative of the family in that time was clearly Thomas Cromwell, chief minister of Henry VIII, despoiler of the monasteries, and in many ways the architect of the Tudor state. It was from Thomas's sister Katherine that Oliver was descended. The son of the marriage of Katherine Cromwell and the Welshman Morgan Williams, Richard, took the name of his powerful uncle Thomas and henceforth was known as Richard Cromwell.

His loyalty brought reward in the form of monastic property and his son, Sir Henry the Golden Knight, consolidated the family position and rebuilt Hinchinbrooke nunnery into a magnificent mansion. His heir, Sir Oliver, Cromwell's uncle, attempted to carry on the traditions, but in his hands they became simply a drain on the family's finances, and he himself affords almost a classic case of a gentry figure falling on hard times as a result of continued but fruitless investment in the court. Though he was often to visit the household of his uncle, young Oliver was born into less exalted surroundings, his father Robert being the second son of the Golden Knight and thus heir to a lesser position. Robert seems to have led a life of relatively modest obscurity, though he sat in Parliament in 1593. His influence on his son does not appear to have been profound, and in any case he died when Oliver was only eighteen.

Three factors in the family situation probably had considerably more impact on Cromwell. Ten children were born to Robert Cromwell and his wife; of those, seven survived infancy, but of them Oliver was the only male. As the only surviving male child in the household, Oliver became from a young age the center of family ambitions, and with his father's death occurring before he was twenty, he was thrust at an early age into a position of family leadership and responsibility. Second, it is clear that his mother doted on him and he on her. And she appears to have been a remarkable woman; years later she was to be described as "a woman of ripe wisdom and great prudence" and even the Royalist historian Clarendon could describe her as "a decent woman." There can be little doubt that she exercised much influence on the growing boy, though the precise nature of that influence cannot now be ascertained. Finally, one should note the important marriage connections made by other parts of the Cromwell family. Two cousins, Elizabeth and Frances, married a Hampden and a Whalley, thus providing the young Oliver with connections with two leading Puritan families. The importance of this was to be shown later at a time when national politics impinged on the life of Oliver. Cromwell's "cousinry" was eventually expanded to include many of the families prominent in the struggle against the Stuarts. Six cousins were imprisoned in the resistance to the forced loan of 1627 and one was among the defendants in the Five Knights Case. When Oliver first went to Westminster as a member of Parliament in 1628, nine cousins of his were members of the House. John Hampden of ship money fame was another cousin, as was Oliver St. John, who defended him. In 1640, Oliver was joined by eleven cousins in the Long Parliament and six more were to be members later. It all underlines the truth of his statement about his social origins. Though he may have come from among the poorer relations of a declining county family, he was no mere commoner; he was related to some of the great men of the nation, and they were men of what may be called the opposition.

The significance of these connections lay in the future. Of the actual details of Cromwell's youth little is known. As is so often the case with those who achieve greatness in adult life, there are many stories and legends about his young days. Few, if any, of them are reliably documented, such as the story that he gave the future King Charles a bloody nose when he visited Hinchinbrooke with his father in 1603. Most accounts do agree that the young Oliver was a lively, indeed boisterous, youth. Whether or not he did dream he would be king, as one biographer asserts, cannot be known, though a persistent legend exists that he was rebuked by his schoolteacher for avowing this and yet, when acting in a play, went beyond his cue, put a crown on his head, "and as if inspired, spoke some big words with great authority." In truth, as Milton was to write, much of the early life of Cromwell is impenetrable. He grew up, as the poet said, "in secret at home . . . [nourishing] in the silence of his own consciousness, for whatever times of crisis were coming, a trustful faith in God, and a native vastness of intellect."

One fact is documented about Oliver's youth, and that is the schooling that nurtured that native vastness of intellect. Following some early instruction at home, Cromwell attended the local grammar school. In such a school, the role of the master was a dominant one, and there can be little doubt that Dr. Thomas Beard exercised a profound influence on the youth, particularly since he was not only Oliver's schoolmaster, but a friend of the Cromwell family and rector of their parish church. Beard was uncompromising in his views, and his Puritan interpretation of history obviously helped to shape the way Oliver would look at things. Before he came to Huntingdon, Beard had published a widely circulated book, *The Theatre of God's Judgements,* which stressed the direct and active intervention of God in the affairs of the world, particularly in punishing those who transgressed. "The works of God are wonderful . . . and such as doth not only demonstrate a divine power to sit at the stern of the world, but also our own weakness, which is not able to comprehend the least part thereof. . . . He is a father in preserving his children and a judge in punishing sinners and those that rebel against him." Beard stressed that particularly upon the mighty did God's judgment bear hard: "God himself becometh executioner of his own justice upon their pates: and in such sort, that every man may perceive his hand to be upon them." Later Beard was to write *A Retractive from the Romish Religion,* a work dedicated to Sir Oliver Cromwell; its denunciation of Catholicism as "the Religion of the great Whore and her paramour Antichrist, who with their cup of fornications and vain pretext of Peter's authority have besotted heretofore all nations of the earth," was a message that the young Oliver doubtless heard both in schoolroom and parish church on frequent occasions.

In an age which has become cynical about institutionalized religion, it is difficult for many to appreciate the reality of the religious word in an earlier age. Cromwell, throughout his active career, was to be both moved and sustained by a profound and sincere belief that God's providences were to be seen directly in this world. There was neither cant nor hypocrisy in this attitude, though many of his detractors have seen it as such. From his very youth, he had been schooled to believe in God from whom, in Dr. Beard's biblical paraphrase, "you have received your sceptres and crowns and who is able (when he please) to bring princes to nothing and make the rulers of the earth a thing of nought." He would have agreed fervently with his teacher that "it is a horrible thing to fall into the hands of the Lord."

Most of Cromwell's early biographers agree that, for all the impact the formidable Beard had on Cromwell's philosophical and religious outlook, he did not inspire the youth in bookish ways. Yet Cromwell was to emerge at least with a love of history; he recommended Raleigh's *History of the World* to his own son as a profitable source of study. It is possible that the influence of Beard is to be felt here too, for Beard felt history was "a very necessary and profitable thing" since "it setteth before us such effects (as warnings and admonitions touching good and evil) and layeth virtue and vice naked before our eyes with the punishments or rewards inflicted or bestowed upon the followers of each of them, that it may rightly be called an easy and profitable apprenticeship or school for every man to learn to get wisdom at another man's cost." Contemporary Royalists were to be scoffing about Oliver's rude learning; particularly they noted his lack of foreign languages and the crudity of his Latin. No doubt there was some truth in this, though he was fluent enough in Latin to carry on discourse in that tongue with foreign ambassadors. In short, Cromwell's schooling, while not leading him toward literary pursuits, was more than adequate, and in Dr. Beard he had found at a very impressionable age a mentor of unusual importance and an adult model of decided character and firmness.

In 1616, Oliver went to Cambridge University. His choice of college, Sidney Sussex, guaranteed that the Puritan influence he had felt at Beard's hands was to be continued. The college was clearly identified with the Puritan wing under its Master, Samuel Ward, a well-known Calvinist. Archbishop Laud was later to refer to it as "a hotbed of Puritanism," a description which would have been equally apt when Oliver arrived as a gentleman-commoner. Virtually nothing is known about his time at Cambridge. Just as is the case with his schooldays, legend and gossip abound, almost all found in blatantly hostile sources. It would appear that he continued the pattern revealed in his schooldays — active and boisterous life, little inclination toward literary pursuits, and a keen interest in other people as people. His tutor, Richard Howlet, is said to have noted in his pupil an addiction to action rather than to speculation, and Royalist propaganda made much of the fact that he seems to have been extremely fond of sport, an inclination one would have thought reasonably natural in a teenage boy.

Cromwell remained only a short time at Cambridge. He probably left after his first year, for in June, 1617, his father died and as the only male in the household, even if he was still a minor, he was needed at home. The fact that he was a minor provided the first documented instance of a brush with the royal authorities; for a short, but worrying period, it appeared that he might become a royal ward, since a portion of the Cromwell lands were held directly from the King by knight service. Had this occurred, Oliver would have incurred financial obligations, not the least of which would have been suing out his livery on reaching his majority, an expensive process which would have been the only way for him to attain possession of his lands. The case went to the Court of Wards and Liveries, where, fortunately for Cromwell, it was decided that his father had already been through the process and there was no need to repeat it .

The three years which followed Oliver's return to Huntingdon from Cambridge are among the most shadowy in his life, and yet they must have been significant and formative ones for the active but somewhat restless young man. He was thrust early into a position of importance within the family; the experience could only have deepened the obviously close and affectionate ties he had with his mother, while at the same time his position as the male of the household must have strengthened his belief in the prevalent patriarchalism of the day. Financially the family had a modest but not uncomfortable life, their income deriving from farming the family lands and perhaps from the operation of a brew-house. It is to this period that the most exaggerated accounts of Cromwell's dissolute style of life belong. Some of what was related about him is probably accurate. He was, after all, an active and young man, and one can well believe Henry Fletcher's comment that his life was "not altogether free from the wildness and follies incident to youthful age." There exists a well-established tradition that he gambled fairly heavily. Royalist propaganda after 1660 embroidered the tradition extensively, portraying him not only as a gambler but as a considerable rake, carouser, and rowdy. James Heath, for example, dismissed him as "a young Tarquin" who accosted women in the streets, terrorized alehouses, and cudgeled others with his quarterstaff. One attack on him, published during his own lifetime, accused him of getting seven women pregnant and noted that he was nicknamed "The Town Bull," but since this author places the events as occurring during Oliver's later married life at Ely, they can be dismissed as malicious fabrications.

In fact, the next firmly documentable event in Cromwell's life was his marriage on 22 August 1620, to Elizabeth Bourchier at St. Giles's, Cripplegate, London. His early biographers record that before this date, he had gone to London to attend one of the Inns of Court, probably Lincoln's Inn. While no firm record of his attendance there has survived, this seems likely enough. It was a common practice for the gentry to spend some period at the Inns of Court, in part as a broadening experience but more importantly to gain some smattering of the legal knowledge essential to a landowner. As Henry Fletcher aptly put it, he went to Lincoln's Inn "that nothing might be wanting to make him a complete gentleman and a good commonwealth man." Here again the decidedly practical streak in Oliver's character seems to have predominated; one author refers to Cromwell as "more reading of men than on the book, as being naturally more inclined and affecting the pratick part than the theorick." His marriage to Elizabeth Bourchier is also suggestive of his attending the Inns of Court, for she was the daughter of a prosperous City merchant, fur-dealer and leather-dresser,

Sir John Bourchier. The evidence is by no means conclusive, because Cromwell could have made her acquaintance in the county society in which he moved as well, for Sir John had bought a county estate in Essex, where he was a neighbor and distant relative of Cromwell's cousins the Barringtons. It should be noted that Sir John was as well a neighbor of the Earl of Warwick, a prominent figure in the parliamentary opposition. Cromwell's marriage not only involved financial advantage for him, but it tied him closer than ever into influential political circles. The marriage likewise gives the lie to the more exaggerated accounts of Cromwell's youthful indiscretions; a man of Sir John's stature and position would hardly have allowed his daughter to marry the ne'er-do-well and rakehell that biased accounts attempt to persuade us Cromwell was.

Cromwell's marriage was close, happy, and fruitful. He wrote to Elizabeth at a later date, "Thou art dearer to me than any creature" and the words ring true. Like Cromwell, Elizabeth was given a bad press by enemies of her husband. Accusations ranged from her being a drunkard (something for which there is no evidence) to being a stingy and mean-minded housewife. Certainly she was thrifty and careful, but these hardly seem major shortcomings, even in the wife of the Lord Protector of England. She was accused, too, of having little sense of fashion and little taste in dress, even when her position had become such that these things might seem important, but this would hardly have concerned Oliver, who attracted attention in his own right for his lack of concern about dress. She appears to have had a somewhat romantic and naïve streak, but it was her solid virtues as woman of the household which appealed to Cromwell. What others dismissed as frugality, he saw as sound economy; what was criticized as overconcern with household management, Cromwell saw as proper care for home, family, and God. Though satirized by those hostile to Cromwell as Protectress Joan, she provided the quiet stability and love that Cromwell needed at all points in his career. That Cromwell did not pen gushing, passionate letters to her, or she to him, means nothing at all. It was not his or her style. The simple eloquence is telling enough. "Truly my life is but half a life in your absence," she wrote to her husband absent on a military campaign. It was a sentiment Oliver would have echoed on his own behalf.

The newly married couple returned to live in the country town of Huntingdon. Their first child, Robert, was born a year later and five further children followed in rapid succession: Oliver in 1623, Bridget in 1624, Richard in 1626, Henry in 1628, and Elizabeth in 1629. It was a happy and close family in its relationships, though events were soon to make Oliver's public life more difficult and turbulent. To the outside world, though, Cromwell appeared at this juncture as the very picture of the modest English country gentleman. Deriving his living substantially from farming, with his property increased in 1628 by the bequest of his childless uncle, Richard Cromwell, Oliver delighted in the pleasures of country life, and would continue to hold those pleasures dear even in his days of political power. His passion for hawking was legendary and the poet Marvell commented upon "his delight in horse fierce, wild deer." These were simple and ordinary traits, but it is a side of Cromwell that should not be overlooked.

A modest, pastoral life was not, however, to be Oliver's future. Though little can be discerned of the process which brought it about, the tilling that Cromwell was to do was increasingly in fields wider and rougher than the flat farmland surrounding Huntingdon. In the same year that he was married, Oliver has left the first trace of his involvement in politics. In November, 1620, his name is found heading the list of fifteen citizens witnessing the indenture of election of members of Parliament for the 1621 assembly. It is worth remarking that both of the members elected can be identified with the opposition group in Parliament; Sir Henry St. John was Cromwell's cousin, while Sir Miles Sandys was the brother of the prominent parliamentarian Sir Edwin Sandys. The "cousinry" to which Cromwell belonged was in the process of asserting itself. Cromwell may have been, as Marvell put it, "living reserv'd, austere, as if his highest plot to plant the bergamot," but in 1628, he was himself elected as a member of the House of Commons as one of the two burgesses for Huntingdon.

For the first time, Oliver's life became genuinely part of the history of the nation. The Parliament that assembled in that year was one of the most momentous of the seventeenth century. Cromwell, of course, arrived as a newcomer and in major part an unknown quantity. On the other hand, he had important and powerful relatives in the House, and he sat as witness to some of the memorable events of parliamentary history. Within three months of going to Westminster, he participated in the passage of the Petition of Right. Its concerns were primarily political and monetary. But religion was also very much an issue in this assembly, and it was in this area that Oliver made his contribution to the Parliament. He became a member of the House Committee on Religion. In that committee he made his first recorded speech, joining in the widespread complaints about the High Church clergyman Roger Mainwaring. Mainwaring was one of the King's preachers, who in 1627 preached a notorious sermon on Divine Right. Despite being censured by the House, he had been given preferment to a rich living by the King. Cromwell joined vociferously in the attack, and used the occasion to speak a word on behalf of his former schoolmaster, Beard, who had been attacked by Bishop Neile of Winchester for preaching against a Dr. Arblaster, who, in Beard's mind and evidently Cromwell's, had delivered a sermon of "flat popery" at Paul's Cross. It seemed to Cromwell all of a piece, royal support for those whose views were unsound, official displeasure toward those who spoke out for godly religion. The committee went on to condemn

Mainwaring, and Neile was censured as one of those "near about the King who are suspected to be Arminians and . . . unsound in their opinions that way."

Cromwell had clearly clashed with authority, clearly identified himself with the opposition. There is significance in the fact that this first entry on the stage of national politics concerned religion. Other sources of grievance were far from unknown to Oliver, but religion lay at the heart of his concern. The Parliament ended in scenes of confusion and violence. Oliver was among those who refused to adjourn and who witnessed the Speaker held in his seat while the opposition propositions were passed. As revolutionary events go, it was a tame scene, yet it cannot but have impressed Cromwell, and it was a portent for what would happen in the future when Parliament assembled again.

Clashes with authority were not confined to the parliamentary arena, and on the local front too Cromwell was to find that his inclinations placed him in opposition to the desires of the court. In the years immediately after his first spell in Parliament, he experienced two such confrontations. Both opposition and court were keenly aware of the importance of controlling the corporations of parliamentary boroughs such as Huntingdon, for through such control ultimately lay control of the House of Commons itself. Neither court nor opposition was in favor of anything approaching democratic control of such seats. The opposition, Cromwell included, was drawn from the privileged orders just as the court group was. But it was in the interest of the court to make local oligarchies as small as possible and as dependent on the court for their position as could be effected. Even before first going to Parliament, Cromwell had attempted to work with Beard to broaden somewhat the political composition of Huntingdon corporation with the intent of making it less oligarchical and more sympathetic to the Puritan position. In 1630, the shoe was on the other foot; the ruling oligarchy in Huntingdon sought assistance from the Crown to tighten its hold on the corporation, an initiative to which the Crown responded with enthusiasm since it coincided exactly with the overall Stuart strategy with respect to parliamentary boroughs. A new charter was issued to the corporation, establishing a government by twelve aldermen and a recorder chosen for life, and a mayor chosen annually from among the aldermen; as was usual in such charters, no chance was taken with the closed group, the first mayor and alderman being named in the charter itself. This government replaced a system which, if far from democratic, had at least been more representative with two bailiffs and a common council of twenty-four elected each year. Cromwell, though his reaction to such a reorganization was predictable, was too prominent a figure locally to be left entirely in the cold by the new arrangement and both he and Beard, who had worked for reorganization in the opposite direction, were named justices of the peace. Within a short period, his objections to the new arrangements had precipitated a local commotion and Cromwell found himself accused of making "disgraceful and unseemly speeches" against the mayor and the barrister and local politician, Robert Bernard; the purpose of those speeches was "to gain many of the burgesses against this new corporation." It was a battle that Cromwell lost. It was eventually referred to the Lord Privy Seal, who, ironically and unfortunately for Cromwell, happened to be the Earl of Manchester, the head of the family that was edging the Cromwells out as the chief family of the district. In the end, the matter was resolved peacefully. The case he argued was declared to be "causeless and ill grounded" and the manner of his putting it was labeled as being "spoken in heat and passion." Cromwell effected a formal reconciliation with the oligarchy of the borough, declaring himself "very willing to hold friendship with Mr. Bernard, who, with a good will, remitting the unkind passages past, entertained the same." It was no doubt a reconciliation brought about under pressure. Perhaps in restrospect a relatively minor affair, it reveals nonetheless something about the developing political temper of Cromwell. He had based his case substantially on a fear that the new charter would threaten the rights possessed by inhabitants of the borough in the common lands. Cromwell, like the vast majority of the gentry, was extremely sensitive to local grievances and very suspicious of any centralizing tendencies on the part of the state. Moreover, the very nature of his reaction was typical of the man. His "disgraceful and unseemly speeches" were clearly impetuous outbursts. It was probably not the first and certainly not the last time that frustration would lead him to such an outpouring, which in cooler moments he might have wished to rephrase.

Cromwell's second confrontation with authority in these years was resolved in equally frustrating fashion for him, although he did make the point of his opposition. One of the fiscal devices resorted to by the King was to levy fines on freeholders whose estates were worth more than £40 a year and who refused to accept the dubious and expensive honor of knighthood. In April, 1631, Oliver was fined £10 for refusing to purchase a knighthood; of the seven men from his neighborhood summoned for repeated refusal to pay, he was the last to submit and it may be possible that his fine was actually paid by someone else. The matter of a £10 fine was no great problem to Cromwell; the nature and implications of the proceedings were, especially since his view of the quality of Charles I's rule had so recently been influenced by affairs in Westminster.

At about the same time Cromwell submitted, he sold his property in Huntingdon and moved to nearby St. Ives, where he became not an independent freeholder but tenant of a farm. Several possible explanations suggest themselves for the move. Clearly Oliver had suffered political defeat in the matter of the Huntingdon charter; as far as any future career in national politics was concerned, his actions had made

Huntingdon an implausible base. Then, too, there is the tradition that some time about this stage in his career he contemplated emigration to New England; the tradition is unconfirmed, but since this was a course followed by large numbers of his coreligionists, there is nothing inherently implausible in the suggestion and certainly his action of converting his property into cash can be construed as the logical preparation for making such a move. Finally, there is some evidence that Cromwell was in awkward economic straits at the time, and the move may be connected with that. Royalist propaganda coupled pictures of his wild and extravagant youth with tales of financial mismanagement; even a relatively fair early biographer commented on his "wasting of some part of that small estate his Father had left him." In any case, the years at St. Ives represented a step down for Cromwell; no longer did he hold public office, nor did he enjoy the status of independent freeholder. The condition persisted until 1638, when he inherited a sizable estate from his childless uncle, Sir Thomas Steward.

While the years may have been awkward ones for Cromwell, they were a time of considerable importance to him. Sometime either shortly before or after he left Huntingdon, Cromwell had a profound religious experience that shaped the course of his future life. It is known from the observations of two doctors that Cromwell was in an extremely depressed and troubled state in the late 1620s. While a member of the 1628 Parliament, he consulted the well-known London doctor Sir Theodore Mayerne, who recorded in his notebook that Cromwell was extremely melancholy. He also consulted a doctor at home, who recalled that he was splenetic, extremely melancholy, and bothered by "fancies." To be sure, Cromwell did display some physical symptoms; his skin was dry and he had persistent pain in his left side. But it would seem that his condition was more mental than physical. He was experiencing the crisis of conversion, the darkness of the soul. He emerged from it with the conviction that he had been called by God to be of the elect, to be one of the saints to whom God's grace is mysteriously given. In 1638, he described the experience in a letter to Mrs. St. John, unfortunately not giving many clues in the process as to the date at which this all important event occurred.

"Truly no poor creature hath more cause to put forth himself in the cause of his God than I. . . . Blessed be His Name for shining upon so dark a heart as mine! You know what my manner of life hath been. Oh, I have lived in and loved darkness and hated the light. I was a chief, the chief of sinners. This is true; I hated godliness, yet God had mercy on me. O the riches of His mercy! Praise Him for me, pray for me, that He who hath begun a good work would perfect it to the day of Christ." The ecstatic and passionate language would be a hallmark of Cromwell's utterances henceforth. Grace had been bestowed on him and he would feel the power of the Lord in all that he did. What he had experienced was the culmination of the process that had begun at Beard's hands.

The years at St. Ives were, for the most part, quiet ones for Oliver, but one instance shows his growing resolve to struggle for the Puritan position. A favorite device of Puritans to secure the preaching they desired was to fund lecturers; the church, especially in the person of Archbishop Laud, attempted to curb such practices, for it knew the strength that the lecturers gave to the Puritan cause. When Thomas Beard died two years after Cromwell had left Huntingdon, Laud quickly abolished his lectureship and when the Mercers' Company of London set up a new lectureship in the town, Laud employed royal intervention to have the Puritan holder dismissed in 1634. Cromwell doubtless witnessed these events with considerable concern, and we can see something of his attitude in the following year when he interested himself in another lectureship. Writing to a Mr.

Storie in London about an endowed lectureship (the precise location of which is not clear from the letter), he urged financial support for the project: "Building of hospitals provides for men's bodies; to build material temples is judged a work of piety; but they that procure spiritual food, they that build up spiritual temples, they are the men truly charitable, truly pious." Whether the intervention was successful or not is unknown, but the attitude is significant.

Cromwell found the 1630s an increasingly troublesome period. Especially was this the case in the matter of religion, for he found the efforts of Laud to produce church uniformity abhorrent. Already the conscience that would argue for considerable freedom of religious opinion was stirred. Some twenty years later in 1658 he recalled those times and the developments he found so distasteful. There were designs, he noted, "to innovate upon us in matters of religion. . . . And so to innovate as to eat out the core and power and heart and life of all religion, by bringing on us a company of poisonous popish ceremonies, and imposing them upon those that were accounted the Puritans of the nation and professors of religion amongst us, driving them to seek their bread in an howling wilderness, as was instanced to our friends who were forced to fly for Holland, New England, almost any whither, to find liberty for their consciences."

In 1638, Cromwell's fortunes took a decided turn for the better. Sir Thomas Steward's bequest to him consisted of land leased from the dean and chapter of Ely and he now moved there with his family, a man of considerable wealth. At Ely he engaged in his most famous confrontation with authority prior to the assembling of the Long Parliament. A critical concern of seventeenth-century England was to increase the amount of land available for cultivation, and one proposed remedy was large-scale drainage of the Fens. But if such drainage produced only benefits for the Crown and major landholders and reduced the rights of those less well off, it had the capacity to inflict considerable harm in the process of trying to do good. When Cromwell interested himself in the question of fen drainage is not completely certain; at least one source states that he had presented a petition to the King against fen drainage as early as 1623, but this seems somewhat unlikely. By 1638, he was clearly deeply involved in the issue. "It was," a complaint noted, "commonly reported by the commoners in Ely Fens and the Fens adjoining, that Mr. Cromwell of Ely had undertaken, they paying him a groat for every cow they had upon the commons, to hold the drainers in suit of law for five years, and that in the meantime they should enjoy every foot of their commons." When the King intervened and undertook to complete the drainage himself, Oliver appeared as the leading spokesman of those who were concerned about the threats to rights in common land; it was reported that he "was especially made choice of by those who ever endeavoured the undermining of regal authority, to be their orator at Huntingdon unto the . . . King's Commissioners of Sewers there, in opposition to his Majesty's most commendable design."

The ultimate working out of this dispute was swallowed up in the increasing public tension leading to the summoning of the Long Parliament. But Cromwell had struck, in very public fashion, a characteristic pose and had sided openly with the less privileged local interests against the encroachments of the Stuart state. His stance was later to earn him from the Royalist press in 1643 the sarcastic nickname "Lord of the Fens"; at the moment, it earned him a considerable local following. There are other signs too that Cromwell was involved once again in national political issues. He was reported to have been "a great stickler against Ship Money," hardly a surprising attitude in a relative of John Hampden, and it was said he spoke in favor of the Scots. Certainly, all sources agree, he was building a considerable reputation in local Puritan and opposition circles, and those circles projected him once more onto the national scene. His extensive web of family relations within the Puritan opposition, his overt struggles against the encroachments of the state, his complete devotion to the Puritan cause, all combined to make him a natural candidate for Parliament when the Short Parliament was summoned. Invited to stand for Cambridge, he became a freeman of that town on 7 January 1640, and two and a half months later was elected as one of its two members. What role he played in the stormy three weeks of the Short Parliament is unknown, though he must have been present to hear the impassioned denunciation of the course of royal policy enunciated by John Pym. When, in October, the elections for the Long Parliament were held he was once again elected.

In the fall of 1640, Cromwell was forty-one years old. He was not any longer a young man, but he was also not what some writers have painted him to be — a relatively insignificant and inexperienced countryman. As the House assembled, his, admittedly, was not a name to be conjured with. But he had important advantages and they must not be forgotten. He had served a valuable political apprenticeship, both in local office as a justice and in national office as a Member of Parliament. He had direct experience of confrontation with authority — over the Huntingdon charter, over enforced knighthood, over the drainage of the Fens. He had lost his early battles, but he had learned from them. He was well related and counted within his cousinry many of the prominent figures of the House. Above all, he was sustained by a deep personal faith. It was a faith that provided him with a sense of mission, a conviction of duty, an unshakable feeling that God was with him and that through God's providences, he would work God's will in a corrupt world that cried out for reform. At least one of his relatives is reported to have recognized the potential for greatness in such a man almost from the moment of the assembling of the Long Parliament. Asked by one of his supporters who Cromwell was, John Hampden replied, "that slovenly fellow which you see before us, who hath no ornament in his speech; I say that sloven if we should come to have a breach with the King (which God forbid) in such case will be one of the greatest men in England." Few political prophecies have touched the truth so closely.

TWO

The First Years
of the Long Parliament

THE SAME DAY that Charles I announced that he would hold
a Parliament, the Lord Keeper ordered the immediate issue
of writs. The general feeling in the country was that the time
allowed, the Parliament being scheduled to meet in November, was very short, but all parties showed a considerable
interest in the elections. Seats were vigorously contested.
Five candidates stood for the county of Kent, four for the
city of York, and the pattern was similar in many other areas.
Of the mood of Cromwell's constituency, Cambridge, something can be guessed from the fact that the representation
changed between the Short and the Long Parliaments. In
the former, Cromwell's fellow burgess was Thomas Meautys,
a man with whom he could have shared little in common
since Meautys was Clerk of the Privy Council and a nominee
of the Lord Keeper. In the Long Parliament, Cromwell was
joined by a man more of his own stamp, John Lowry, who
was later to be a colonel in the parliamentary army and was
nominated to be one of the King's judges in 1649. With such
a striving for seats and with feelings running so high, it is
hardly surprising that there were a number of disputed

returns, but here again the opposition held the upper hand. Disputes were referred to a committee of privileges of the House of Commons when it assembled; the committee had been suitably packed by the House of Commons leaders, and in case after case it decided in favor of the opposition candidates.

The House which assembled in late 1640 was initially united in its main aims: to bring arbitrary government to an end, to punish those thought to be responsible for it, and to see to it that it was impossible for the Stuart system to be resurrected. Pym spoke for more than himself when he commented that "they must not only sweep the house clean below, but must pull down all the cobwebs which hung in the tops and corners." The near unanimity of opinion in the first session of the Parliament meant that the destruction of the apparatus of the Stuart state was accomplished with relative ease, guided by Pym and his confederates and enthusiastically joined in even by such future royalists as Sir Edward Hyde. The King, in a very real sense, was powerless to resist; with that portion of the ruling class which was represented in the Parliament substantially bent on reforming his government, Charles had very little room in which to maneuver. The events that the process of reform unleashed proved in the long run to be revolutionary, but it would sadly misconstrue the attitudes of those assembled at Westminster in 1640 to think they saw themselves as revolutionaries. If they thought in such terms at all, they would have seen themselves as counterrevolutionaries. They came to Parliament with a strongly held conviction (for which, admittedly, historical fact was more noticeable for its absence than presence) that there had been a time when the ancient mixed constitution of king, lords, and commons had functioned smoothly and cooperatively. Their reading of the first years of the seventeenth century was that this ancient balance had been disrupted by the Stuart kings, who had centralized government, threatened local autonomy, upset religion, ignored the House of Commons, employed dubious justice, and imposed arbitrary and illegal taxation that threatened their possession of property. If there was a revolutionary force loose in the land, they would argue, it was the innovations of Laud and Sir Thomas Wentworth, the King's leading secular adviser. Their role was to restore the ancient constitution, to guarantee their ancient rights and liberties; it was, looked at in this way, a very conservative program. It was also a program in which, predictably, there was far more consensus on the negative side than there was on the positive. There was near unanimity about what ought to be abolished, but since the ancient constitution they were allegedly restoring was itself a myth, there was little agreement about what if anything should replace dismantled structures. From the start, then, it was a revolutionary program that saw itself as conservative restoration, and it was deeply flawed because it lacked any clear consensus where it was going. Cromwell himself caught the mood as well as any: "I can tell you, Sirs, what I would not have but I cannot what I would."

Among the initial moves of the Parliament, the greatest gamble was a full-scale assault on Strafford (as Sir Thomas Wentworth had now become) and Laud. Both were impeached in early November. Pym calculated that if Strafford were removed, the King would be powerless to halt the move for reform. Should, however, the attack fail, the opposition would be cruelly exposed. With great skill, Pym marshaled the attack, steering more radical members away from controversial issues such as church reform to keep them focused on the main point. The attempts to impeach Strafford failed; when he was brought to trial he effectively refuted the vague charges of treason raised against him. But Pym was not to be halted. In April, 1641, just as the Lords were about to abandon the trial, a bill of attainder against Strafford was introduced in the House of Commons by Sir Arthur Hesilrige, an associate of Pym; it was passed ten days later, and in May Strafford went to the scaffold.

The failure of the King to save his greatest secular servant seriously weakened what was left of the monarch's cause, as Pym had calculated. In the ensuing weeks, a number of royal followers made their peace with King Pym, who seemed, for the moment at least, to call the tune more effectively than King Charles. The process of reform went steadily on. A Triennial Act had been passed, allowing for the summons of a Parliament at least every three years, whether the King had called it or not. The King agreed too to a bill by which the current Parliament could not be dissolved against its own will. In June an act regulated tonnage and poundage according to the parliamentary desires, and in July, the prerogative courts of the Crown, which had been used increasingly to back up the despotism of the personal rule, were all abolished. Star Chamber, High Commission, the Councils of the North and Wales all went by the board along with the power of the Privy Council to give judgment in lawsuits. In August, the financial expedients of the personal rule (ship money, distraint of knighthood, revived forest laws) were declared illegal and abolished. The weakened position of the King was further indicated by his taking into his government some of the opposition, including Oliver St. John, who became Solicitor General, and the Earl of Essex, who became Lord Chamberlain. In like manner, the anti-Laudian Bishop Williams found himself promoted to the archbishopric of York. To this time Parliament had been united and effective, in major part because Pym had skillfully steered the business clear of the most controversial issues. When the first session came to a close, members could congratulate themselves on a work of demolition well done; in the eyes of many, the ancient constitutional balance had been restored.

In previous Parliaments, Cromwell had been a relatively quiet member. In the Long Parliament, however, he quickly emerged both as more vocal and more busy. The impression he made in those early days of the Long Parliament was well caught by a hostile witness, the future Royalist Sir Philip Warwick, who recorded in his memoirs: "The first time I ever took notice of him was in the beginning of the Parliament held in November, 1640. . . . I came into the House one morning, well clad, and perceived a gentleman speaking whom I knew not, very ordinarily apparelled, for it was a plain cloth suit which seemed to have been made by an ill country tailor; his linen was plain, and not very clean, and I remember a speck or two of blood upon his little band, which was not much larger than his collar; his hat was without a hatband; his stature was of good size; his sword stuck close to his side; his countenance swollen and reddish; his voice sharp and untunable, and his eloquence full of fervour." The issue which so agitated Cromwell was the case of John Lilburne, who was later to be one of his most implacable enemies. At the moment, however, Lilburne languished in prison under sentence from the Court of Star Chamber for distributing unlicensed pamphlets, including one by the popular Puritan hero William Prynne. The cause was of deep moment to Cromwell; one of the pamphlets had been against the bishops, and to his mind Lilburne was nothing less than a martyr to the high-handed action of the Stuart king. Warwick had little sympathy with the cause Cromwell was arguing. "The subject matter," he commented, "would not bear much of reason." On the other hand, he was deeply struck by the power of argument used by this man unknown to him; "he aggravated the imprisonment of this man by the Council table unto that height that one would have believed the very government itself had been in great danger by it." And Warwick's concluding comment shows that he was not alone in being impressed by the force of Cromwell's speech: "He was," Warwick noted, "very much hearkened unto."

The incident was typical of Oliver's activity in the House

in the period up to the outbreak of hostilities. Not exactly in the forefront of affairs on most occasions, he was nonetheless an active member of the House, and labored strenuously on behalf of Pym's group. Warwick's account suggests that he was a dynamic, if perhaps somewhat crude, speaker, but his rough approach had its benefits and there is no doubt he was increasingly listened to, not least of all because of his close family ties with more visible members of the opposition. A good deal of his activity is now lost from the historical record, for much of what Cromwell did, he did in committee. But this was precisely where his services could be most valuable, and the wide range of his committee activity is a fair indication of his growing importance to the opposition cause. It is not surprising to find some of his activity linking up with earlier struggles. He became, for example, a member of a committee to consider claims arising from the Fens dispute, and in May and June, 1641, he pursued the issue with the same tenacity and fervor he had shown in 1638.

The incident is thoroughly consistent with what is known about Cromwell's earlier forays into political disputes. On matters that were of importance to him, he was forceful, direct, rude, and often impetuous. There was nothing of discretion or subtlety here; these were political arts that Cromwell would learn through experience. For the moment it was direct, passionate and wholly of a piece with his earlier confrontation with Bernard and the mayor in Huntingdon.

The altercation over the Fens was not one of the major interests facing the Commons, nor was it representative of Cromwell's most deeply felt concerns. It is sometimes argued that, because the major contentious issues of the first session of the Long Parliament were largely connected with the structure and functioning of the Stuart state, religion was not a leading cause of the outbreak of hostilities. There is some truth in this, but two points are important to remember. In the first place, religious issues clearly did emerge in the first session; since they were, by their very nature, divisive,

Pym labored to keep them in the background, but they were there. In the second place, they were issues of primary importance to Cromwell, even if other areas of dispute were more significant to other members. Looking back on those years, Cromwell commented, "Religion was not the thing at first contested for, but God brought it to that issue at last . . . and at last it proved that which was most dear to us." There is doubtless some hindsight in the statement, reflecting Cromwell's way of seeing God's providence at work in the passage of human events. But there is also acute perception. Some have taken the comment to be a confession by Cromwell that religion was not the main issue, but surely it is just the contrary; to him religion was the main issue, even if it had taken some time to reveal this.

Cromwell's whole busy pattern of activity as a member of the House reinforces the view that matters touching religion were the ones most likely to stir his passions and elicit his keenest interest. He was, of course, involved in some of the essentially constitutional issues. He was among those, for example, who clamored for reform of the Exchequer and he moved the second reading of a bill for annual parliaments. But overall, the pattern of activity was dominated by religious matters and in pursuing these, Cromwell, as might be expected, revealed himself as opposed to the episcopal hierarchy in general and to Laudian influences in the church in particular. He was very active in pursuing complaints against Matthew Wren, the Laudian bishop of Ely, a notorious anti-Puritan. On occasion, his enthusiasm for the cause led him to outspoken expression. His attack on Sir John Strangeways in February, 1641, over the issue of bishops caused him to be reproved for unparliamentary language. It is perhaps significant with respect to Cromwell's priorities at this time that he took only a minimal part in the proceedings against Strafford; his one recorded intervention in those events involved religion and, in the process of blaming Strafford for the ills of Ireland, suggested that the House should take under discussion methods to "turn the Papists out of Dublin."

The position that Cromwell took with respect to religion involved him from the very first in some difficulty. While his basic political instincts were conservative, his religious conceptions were, in the context of the time, radical. This had already been shown in his interchange with Sir John Strangeways, who raised an argument Cromwell was to encounter often in the coming years (and one which he turned himself against those whose religion was more radical than his own in the 1650s). Strangeways objected to Cromwell's attacks on the bishops on the grounds that effecting parity within the church would have wider implications about effecting parity throughout the Commonwealth. Assaults on established forms of office and possession could, many feared, be extended to attacks on other forms of property. In 1641 in the case of the bishops, Cromwell swept the argument aside brusquely. Cromwell's division from many of the more conservative members of the House was shown very clearly in his association with the so-called Root and Branch Bill. Following up an earlier petition, the bill proposed the total abolition of the bishops and all their "dependencies, roots and branches." The bill was presented to Parliament not by Cromwell, but rather by Sir Edward Dering. Dering, however, later revealed that he had received it just before the debate from Sir Arthur Hesilrige, who in turn had got it from Cromwell and Sir Henry Vane the Younger. The actual authorship of the bill is not definitively known; Clarendon credited it to Cromwell's cousin Oliver St. John, but there is considerable plausibility to Dering's account. In any case the bill, which alarmed a number in the House, stemmed from the circles within which Cromwell moved, and its radical proposals were among the pressures that began to edge some of the cautious revolutionaries of 1640 toward support of the King.

Cromwell's religious attitudes are likewise revealed in his

attacks on the Book of Common Prayer, which he dismissed with the comment that "there were many passages in it which divers learned and wise Divines could not submit unto and practice." Likewise, in the matter of preaching, Cromwell showed characteristically Puritan sympathies when he successfully introduced a motion on the subject of sermons, permitting the parishioners of any parish to elect a lecturer and providing for the charge to be met by the parish.

Cromwell's position naturally enough alarmed the conservatives, but even in these early days of the Long Parliament, he experienced problems with some of his potential allies as well. The Scottish Presbyterians were as little inclined to accept the institution of episcopacy as Cromwell was. But their demands in religion raised doubts in Cromwell's mind. Their conditions for a firm settlement with the King involved "uniformity in religion," by which they meant the establishment of Presbyterianism on the Scottish model as the state religion. Though Cromwell had not yet fully formulated his ideas on religious toleration, the concept of enforced uniformity, even of a clearly Puritan sort, troubled him. In February, 1641, he wrote to a Mr. Willingham in London for some material relating to the Scottish demands for uniformity in religion so that he could study it further before debate on the matter took place.

Of course religion and political affairs were inextricably entwined, and thus we find Cromwell active in the House too in a number of matters of essentially political import. The interconnection of religion and politics was shown very strikingly by Cromwell's involvement in the endorsement of the Protestation assented to by both houses in early May, 1641. If anything, the surviving evidence suggests that he would have liked the document to have been even stronger than it was. As it stood, the Protestation was an unambiguous condemnation of the practices of the King in both politics and religion with its accusations of subverting the fundamental laws of England and Ireland and its suggestion that there had been attempts "to introduce the exercise of an arbitrary and tyrannical government." There were likewise references to the subversion of the true Religion and dark allusions to "Jesuits and other adherents to the See of Rome." The oath which concluded the Protestation tied religion and politics closely together, for it not only swore allegiance to the King but promised to uphold the true reformed Protestant religion and the "power and privileges of Parliament, the lawful rights of the subjects." Cromwell was very active in securing the assent of the House, and he followed this up by writing back to his constituency of Cambridge, noting to the mayor and aldermen that the Protestation was "not unworthy your imitation." Then, Cromwell added, "the result may (through the Almighty's blessing) become stability and security to the whole kingdom" for "combination carries strength with it; it's dreadful to adversaries."

The first session of the Long Parliament ended in something of a mood of euphoria. At the end of the summer of 1641, it seemed that the desires of Parliament had been achieved, that indeed it was an *annus mirabilis* that would lead to a resurrection of church and state. In August the King went to Scotland, accompanied by much suspicion on the part of Pym and his followers like Cromwell, who asked pointedly whether the trip was necessary. They were suspicious, and rightly so, that the main purpose of Charles's trip was to try to find support in his northern kingdom to stem the tide that seemed so clearly to be running against him in England. But peace was signed with Scotland on 7 September without the King having gained the Scottish support he hoped; indeed, the discovery of a plot by supporters of the King to murder some of the chief Scottish leaders — the so-called Incident — obviously did not strengthen his position there. Yet the parliamentary leaders, for all the enthusiasm of their preachers, had cause to be concerned. The work of destruction done, their unity was beginning to crack; moderates were beginning to press for understanding with the

King and as Charles made seeming concessions from his side, those who were in the van of the attack faced the danger of being left in an exposed position. Religion was clearly one of the divisive issues, but there were clearly further causes, too, for the beginnings of defection from the parliamentary ranks. They are illustrated in the career of Edward Hyde, the later Earl of Clarendon, who moved slowly from the position of reformer to leadership of the King's party. His main concern was to save and consolidate the legislative work of the first session of the Parliament. By the end of that session, the victory of Parliament a d the common law over the instruments of prerogative government had seemed complete. The obvious course for the parliamentary party at this point, as Hyde saw it, was to abate the political confusion and seek a reconciliation with the King, but as the radicals pressed on in matters like religious reform it became increasingly difficult to be both a parliamentarian and a favorer of reconciliation. Hyde and others began to filter to the Royalist side. To Cromwell, for whom religion had been a central issue from the start, their actions were inexplicable.

The whole nature of the political situation was radically altered by the Irish rebellion of October, 1641. At a stroke it shattered whatever hopes there were for a stabilizing reconciliation and immensely strengthened Pym's hand. With the controlling hand of Strafford removed, a revolt of the Gaelic Irish in Ulster quickly spread into a far wider conflict, with the Catholic Old English settlers of the Pale joining their coreligionists. The English reaction to the news from Ireland was one of horror. Anti-Catholic feelings were easily aroused, and in this case they were fanned by widespread reports of a general massacre of the English in Ireland. Certainly many English settlers were killed and there was extensive suffering. But the accounts which reached England were horrific in the extreme. Though there is no evidence that a deliberate massacre of the English did take place, the truth of the allegations was assumed without question in

England and casualty figures in excess of 200,000 were widely accepted. Great stress was made of the barbarity of the Irish; those massacred were, as one contemporary noted, "like so many human sacrifices to their superstition" and tales spread of children slain before their parents, of men roasted and eaten, of women violated before suffering death. Behind it all, it was alleged, were the treacherous and evil machinations of the Catholic clergy. That the reports were exaggerated mattered not at all; people believed they were true and they conducted themselves accordingly. At no time in the seventeenth century did the English hold a high view of the Irish, but the events of October, 1641, seemed to more than confirm the worst opinions. The revelations profoundly affected Cromwell; his whole view of the Irish was fundamentally framed by the reports he heard in 1641 and his subsequent carriage toward them finds its roots, if not its justification, in that year.

The Irish rebellion raised at once an issue of momentous importance. No one disputed that armed intervention was necessary to put it down, but who was to control the forces raised for the purpose? The issue was further clouded by the fact that it was widely believed that the rebels were acting at the orders of the King, especially since one of the Irish leaders prominently displayed a spurious "commission" from the King authorizing the restoration of the Roman Catholic religion. It had been feared earlier that Strafford might bring an Irish army over to curb the opposition; now it was to be feared that the King with an army at his command might make an accommodation with the rebels and achieve the same result.

The Grand Remonstrance was the upshot of these concerns and the revived sense of urgency they created in the House. The document was a lengthy and all-embracing assault on the iniquities of Stuart rule, ranging from demands that the King rid himself of his "evil councillors" and "take such as might be approved by parliament" to an article relating to the taking of common lands in the Fens from the subjects, for which Cromwell was responsible. Pym used the revelations from Ireland to great effect in pushing the Remonstrance forward; the events in Ireland, he maintained, proved how untrustworthy the King was, how impossible it would be to trust such a man with an army which he might turn on the Parliament instead of the Irish rebels.

The debate over the Grand Remonstrance was a critical point in the process by which civil war came about. Its very comprehensiveness and sharp language guaranteed that it would be controversial. In one sense Pym won his fight, for not only did the Remonstrance pass, but on Hampden's motion Pym's forces were able to secure a second vote ordering it to be printed. The latter was an unprecedented and deeply divisive move. It was a deliberate appeal to the people, and carried the fight outside the House to a far wider audience. It was only to be expected that many would see in this action of King Pym a flagrant disregard for the established rights of the crown and a deliberate fragmentation of the traditional ruling classes. In another sense, the passing of the Grand Remonstrance revealed something quite different. Clause after clause was fiercely opposed by Hyde and others and on the night of 22–23 November, after fifteen hours of violent debate, it passed by only eleven votes. That close vote was a clear indication that the unity of the House of Commons was finally, definitively, and decisively split. Charles for the first time had a large party of his own in the House, and it was this factor which served as the precipitant to actual fighting. Had the House of Commons remained united in opposition as it had been during the first session, Charles could have done little but intrigue and finally submit; once unity was broken and he had a large following of his own, the groundwork was laid for a military solution. Some years later James Harrington commented, "It was not the war that caused the dissolution of this government, but the dissolution of this government that caused this war."

His assessment was perfectly correct, and in the process by which the ruling classes found themselves divided and at loggerheads, the vote on the Grand Remonstrance was more than a symbolic culmination.

What part had Cromwell played in these stirring and disruptive events? Needless to say, he was firmly in Pym's camp and pressed vigorously for the passage of the Remonstrance. In fact, he was so fully within the camp, so convinced of inequities that needed rectification, so passionately involved in the issue at hand, that he seems naïvely to have been almost wholly oblivious to the political realities of this explosive situation. He seems to have had almost no sense at the outset of the ferocity with which the Remonstrance would be fought and the extent to which it would divide the House. He was simply anxious to get on with it, convinced that what he saw as its essential rightness would triumph without difficulty. He was appalled on 20 November when a delay in proceedings was granted to opponents to consider it further; "That day," he confidently predicted, "would quickly have determined it." He went so far as to tell Lord Falkland that the debate on the Remonstrance would be "a very sorry one" since there would be few who would oppose its passage. At the other end of the process, he was no less passionately committed to the Remonstrance, but he had seen at first hand the strength of the opposition and through it had come to appreciate the crucial nature of its passage. Following the passage of the motion to have the Remonstrance printed, he solemnly confided to Falkland the importance the events had for him. "If the Remonstrance had been rejected," he is reported to have told Falkland, "he would have sold all he had the next morning, and never have seen England more; and he knew there were many other honest men of the same resolution."

The months immediately following the passage of the Grand Remonstrance witnessed an uneasy sparring between the two camps and attempts by both to consolidate support on their side. Critical to Pym's cause and that of Parliament were the City elections of January, 1642, in which parliamentary supporters came to the fore; to that time, the ultimate inclinations of London's governors were no certainty. The King's bungled attempt on 5 January to arrest five leaders of the Parliament further heightened tension. The words of Speaker Lenthall on the occasion, indicating that he was a servant of the House and not of the King, were one portent of the way matters had developed: "I have neither eyes to see nor tongue to speak in this place but as the House is pleased to direct me, whose servant I am here." The fact that the five members (Pym, Hampden, Hesilrige, Holles, and Strode) fled to the City of London for safety was another. These were the days when, as Bulstrode Whitelocke recalled, the country "insensibly slid into this beginning of a civil war by one unexpected accident after another."

Cromwell played his part in the political maneuvering during those increasingly tense days. Still clearly not in the front rank, he was nonetheless zealous on behalf of the advanced party. It is apparent that his group was well aware of the importance of controlling elections to the House, for Cromwell sat along with Pym on a committee which investigated an attempt by the Earl of Arundel to influence a parliamentary election in Arundel. In a sense it was a minor measure of how things were changing. In writing to the corporation, the Earl of Arundel was not doing anything different from what men in his position had been doing for years, but the order which resulted from the hearing stopped the election. It is clear too that Cromwell had, along with his colleagues, a keen sense of the possible danger to them of an army plot with the Crown; his attack on the Earl of Bristol in December aimed at removing him from the Privy Council because of fears of this sort. In one key sense, Cromwell was in advance of many of his colleagues; he saw at an early date that decision was to be reached by the sword rather than the council table. This is not to say that he favored recourse to arms as the way of settling the kingdom, only that he perceived there was to be no other way. On 14 January, he moved, and it was ordered, that a committee should be named to look to putting the country into a posture of defense; he was equally involved in work relating to the pacification of Ireland, advancing money to aid Dublin and investing over £2,000 by July, guaranteed against Irish land, to further the English cause. Where precisely he stood on some of the major issues at stake cannot be wholly documented, but it seems safe to assume he backed the position sketched out in the 19 Propositions presented to the King at the beginning of June. These were the most advanced statements of the parliamentary cause made to date, and if implemented, would have established a firm parliamentary sway over the monarchy through such demands as that the Privy Councillors were only to be appointed with parliamentary approval. The King, who had long since left London for the North, rejected them out of hand. In his rejection, he nicely turned the arguments of previous years on the parliamentarians themselves; he pointed out that acceptance of the 19 Propositions involved abandoning the treasured concept of a mixed government which Parliament had so long claimed it was attempting to defend. His answer was a shrewd propaganda stroke; it was also essentially correct. The logical culmination of the parliamentary position, whether its adherents wished to admit it or not, involved considerable alteration in the existing framework of government. Cromwell sat on the committee to consider the King's answers, and such thoughts must have been in his mind.

Some clues as to Cromwell's attitude can be gained from the pattern of his committee work. His activities with respect to Ireland, his concern for the safety of the Tower of London, his worries about the loyalties of the Lord Mayor of London all suggest that he had accepted the drift of events. More dramatic proof of his position was given by overt action outside the House. As was frequently the case with Cromwell, his position was indicated by deeds, not words. As burgess for Cambridge, Cromwell was well aware of the wealth in plate possessed by the individual colleges. As an actual struggle grew nearer and nearer, it became increasingly important to the Parliament that this treasure not fall to the King and swell his war coffers. In late July the King had, in fact, suggested that the silver be sent to him at York for protection. By the middle of the month, Cromwell had already shown concern for the defense of his constituency by seeking an order that two companies of volunteers be raised there; he himself contributed money toward their supply of arms. By August he was in Cambridge with his brother-in-law Valentine Walton to guarantee that if college silver left Cambridge it would be directed to the Parliament and not to the King. When a Royalist captain arrived in August to take the silver to the King, he met armed resistance. Acting on his own initiative, though later indemnified by the House of Commons for his action, Cromwell had stopped perhaps £20,000 of valuable support reaching the King. The action, taken before the actual outbreak of hostilities, was characteristically precipitate, but it was of great importance. A contemporary, Thomas May, noted that many of the gentry and men of rank in the area were disaffected to the Parliament and that there had existed considerable danger that those counties might have fallen "into as much distraction and sad calamity as any other part of the land had felt" had prompt action not been taken. In particular he cited in this respect "the successful services of one gentleman, Master Oliver Cromwell of Huntingdon."

Only a few days later, on 22 August, the King set up his standard at Nottingham. With a nice touch of both prophecy and irony, it was blown down shortly afterward. The dispute had moved to the battlefield.

In August, 1642, Cromwell was still not in the forefront of the parliamentary party. But because he had put aside introspection for action at Cambridge, he had taken a major step toward such prominence. In two years, he had gained immensely valuable political experience. No one could have worked as one of Pym's lieutenants without learning something. As an active committeeman, as an increasingly frequent speaker, as a messenger between the two Houses, Cromwell had an intense political education in that short period. The political skill he was to display in coming years was no sudden or accidental gift. It was formed in two years of hard, time-consuming work at the behest of King Pym. Added to the skill was a firm faith that gave meaning and direction to what he did. He was about the Lord's work and the terrible providence of the Lord would determine where that work led.

THREE

The Eastern Association

BOTH CROMWELL'S POWER and much of his ultimate fame depended on his ability as a military commander. His successes are almost unparalleled in the history of warfare and they stand as the more astonishing since he came to a military career with a total lack of experience. The fact that many of the other soldiers of the English Civil War were equally unprepared and that England suffered from a war fought by amateurs does not diminish the magnitude of his achievement. He was not a faultless commander and there are occasions on which criticism must be leveled against his conduct of affairs, but, on balance, the record is a remarkable one. Cromwell himself, from the very first, attributed the successes of himself and his men to the power of God; each successive victory deepened the impression in his mind that he was an actor in a drama orchestrated by divine providence. In examining his military career, one cannot help but admit more ordinary, earthly influences were at work: brilliantly conceived tactics, a high degree of organization, discipline and, above all, morale. Both his contemporaries and later historians have sought in vain to document more tangible reasons for his military success. Experience appears to have been his great teacher, and innate genius his most considerable strength.

Since Cromwell had already engaged in belligerent action before the King raised his standard, it should occasion no surprise that he was quickly and aggressively engaged in the process of raising a fighting force. Others may have had misgivings and second thoughts about the turn events had taken and thus responded to the crisis in lackadaisical or even overtly neutralist ways, but Cromwell apparently never faltered, once the course was set. In late August he mustered a troop of horse at Huntingdon, aided in the effort by his brother-in-law John Desborough, who served as his quartermaster. If the words of the Royalist historian Clarendon are to be trusted, Cromwell was blunt and unambiguous to those who volunteered under his service. Officially forces were being raised to fight for King and Parliament, a convenient slogan to ease the consciences of those who could not face up to warfare against their anointed monarch. Many of the parliamentary forces marched to battle under this fiction that they were fighting for the King against the evil councillors who had misled him. According to Clarendon, Cromwell had none of this: the slogan was to him a "perplexed and cozened expression" and he assured those at Huntingdon that if the King charged him in battle, he would shoot him as he would any other man. He noted that he expected the same attitude from those under his command and urged them not to volunteer if they felt squeamish about it. Years later Thomas Tany recalled this scene at the market house in Huntingdon, at which he had been present, and recorded Cromwell as having promised "to stand with us for the liberty of the gospel and the laws of the land."

As the political dispute deteriorated to actual fighting, it was clear that Parliament possessed some key advantages. The rough geographical division of the country in a Royalist North and West and a parliamentary South and East meant that Parliament had at least the potential command of the richer part of England, and especially that it had at its disposal the resources of London. It was the sort of factor that would weigh more heavily the longer the fighting lasted; hence it was clearly in the interest of the King to gain a quick victory. Inexperience and indecision prevented that end from being achieved. Cromwell was far from alone in his lack of experience. A plaguing problem for both sides in the war was the lack of trained and skilled officers. Warfare had not been a part of English life in recent memory, the last serious campaigns undertaken by English troops being those in Ireland at the end of the Elizabethan period. There were some professional soldiers who had seen action on the continent, but in the initial stages of the war they were not used effectively by either side. If anything, in the first stages of the conflict, the advantages in terms of trained officers lay on the Royalist side, but since a number of these men were Catholics, the King necessarily used them as inconspicuously as possible to avoid abetting parliamentary propaganda, which frequently sought to counter the Royalists by evoking popular fears and hatreds of Catholicism. The Royalist advantage in this respect was, however, directly reflected in their command structure. The Royalists conducted the war through the agency of a council of war predominantly military in its composition. Parliament attempted to control its forces through a committee of the Lords and Commons for the safety of the kingdom. While they had a commander-in-chief for their forces, the Earl of Essex, he really acted not as the directing force, but as general of the main field army. Ultimate control rested with the committee in London, which attempted to dictate strategy not merely as amateurs but also by remote control. Both sides suffered from lack of discipline, much of it stemming from the fact that many of the troops who were raised were private companies drawn from the tenants and followers of individual noblemen and gentlemen. Discipline was a matter that particularly concerned Cromwell, and as the war progressed his soldiers were to be notably distinguished by his attention to this factor.

In October, 1642, the Royalist army began an advance from Shrewsbury toward London. At Edgehill near Kineton in Warwickshire, they clashed with the forces of the Earl of Essex in the first significant battle of the war. It was, on the whole, an indecisive conflict; only the Royalist cavalry under Prince Rupert had undisputed success, but in their zeal to follow up a fleeing enemy, they galloped on to Kineton and removed themselves from the field of battle, thus allowing the parliamentary foot to make a useful counterattack. Essex, who was supposed to be covering London, fell back on Warwick, and the King pushed on to Oxford, his headquarters for the remainder of the war. Both sides claimed the victory. Cromwell's role in the battle is shrouded in mystery. He was certainly there, as was his eldest surviving son, Oliver, who was serving as a cornet in Oliver St. John's regiment. But it would appear that he only took part in the latter stages of the battle, in the counterattack against the Royalists. Cromwell himself remarked that "he had been all that day seeking the army and place of fight." A local tradition at Burton Dassett has it that Cromwell climbed the tower of the church there, which overlooks the battlefield, to see how the engagement was going and then in his excitement slid down one of the bell ropes in his haste to gain the battlefield. The Royalist Sir William Dugdale related a similar story, though he suggested Cromwell climbed the tower in order to avoid the battle. Dugdale is not alone in stating that Cromwell betrayed cowardice on the occasion; Denzil Holles in his *Memoirs* wrote that Cromwell deliberately avoided the battle. One need not believe these accusations. Cowardice in battle was wholly out of character with Cromwell. If the story of his climbing the church tower is true, it was doubtless done to get some perspective on what was, by all accounts, a confused battle.

The first indecisive campaign of the war drew to a close in the following month. The King missed his chance to nip rebellion in the bud by the slowness of his advance on London. By the time his troops reached Brentford on 12 November, Essex had led his army back to London. His troops, reinforced by the London trained bands, once again faced the Royalist army at Turnham Green. The King, realizing he was hopelessly outnumbered, withdrew, and with the unfought battle of Turnham Green, London was, for the moment, safe.

Cromwell was deeply impressed by this first campaign, particularly by the battle of Edgehill. Two things stuck in his mind. First, he could not help but be impressed by the charge of Rupert's cavalry, but even more so by the fact that the impact of that charge was blunted by the inability to rally these forces after the initial charge and keep them involved in the battle, instead of tearing off to Kineton. Second, he was deeply impressed by the spirit shown by Rupert's soldiers. It was lacking and sorely needed on the parliamentary side. Just after the battle, he discussed the latter point with John Hampden. "Your troopers," he commented, "are most of them old decayed servingmen and tapsters and such kind of fellows . . . and their troopers are gentlemen's sons, younger sons, persons of quality. Do you think that the spirits of such base and mean fellows will be ever able to encounter gentlemen that have honour and courage and resolution in them? . . . You must get men of a spirit . . . that is likely to go on as far as a gentleman will go, or else I am sure you will be beaten still." Hampden was frankly skeptical and thought the suggestion impractical, but it was an article of faith on Cromwell's part that a godly army could be built and that it would have such a spirit. The subsequent development of his own forces reveals that his vision was both greater and more realistic than that of his cousin.

The opening stages of the war contained little of comfort for men of Cromwell's frame of mind. Already members of the House were having second thoughts; a peace party within the House, led by Denzil Holles, sought to upset the primacy of Pym. Cromwell's feelings on the matter were shown clearly when he acted as a teller for the Noes when an act was proposed that would have granted indemnity to the followers of the King. As was often the case, his actions, too, spoke louder than words. At the end of 1642, Parliament set about creating regional associations to give it a more cohesive fighting force. In the formation of both the Eastern Association and the Midlands Association, Cromwell played a significant role. Such associations were vital to Parliament, not only to raise more troops and supplies, but also as a counter to the prevalent localism that marked the conflict. It might be said that, from the start, the Parliament and many of the components of the associations were at cross-purposes. It is clear that from the perspective of the counties involved, the Eastern Association was seen primarily as a mechanism for local defense, brought together by the necessities of the time rather than stemming from any inherent sense of unity or shared ideological perspective on the part of the participants. From Pym and Cromwell's perspective, it was intimately connected with the formation of a national field army.

In returning to the eastern counties, Cromwell faced two main tasks. One was impressing Parliament's determination on the localities, by rallying the faithful and harassing the fainthearted. Cromwell had little hesitation about indulging in the latter. When the sheriff of Hertfordshire denounced Essex and his followers as traitors, Cromwell's troops arrested him and sent him to London despite extensive local objections. When he heard that his former antagonist at Huntingdon, Robert Bernard, was "active against the proceedings of Parliament and for those also that disturb the peace of this country and the kingdom," he dispatched troops to visit him as well. When Bernard protested, Cromwell replied with a thinly veiled threat: he came, he said, not to hurt any man, "nor shall I you. I hope you will give me no cause. If you do, I must be pardoned what my relation to the public calls for."

Cromwell's main task was, however, the consolidation and enlargement of his own troop. By degrees, the troop grew into a regiment. And it was a regiment with a very distinctive character, for in building it, Cromwell was guided directly by the advice which he gave John Hampden after Edgehill and which Hampden had been inclined to dismiss with skepticism. In January, Cromwell had become a colonel and had made enough impact on the parliamentary side to deserve the sobriquet "noble and active Colonel Cromwell," which John Vicars bestowed on him. Cromwell's concern in putting together his force was to recruit men who were committed to the task at hand, who could act visibly as a godly regiment. It was character and spirit that mattered to him, not rank or social origins. Richard Baxter remarked on how from the very first Cromwell was concerned to get religious men into his troop. Such a procedure for raising soldiers was by no means universally praised; Hampden may have thought it impractical, but others viewed it as genuinely subversive of the social order. At a later date, Manchester, for example, claimed that Cromwell's officers were "not such as were soldiers or men of estate, but such as were common men, poor and of mean parentage, only he would give them the title of godly, precious men"; they were, Manchester derisively added, "such as have filled dung carts both before they were captains and since." A striking example of the antagonism Cromwell's methods aroused and of his forthright rejection of such criticism was provided by the case of Ralph Margery. Margery had raised a troop of horse for Parliament, but had been removed from his command by the Suffolk committee on the grounds that he was not a gentleman and hence incapable of holding such a post. Cromwell's answer was to absorb Margery's troop in his own forces. In September, 1643, he put his reactions to the case against Margery in words that have often been quoted and that sum up a good deal of Cromwell's attitude about the relationship between social class and military command. "It may be it provokes some spirits to see such plain men made captains of horse. It had been well that men of honour and birth had entered into these employments, but why do they not appear? Who would have hindered them? But seeing it was necessary the work must go on, better plain men than none." Elsewhere he commented, "I had rather have a plain russet-coated captain that knows what he fights for and loves what he knows than what you call a gentleman and is nothing else." Cromwell's rationale for the position was simple and direct. If the gentry would not join in God's battle, substitutes must be found, and in that search commitment to the godly cause was sufficient to override traditional social considerations. Besides, Cromwell urged, only committed officers can lead men vigorously. Fainthearted men will communicate their unwillingness to their men; on the other hand, he noted, "A few honest men are better than numbers. . . . If you choose godly honest men to be captains of horse, honest men will follow them."

Closely allied to Cromwell's views on the social origins of his officers were his views about their private opinions and persuasions. Cromwell had already, on more than one occasion, shown that he was deeply troubled by outside interference with a man's conscience. He carried that attitude into the army; indeed, it is likely that it was his army experience which consolidated his views on religious toleration into a position in favor of freedom of conscience far in advance of the majority of his contemporaries. It was to be expected that the Royalists would attempt to portray the parliamentary army as composed substantially of dangerous sectarians. Charles I had, in fact, told his followers that the enemy was mostly "Brownists, Anabaptists, and atheists, such as desire to destroy both church and state." It made little difference that the description was far from accurate;

"Brownists" and "Anabaptists" were convenient smear words and particularly the latter conjured up lurid images of depravity and social revolution. But Cromwell faced such criticisms not only from the enemy but also from his own side. John Hotham, for example, rightly reproved and imprisoned for irresponsible conduct, complained to the Speaker of the House that Cromwell had used an Anabaptist against him as well as employing another officer who was only a yeoman. Cromwell felt sufficiently harassed in September, 1643, to appeal for aid to his cousin Oliver St. John; "I have a lovely company. . . . They are no Anabaptists; they are honest, sober Christians; they expect to be used as men."

In the following year, shortly after Cromwell was promoted to lieutenant general, the matter was even more directly out in the open. In the spring of 1644, Cromwell clashed openly with Manchester's Major General Laurence Crawford over the issue of insisting on religious conformity among the troops. Crawford was a Scottish Presbyterian and had no use for Anabaptists, and indeed little enough for men of an Independent conviction such as Cromwell. Trouble first surfaced over Lieutenant William Packer, who was a known Baptist. Crawford had him arrested, probably on religious grounds, and Cromwell rose to his defense, insisting he was a godly man. Subsequently one of Crawford's own officers, Lieutenant Colonel Henry Warner, fell under similar displeasure because he refused to subscribe to the Solemn League and Covenant, a test of Presbyterian orthodoxy, on religious grounds. Cromwell was outraged that a man loyal to the cause should be cashiered on sectarian grounds. "Ay, but the man is an Anabaptist," he wrote to Crawford. "Are you sure of that? Admit he be, shall that render him incapable to serve the public. . . . Sir, the state, in choosing men to serve them, takes no notice of their opinions, if they be willing faithfully to serve them, that satisfies. I advised you formerly to bear with men of different minds from yourself; if you had done it when I advised you to it, I think you would not have had so many stumbling blocks in your way." His final warning to Crawford went directly to the point: "Take heed of being sharp or too easily sharpened by others against those to whom you can object little but they square not with you in every opinion concerning matters of religion." It was an eminently modern and reasonable stand, but in the seventeenth century it could only be viewed as revolutionary by those conditioned to believe that stability in the state required uniformity in religion.

If Cromwell accepted a certain degree of social democracy in selecting his officers and refused to question their consciences so long as they were overtly committed to the cause, he was, as a good commander should be, very much concerned about the morals and discipline of his men. Suitable preachers were provided for the troops so they might, as a saying had it, "have the praises of God in their mouths and a two-edged sword in their hands." But it was notably in the matter of discipline that Cromwell's troops stand out in contrast to the general practice of the time. When two troopers tried to desert in April, 1643, Cromwell ordered them to be whipped in the marketplace at Huntingdon, as a punishment to themselves and an example to others. Such rigidly enforced discipline had its results. A parliamentary newspaper reported ecstatically in the following month that Cromwell had under his command "2000 brave men, well disciplined; no man swears but he pays his twelve pence; if he be drunk, he is set in the stocks, or worse, if one calls the other 'Roundhead' he is cashiered, in so much that the countries [i.e., counties] where they come leap for joy of them, and come in and join with them." No doubt the picture is somewhat exaggerated, yet every evidence suggests that Cromwell's troops were indeed better behaved than most engaged in the Civil War, and the newspaper's concluding comment, "How happy it were if all the forces were thus disciplined," has the authentic touch of heartfelt desire.

The force that Cromwell had built was formidable in

numbers as well. What had started as a single troop of horse had become a regiment of five troops by March, 1643; by the following September it had doubled in size and by the spring of 1644 it appears to have included fourteen troops. His family connections provided him with a number of the officers. In addition to Desborough who had been with him from the start, and his son Oliver, who had been at Edgehill, Cromwell was also joined by his cousin Edward Whalley and his young nephew Valentine Walton.

Discussion of Cromwell's regiment cannot avoid raising the subject of its alleged iconoclasm. Indeed Cromwell himself has long been burdened with the reputation of being a destroyer and desecrator. His image in folklore is that of a Puritan fanatic who set about the fabric of England's churches with a nearly unparalleled ferocity. The reputation is much exaggerated and equally much misunderstood. That there was iconoclasm during the war, much of it conscious and premeditated, is perfectly true, yet a goodly portion of that for which Cromwell was blamed was done by others, significant parts of it before he was even born, much less embarked on a military career. There is, for example, a good deal of confusion in the popular mind of the destruction that occurred at the time of the Reformation under Thomas Cromwell and the actions of Oliver and the parliamentary troops. The sorts of actions attributed to Cromwell were, in many cases, nothing new. The stabling of horses in churches and cathedrals undoubtedly occurred, though probably not so frequently as legend would have it. But it had happened before Cromwell and would occur afterward; in 1264 Simon de Montfort's soldiers had stabled their horses in Rochester Cathedral, while in 1685 Wells Cathedral was similarly treated by the followers of the Duke of Monmouth. The stories, nonetheless, abound. At the end of the eighteenth century, a Colonel Byng, traveling through Oxfordshire, noted how common the rumors were when he commented, "Whenever I enquire about ruins, I always get the same answer, that it was some popish place and destroyed by Oliver Cromwell, to whose share is laid even more devastation than he really committed." The Royalist newspaper *Mercurius Aulicus* was prone to such attacks on Cromwell. In March, 1643, it reported that he had committed "many outrages" in Cambridge and had "caused the Heads of Houses to take down their organs and all the furniture of their Chappels," while in the following month it waxed even more indignant about alleged desecrations perpetrated in Peterborough, where Cromwell, it said, "did most miserably deface the cathedral church, break down the organs, and destroy the glass windows, committing many other outrages on the house of God which were not acted by the Goths in the sack of Rome, and are most commonly shown by the Turks when they possess themselves by force of a Christian city." In fact, the vast majority of these stories fall apart on close examination. For example, Cromwell has been credited with destroying the tower and transept of Ely Cathedral, but the truth was that the tower had fallen down in the fourteenth century. As to the alleged horrendous scenes at Peterborough, the only evidence of personal iconoclasm by Cromwell is the breaking of a crucifix, and even that story comes from a 1686 source and thus cannot carry complete conviction.

That much said, it must be admitted that Cromwell's mind was not totally out of touch with the iconoclastic spirit. He shared fully in the Puritan desire to return to the simplicity of the New Testament religion; he feared and disliked any ceremonial that seemed to smack of the church of Rome, and he was anxious to preserve in as pure a form as possible free and direct communion with his God. The liturgical practices of the Anglican church deeply offended him on all three of these counts, and he reacted strongly against them. There are, for example, the reasonably well documented accounts of what happened at Ely Cathedral in January, 1644. There the Anglican clergyman Hitch persisted with the choir service despite the objections of the parliamentary soldiers. Cromwell himself, it must be noted, was deeply fond of music and had no objections to organs; indeed, he later installed one at Hampton Court when he was Protector. But he felt strongly that they were out of place in a church as part of the worship of God. As the governor of Ely he was forced to react to the persistence of Hitch, but it is noteworthy that he did not do so in the spirit of fiery iconoclasm. Instead he wrote a letter to Hitch warning him that if he persisted in his practices, the soldiers were likely to take matters into their own hands in a tumultuous and destructive way. It was only when this failed that he took more direct action. Arriving in the middle of a choir service, he told Hitch, "I am a man under authority and am commanded to dismiss this assembly." When Hitch ignored even this, Cromwell finally placed his hand upon his sword, told Hitch to "leave off his fooling and come down" and expelled the congregation. The actions are not those of a fanatic, but of a man who finally takes firm action after a series of what he considered reasonable requests had been ignored. It was completely in character. He did continue to object to what he saw as idolatrous forms of worship; he referred caustically at a later date to "these men that live upon their mumpsimus and sempsimus, their masses and service-books, their dead and carnal worship." "No marvel," he added, "if they be strangers to God." Yet in dealing with them, more often than not, he followed his own precept: "In things of the mind, we look for no compulsion, but that of light and reason."

The force that Cromwell had carefully built up, a disciplined and godly force, as it is so often referred to, had early and dramatic success near Grantham in Lincolnshire in May, 1643. Marching toward the town, he found himself suddenly face-to-face with the enemy. According to his own account, he was badly outnumbered, facing twenty-one troops of horse and three or four of dragoons with only twelve troops, "some of them so poor and broken that you shall seldom see worse." After exchanging musket fire and waiting for half an hour for the enemy to make a move, Cromwell suddenly charged. The shock tactics worked and the Royalists were scattered. At the loss of only two men, Cromwell had obtained his first notable victory. Characteristically, Cromwell saw in it the powerful hand of God. It was God, he wrote, that "hath given us, this evening, a glorious victory over our enemies."

Throughout the summer Cromwell bent himself to his task. Clearly he wished to raise as powerful a force as possible and with it prosecute the war energetically. Already, he showed definite signs of impatience with those of his colleagues who were unwilling to press on so vigorously and chose to drag their feet instead. His complaint to the Association at Cambridge about the delay of another commander in joining him in the field was characteristic: "This is not a time to pick and choose for pleasure. Service must be done. Command, you, and be obeyed." His string of successes continued, despite the lack of cooperation. He captured Stamford and defended Peterborough from Royalist attack. He took Burghley House and, despite the rules of war at the time, which would have allowed him to kill the garrison for refusing to parley, he took two hundred prisoners instead. At Gainsborough, he fought an action which was styled by one of his eighteenth-century biographers the foundation of his future greatness. The engagement at Gainsborough reveals a good deal about Cromwell's capabilities as an officer. He carried off successfully a difficult offensive movement against a well-placed enemy force. He did so with characteristic dash and bravery. At the moment of victory, he did not allow his force to be dissipated, as Rupert had done at Edgehill, and then he executed with skill and discipline that most difficult maneuver, retreat in the face of a fresh and numerically superior force. If it was God's providence again at work, that providence had an unusually able agent in the person of Oliver Cromwell.

By the end of July, Cromwell had become governor of the Isle of Ely and one of the four colonels of the Earl of Manchester, who had been placed in command of the eastern counties. For all the success that Cromwell himself had had, the military situation remained precarious for the Parliament. The forces of Newcastle, having moved from the North, were an ever present danger to the eastern counties, while Essex had abandoned any intention of besieging the King in Oxford after the parliamentary defeat at Chalgrove Field in mid-June. Cromwell showed solicitous care, indeed anxiety, that his forces not be allowed to decay through parliamentary neglect. Throughout the summer and autumn he pleaded with various authorities for more money and for reinforcements. At points, he was reduced to paying for supplies out of his own pocket, though he complained to the Deputy-Lieutenants of Essex, "I think it is not expected that I should pay your soldiers out of my own purse." To the Commissioners at Cambridge he complained that the money provided for his soldiers was far from adequate; "it will not half clothe them, they are so far behind." Above all he was concerned that neglect of his men would lead to a collapse of their spirit and morale. "If we have not more money speedily they will be exceedingly discouraged . . . make them able to live and subsist that are willing to spend their blood for you." To his cousin Oliver St. John he wrote in September that his soldiers were still ready to venture all though the situation was becoming desperate; "lay weight upon their patience, but break it not. . . . The force will fall if some help not. Weak counsels and weak actings undo all. . . . All will be lost, if God help not. Remember who tells you."

It was not until the beginning of the following year that such concerns were fully met, but as early as the fall things began to look better in a military sense for the parliamentary cause. Hopes of Scottish assistance were in the air, though Scottish insistence on a Presbyterian settlement as the price for agreement was a genuine stumbling block. Essex had reached Reading and again cut off the King from London. It was at this point that Cromwell was ordered north to join forces with the parliamentary commander there, Sir Thomas Fairfax. On 10 October, they had notable success in their first collaborative effort at Winceby.

The key action of this northern campaign occurred in the spring of 1644. Newcastle was by then apparently trapped in York. The alliance with Scotland had been achieved by Parliament, and Scottish troops under Leven had pushed as far south as Durham. Fairfax and his father had captured Selby. If Prince Rupert could be prevented from relieving Newcastle at York, the parliamentary prospects looked very encouraging. Cromwell and Manchester secured the eastern Midlands against possible threats from Rupert and then headed north themselves. While York stubbornly held out, the apparently favorable situation was suddenly reversed by a series of victories on Rupert's part, first at Newark, then at Lathom House; they were victories which made possible that which the parliamentary command had most cause to fear, the relief of York and the joining of Newcastle's and Rupert's armies. In a state of some confusion, not the least aspect of which was a lack of precise information concerning Rupert's movements, the parliamentary commanders decided to abandon the siege at York and take up a position on the Knaresborough-York road in an attempt to cut off Rupert's advancing troops. With a brilliant and rapidly executed march, Rupert, however, completely outmaneuvered the parliamentary forces and relieved York from the northwest instead of using the main road. Then, somewhat rashly, he set out to pursue the parliamentary army, which was falling back toward Tadcaster. On 2 July 1644, his advance guard of horse came within sight of the rearguard of the parliamentary army under Cromwell, Fairfax and the Scot Leslie. Leven and the parliamentary foot had gone on toward Tadcaster but a frantic message had them back on the field by the latter part of the afternoon. At four o'clock the two armies faced each other over Marston Moor, and the stage was set for the largest battle, in terms of numbers, fought on British soil. It was a battle that had a personal element to it as well. The two most successful cavalry commanders of the war — Prince Rupert and Oliver Cromwell — faced each other. The story is told that Rupert personally interrogated a captured trooper from the parliamentary forces to find out if Cromwell was there; when the man was released and told this to his parliamentary colleagues Cromwell tersely commented, "By God's grace he shall have fighting enough."

The prophecy was apt. In the battle that followed, Parliament won a notable victory and Cromwell a considerable measure of renown. Rupert, in fact, decided not to offer battle that day and, convinced the parliamentarians would not attack, retired behind the lines for his evening meal. But the parliamentary forces, bolstered by their superiority of numbers and encouraged by the fact that the topography of the field favored them, had decided on attack. It came shortly after seven o'clock in gathering darkness and drenching rain in the form of a rapid, controlled charge by Cromwell's horse. Cromwell's charge from the left wing went very well, aided admittedly by the premature advance of the Royalist Lord Byron, which had as its chief effect masking the fire of his own musketry behind him. Equal success was not met elsewhere on the field. The center moved ahead as planned, but the right, under Sir Thomas Fairfax, was in immediate difficulty and Fairfax was himself cut off by the enemy horse. Indeed Cromwell's initial success on the left was not long sustained. Rupert, rushing to the field, broke through, scattering those before him. The situation was relieved only by the second line of parliamentary horse under Leslie. It may be that Cromwell was absent from the field at this point, wounded in the neck. He returned in time for a second major assault by the left, one which thoroughly routed Rupert's cavalry and sent them flying away. Just as at Gainsborough, Cromwell again displayed the lesson of Edgehill. Instead of pursuing Rupert on toward York, he kept his men "close and firm together in a body" and turned his attention to other parts of the battlefield.

It was a critical and decisive action, for elsewhere the battle was going badly for the parliamentary forces. Fairfax himself had made it to Cromwell's lines, but the parliamentary right was in confusion. The center too had caved in and the Scottish general, Leven, had commenced a rapid withdrawal there that was not to end until he reached Leeds. Manchester and two remaining regiments of Scots held on bravely, but their situation was clearly precarious. The intervention of Cromwell's cavalry changed all. Charging from a wholly unexpected quarter (in effect out of what had been the Royalist woods at the beginning of the battle), they saved the right and by that saved the center as well. Victory had been snatched from defeat, and it had been done by Cromwell's unique talent in rallying his cavalry after a charge. The slaughter had been heavy; some estimated that the casualties ran as high as 7,000 on the Royalist side and there were some 1,500 prisoners. Parliamentary forces suffered far less; despite numerous men wounded, they sustained only about 300 casualties. Among the dead was Cromwell's nephew Valentine Walton. Cromwell wrote a moving letter, strong in Puritan faith, to his brother-in-law to tell him of the death of his son.

Cromwell gained great fame for his role in the battle. It is typical of the way many have historically viewed him that this letter to Walton, written in condolence to a friend, has been so often cited as proof that Cromwell deliberately played up his own role and minimized that of the Scots. To be sure the account of the battle contained in the letter made only scant reference to the role played by the Scots: "The left wing, which I commanded, being our own horse, saving a few Scots in the rear, beat all the Prince's horse. God made them as stubble to our swords; we charged their regiments of foot with our horse, routed all we charged." Whether or not Cromwell did puff up his role in the battle (and the letter to Walton is no proof that he did, since he was deliberately brief about the battle), others were quick to recognize the critical role he and his men had played. Rupert gave the nickname "Old Ironsides" to Cromwell after the battle, and it was quickly enough passed on to his men. In Edinburgh Major Harrison, much to the annoyance of the Scots, persisted in spreading the view that "Cromwell alone, with his unspeakably valorous regiments, had done all that service."

The great victory of Marston Moor was not followed up in any conclusive fashion. A number of factors intervened. While a joint command had been successfully employed on the field of battle, the strong localism that marked the conflict quickly reappeared. Leven went off with the Scots to attend to the town of Newcastle. The Fairfaxes restricted their attention to Yorkshire, and Manchester slowly withdrew toward the territory of the Eastern Association. In the latter commander, the will to push things to a military solution was noticeably lacking, and because of this, tension grew between him and Cromwell. That tension was illustrated by Manchester's threats to hang John Lilburne for taking Tickhill Castle against orders; Cromwell intervened on Lilburne's behalf. The problems were to be found not only at the command level, but in the wider political scene as well. Tensions between the Presbyterians and the Independents (neither of them any more simply religious groupings, the "Presbyterians" including those who might be called the moderates or the peace party and the "Independents" the radicals or war party) had been greatly intensified in recent months. Because of Cromwell's own inclinations and the reputation of his men, his forces were increasingly viewed with suspicion by more cautious men. Such suspicions were in no way eased by reports of what

Cromwell allegedly said in this regard. He was reported as saying "I desire to have none in my army but such as of the Independent judgment" and with respect to the Presbyterian Scots, he is said to have commented, "In the way they carry themselves now . . . I would as soon draw my sword against them as against any in the King's army."

Cromwell's obviously deep felt frustration was further heightened by the developing military situation and his commander's reaction to it. The defeat of Marston Moor was offset by major Royalist victories over Waller at Cropredy Bridge and over Essex at Lostwithiel. In the South and the West, the tide seemed to have turned to the King and Cromwell felt strongly that Manchester was duty bound to use his forces to help their beleaguered comrades and to get between the King and London. Manchester, as always, hesitated and expressed irritation when pressed by Cromwell to action. For his part, Cromwell had a powerful weapon to hand which he did not hesitate to use; he was still a Member of Parliament as well as a military commander, and as M.P. he could levy criticism and seek solutions in a way that was not open to him simply as a soldier. Cromwell had periodically visited the House during lulls in the campaigning. In November, 1642, for example, he had been named to the Committee for Plantations to consider policy toward the New World colonies. It was a measure of his importance within the House that he was named to the Committee of Both Kingdoms in February, 1643, after the Scottish alliance was formed. He had already used the House as a forum to attack what he considered the inept handling of the war effort. In January, 1642, he had launched a strong attack on Lord Willoughby for his conduct at Gainsborough and also for what Cromwell considered "the very loose and profane commanders" that Willoughby tolerated within his staff. Now in 1644, he turned to the same forum again with two aims in mind, forcing Manchester into action and securing some guarantees for the religious opinions of his troops.

Cromwell was increasingly convinced that Major General Crawford, with whom he had already had violent disagreements, was exerting unfortunate influence on Manchester. He threatened that all Manchester's colonels would resign if Crawford was not removed and carried the case to the Committee of Both Kingdoms. Then with a nice sense of political timing he withdrew the threat in return for a guarantee that Manchester would immediately march west to engage the Royalist forces. In September, he took care of his second concern in the House, speaking out strongly on behalf of the Independents and at the same time lending support to a motion offered by Oliver St. John that a joint committee of the Lords and Commons should "endeavour the finding out some way, how far tender consciences, who cannot in all things submit to the common rule, which shall be established may be borne with according to the Word."

The forcing of Manchester to move west did not produce the results Cromwell hoped for; indeed, all the campaign did was to deepen his sense of dissatisfaction and frustration. Manchester's westward progress was slow and reluctant. When he did finally engage the King's forces near Newbury on 27 October, it looked initially as if the opportunity had been provided for another victory as shattering as that of Marston Moor, for the parliamentary forces outnumbered those of the King two to one. It was not to be. The battle was an ill-managed affair of inconclusive result, and the opportunity was wasted. At a council of war held on 10 November, the divergence between Cromwell and his commander broke into open acrimony. Cromwell pressed for a vigorous continuation of the war despite the season and the condition of the army. Manchester urged no further action. Indeed, he went so far as to indicate no desire to defeat the King. "If we beat the King ninety-nine times, he would be King still and his posterity, and we subjects still, but if he beat us but once we should be hanged and our posterity undone." Cromwell was outraged; "My Lord, if this be so, why did we take up arms at first? This is against fighting hereafter. If so, let us make peace, be it never so base." It was time, in Cromwell's judgment, to carry the dispute to a higher forum once again.

Cromwell's life for the past two years had been predominantly that of a soldier. He had forged a military machine, remarkable in its makeup and spirit alike and he had gained a great personal reputation as a cavalry leader. In these years, he had had little time for domestic concerns, yet they never can have been absent from his mind. There had been, in the lulls of the campaigning, moments of domestic happiness, crowned by the courtship of his eldest daughter, Bridget, by Henry Ireton, an intellectual soldier who was to become one of Cromwell's closest confidants. There had been, too, moments of dark tragedy, of which the chief was the death from smallpox of his eldest surviving son, Oliver. (Robert had died five years earlier at Felsted School.) And continuing throughout all was concern how the household could manage, with the master away on campaign. In April, 1644, Cromwell ordered that some of the money due to him should be paid to his wife; the £5 a week he so allocated was later taken to be an example of how he used his official position for corrupt purposes, but it was clearly nothing of the kind, only the effort of a concerned husband trying to look to the needs of his family. Such cares were never far from his mind, but for the moment, his chief concern had to be the faltering of the war effort and the disintegration of the allied parliamentary front, and he knew that he must gamble on decisive action at Westminster to set these right.

FOUR

The New Model

CROMWELL'S DISSATISFACTION with Manchester was of long standing. It is possible that some of the difficulty may have been connected with the county rivalry of the two families, but as Cromwell prepared to confront his commander directly, it was with wider concerns in mind. Cromwell knew that if a peace was concluded before the King was defeated, the Independents stood to lose the most. Moreover, he obviously did not share the reluctance and essential defeatism of Manchester. That his thoughts were on broader issues — the creation of a fighting force not bound by localism and motivated by the spirit that marked his own troops and the vigorous prosecution of the war itself — rather than on a simple personal attack on Manchester is revealed by the fact that, for all his dissatisfaction with Manchester, he was quite prepared to defend him when he felt he was accused on ill-informed grounds. The Committee of Both Kingdoms had been very critical of Manchester for not attacking Basing House, that powerful Royalist stronghold in the South, as they had ordered. On this count, Cromwell defended his commander and, in doing so, cast thinly veiled doubts on the wisdom of having the war effort directed by a central civilian authority instead of by the men in the field. In a broad sense, Cromwell was attacking the central parliamentary strategy. Instead of concentrating on sieges and the defense of fortresses, he favored a more openly attacking posture.

To appreciate the importance and the risk of what Cromwell was now undertaking, it is necessary to recall the military and political situation. Looked at in one sense, the Royalist cause did seem shaky. The great defeat at Marston Moor and the evaded possibility of another such defeat at Newbury were disturbing portents. On the other hand, the King realized how divided and distracted his parliamentary opposition was. The tension between the Scots and the English did not diminish; the division which we label Presbyterians versus Independents was serious and growing and was reflected in the increasingly uneasy cooperation between those who would accept peace at nearly any price and those who wanted to prosecute the war to a full and final conclusion. A parliamentary commander with no love for the Independents, Sir Samuel Luke, summed it all up nicely: "I fear fair words will endanger us more this winter than all the force of the enemy has done this summer." One further source of friction and conflict should be noted; in using his position as a member of the House of Commons to attack Manchester, Cromwell was casting doubts on the suitability for command of a member of the House of Lords and thus was threatening what remained of the working relationship between the two Houses of Parliament.

At the end of November Cromwell presented his charges against Manchester to the House of Commons at their invitation. The main point of the attack was simple and direct: "The said Earl hath always been indisposed and backward to engagements, and the ending of the war by the sword, and always for such a peace as a thorough victory would be a disadvantage to — and hath declared this by principles express to that purpose, and by a continued series of carriage and actions answerable." Manchester's response to the charges was predictable; three days later he made an extended statement in the House of Lords. It was, in essence, a long diatribe against Cromwell, attributing to him all sorts of dangerous and radical positions. His charges ranged from embezzlement, for which he produced as evidence the £5 a week Cromwell had arranged to have paid to his wife, to accusations of seeking to upset the social order. In words clearly calculated to arouse the House of Lords, he alleged that Cromwell had expressed a hope "to live to see never a nobleman in England and that he loved such better than others because they did not love Lords"; Cromwell, Manchester said, had even made the attacks *ad hominem,* for he had told Manchester himself "it would not be well till he was but Mr. Montagu." In his *Narrative,* which he likewise issued, Manchester moved the argument on to more military grounds, but the bitterness toward Cromwell was in no way abated. He saw his capacity as a military commander constantly threatened by the pressures exerted by "Cromwell and his junto" and he portrayed Cromwell as an ambitious man, anxious for his own personal glory, "attributing all the praise to himself of other men's actions" (a comment that would clearly strike a responsive chord among the Scots). Faced with these sets of accusations, both Houses referred the matter to committees.

The consternation that Cromwell's outspoken opinions caused is revealed by the fact that his opponents within the parliamentary side were willing to consider extraordinary means to set him aside. In December, Essex consulted with some lawyers to see if, after consultation with the Scots, they might not be able to charge him with being "an incendiary." The scheme came to nothing. It was pointed out that Cromwell had a wide popularity and that such an attack might do more damage than good to the parliamentary cause. But the very fact that this approach was considered shows how deep were the divisions within the parliamentary ranks.

Those who maintain that Cromwell was a soldier only and not an adroit politician should consider the skill of his next move. In much the same way as he had applied force earlier to Crawford and then withdrawn it, having forced Manchester to move his army westward, Cromwell now, having raised the issue by the virulence of his attack on Manchester, suddenly shifted ground and placed the argument on a new and more constructive level. On 9 December 1644 he made a memorable series of speeches in the House: "It is now time to speak or forever hold the tongue. The important occasion now is no less than to save a nation out of a bleeding, nay, almost dying condition, which the long continuance of this war hath already brought it into; so that without a more speedy, vigorous, and effectual prosecution of the war . . . we shall make the kingdom weary of us and hate the name of a parliament." He went on to note that not only the Royalists but many who were friends to Parliament at the beginning of the struggle accused the Parliament men of prolonging the war to their own benefit; they said, he reported, "that the members of both Houses have got great places and commands, and the sword, into their hands; and, what by interest in the Parliament, what by power in the army, will perpetually continue themselves in grandeur, and not permit the war speedily to end, lest their own power should determine with it." Cromwell was at pains in his speech to insist he was not reflecting on any individual person; "I know the worth of those commanders, members of both Houses, who are yet in power." Even though the whole setting was occasioned by his attack on Manchester, he maintained it was not his part "to insist upon complaint or oversight of any Commander-in-chief upon any occasion whatsoever; for as I must acknowledge myself guilty of oversights, so I know they can rarely be avoided in military matters." The solution he offered was both simple and sweeping. "If I may speak my conscience without reflection upon any, I do conceive if the Army be not put into another method, and the war more vigorously prosecuted, the People can bear the war no longer, and will enforce you to a dishonourable peace." He concluded his arguments by an appeal for self-denial in the service of the wider cause. "Let us apply ourselves to the remedy; which is most necessary. And I hope we have such true English hearts, and zealous affections towards the general weal of our Mother Country, as no members of either House will scruple to deny themselves, and their own private interest, for the public good."

The idea of a new model for the army was not original with Cromwell. In June, 1644, Waller had said pointedly to the House, "Till you have an army merely your own, that you may command, it is impossible to do anything of importance." In November, the House had expressed much agitation about offices of profit being held simultaneously by its members. But the speech was a masterly stroke; the personal quarrel with Manchester had been altered to a general point of principle and the upshot was the Self-Denying Ordinance which provided that "during the time of this war, no member of either House" was to hold a military command from forty days after its passage. The conjunction of forces that led to the passing of the ordinance reveals the mixed motives in the House. The proposer of the ordinance was a staunch Presbyterian and opponent of Cromwell, Zouch Tate; the seconder was Sir Henry Vane the Younger. Tate doubtless saw it as a way to remove Cromwell the M.P. from command, while Vane saw it, as Cromwell did, as a right reordering of the army to further the cause of the aggressive party. The enthusiasm of the House of Lords, which was presented with the ordinance on 19 December, was noticeably less impressive. They still were angered by the attack on Manchester, one of their members, and they saw that passage of the ordinance would effectively disbar any member of their House from military command, there being at the time no legal way to resign a peerage; on the other hand, a member of the House of Commons could presumably resign his seat and retain his military command.

The fact that Cromwell retained in the end both his seat and his military command has led many then and since to be unduly cynical about the role he played at the time. It has been darkly hinted that he had foreknowledge of the fact that he would be retained, but there is no evidence of this. Surely Cromwell's friends and supporters hoped that he would survive as a military commander, but such hopes should not blind us to the scope of the gamble Cromwell was making. Everything in his conduct in the uncertain period after the House of Commons passed the Self-Denying Ordinance suggests that he was willing to pay the price of letting go his command if that was necessary to achieve an army of spirit that could win the war. In his second speech on 9 December, he openly stated his willingness to lay down his commission, and there seems little reason to doubt his sincerity. It was not until 10 June that his official role in the New Model was confirmed and even that was given a time limit. In the intervening months, he did soldier on behalf of the Parliament because military necessity dictated that they call on him. But his conduct was impeccably correct. When he served with Waller in a campaign in the West to hold back the Royalist general Goring, the terms of the Self-Denying Ordinance had not, in fact, come into force because of the slowness with which the Lords handled it. In this campaign Cromwell served under Waller's command, and it was reported that he carried himself as an obedient officer and did not question his superior's orders. At the end of the campaign, he returned as he was supposed to on 17 April to Windsor to surrender his command, as the terms of the Self-Denying Ordinance required. Again military necessity intervened, it being necessary to prevent the King from joining his forces with those of Prince Rupert. In the circumstances Cromwell was ordered by the Committee of Both Kingdoms to a campaign in the region of Oxfordshire. It was his first command in the New Model Army, and he took his chances successfully. But his awareness that this might well be a temporary situation is indicated in his letters to the New Model commander Fairfax; he refers to himself as leading "your honour's regiment (lately my own) ." In fact until very shortly before the battle of Naseby, the New Model Army was without a lieutenant general of horse. It was Fairfax in conjunction with the City of London who petitioned for Cromwell's appointment, Fairfax stressing "the general esteem and affection which he has both with the officers and soldiers of the whole army, his own personal worth and ability for the employment . . . [and] the constant presence and blessing of God that has accompanied him." It was only four days before Naseby that the House of Commons agreed and the House of Lords did not follow suit until after that battle and then confirmed his commission for only three months.

In the interval between his speeches on 9 December and the battle of Naseby Cromwell did, however, play a significant role in helping to shape the New Model. Many of his cares and concerns were predictable. In view of the tight discipline within his own regiment, it is not surprising to find him critical of the lack of such discipline elsewhere in the army and insisting that this must be rectified in the New Model. He referred feelingly to "the prophaneness and the impiety and absence of all religion, the drinking and gaming, and all manner of license and laziness" and he indicated without qualification his belief that "till the whole army were new modelled and governed under a stricter discipline, they must not expect any notable success in anything they were about." He served very actively on a subcommittee of the Committee of Both Kingdoms to consider the reorganization of the army. As sketched out, the New Model was to have ten regiments of horse (later increased to eleven), twelve foot regiments, and a regiment of dragoons; their pay was to be guaranteed by a monthly levy on the parliamentary territories. He was active in securing the selection of Sir

Thomas Fairfax as the commander in chief; he and Vane were the tellers for the Yeas on the vote. Particularly Cromwell seems to have been concerned that the army command should not be unduly hampered by parliamentary control; he felt strongly, for example, that the commander should have the right to appoint his own officers rather than have Parliament designate them. He did not entirely win that battle, but did achieve a compromise that allowed Fairfax to make appointments subject to subsequent parliamentary approval. He objected vigorously to the application of any sort of religious tests to the officers, a point on which he had insisted from early in his own command.

By April the New Model was ready and by May it was in the field. It is necessary to stress that it was a very unproven quantity. One near contemporary remarked that "upon this new establishment, the King's party were very much heightened, thinking it an easy matter now to subdue the Parliament's army, being thus chopped and changed, and many eminent commanders (including Manchester, Essex, and Waller) laid aside and discontented." John Vicars, writing a year after the formation of the New Model, had much the same point to make. "O the wonderful, base and despicable esteem that was thereof, not only in the King's army and malignants, but even among very many seeming friends among us, and those no mean ones too! O how did they disparage, undervalue, and contemn, as it were, this New Modelled Army, calling it a New Nodelled Army, jeering them as a company of young Tyroes, or fresh-water soldiers." Cromwell's view was, needless to say, quite different. He appreciated the importance of the new officers and the removal of those who had scruples about actually defeating the King. He understood the importance of the fact that this was a national army that could transcend the localism that had hitherto hindered effective military strategy. He knew the importance of discipline and of pay. And perhaps most significantly to a man who looked for the approbation of

God, he saw in the initial victories he achieved near Oxford at Islip and at Bletchingdon House in April, the tangible sign that God's providence was with this army. "This was the mercy of God and nothing more due than a real acknowledgement; and though I have had greater mercies, yet none clearer." Because the army had become godly and fought a godly cause, Cromwell indicated to the Committee of Both Kingdoms, providence was with them. "Surely God delights that you have endeavoured to reform your armies; and I beg it may be done more and more. . . . I wish to be of the faction that desires to avoid the oppression of the poor people of this miserable nation upon whom who can look without a bleeding heart."

The spring campaign in 1645 began in an atmosphere of some confusion, occasioned by the fact that the parliamentary leadership was uncertain as to the intention of the King's moves. He was known to be heading generally north, but was he aiming to engage the Scots or was he making for the Royalist stronghold of Chester, besieged by parliamentary forces under Sir William Brereton? Brereton, in fact, had conceived an ambitious scheme for the defeat of the King's army. While he held on at Chester and joined up with the Scottish army, Cromwell and Fairfax should also join and pursue the King from the rear. If all fell right, Brereton noted, "this should be the last game they should ever play." Brereton shared his plan both with Cromwell and the committee in London. It is a measure of Cromwell's grasp of the military situation that he saw the advantages in such a plan, but the committee in London was less favorably inclined and the scheme came to naught. It is likewise a revealing commentary on Cromwell's basic loyalty to the command structure that he dropped back without question when the committee ordered him to do so. By the end of May, he was in East Anglia, protecting the area of the Eastern Association.

When the King and Prince Rupert sacked and took Leicester on 1 June, even the cautious committee in London could not ignore what was happening in the Midlands. It was plainly foolish to tie down Cromwell in East Anglia while the King marauded in the Midlands; still less did it make sense to let his military commission lapse. It was at this point that Fairfax finally had his way and Cromwell was appointed to the vacant post of lieutenant general of horse in the New Model. The war in the Midlands had followed a dance of evasion. The two main armies moved about, not always fully aware of the other's location. It is apparent that the King, despite the success at Leicester, had little intention of engaging Fairfax, particularly since his cavalry was depleted by the absence of Goring and his horse. Instead, he resolved to make for Newark. Fairfax, on the other hand, was determined to force the King to battle once he was joined by Cromwell and his men; he was well aware of the fact that his forces, especially with the addition of Cromwell's men, vastly outnumbered the King's army, for he had captured papers that revealed Goring's delay in bringing his horse from the West. Cromwell joined Fairfax on 12 June, while the King's army continued on its way to Newark, apparently quite unaware of the danger it was in. On 13 June, the King's army stopped for the night at Market Harborough. It is indicative of the failings of the Royalist intelligence that they were calmly eating supper when the news reached them that parliamentary troops had captured a rearguard outpost left at Naseby, some seven miles away. The King's hand was well and truly forced. He could either retreat to Leicester in what could only have been perilous conditions, or he could stand and fight. He chose the latter course. In retrospect, it is easy enough to criticize his decision, given the odds he faced and the crushing defeat he suffered. On the other hand, the fact he was facing a largely untried army clearly colored his thinking. He would have agreed completely with the parliamentary supporter who, seeing the New Model march to war, commented, "Never did any army go forth to war who had less of the confidence of their own friends or were more the objects of the contempt of their enemies." He had little doubt that his troops could defeat "the rebels' new brutish general" just as they had beaten Essex.

Cromwell had no doubts in his own mind about how the battle would go. Several sources indicate a mood of elation came over him as the battle approached; one who was there remembered him having "a fit of laughter" just before the battle, an incident that at least one biographer of Cromwell has taken to indicate he was in something of a manic state. A month after the battle, Cromwell recalled those moments in words which testify to his supreme faith in God to tip the balance his way. "I can say this of Naseby, that when I saw the enemy draw up and march in gallant order towards us, and we a company of poor, ignorant men, to seek how to order our battle — the General having commanded me to order all the horse — I could not, riding alone about my business but smile out to God in praises, in assurance of victory, because God would, by things that are not, bring to naught things that are, of which I had great assurance, and God did it."

For all of the numerical superiority of the parliamentary forces, the battle was, however, no foregone conclusion. Few battles in the seventeenth century were. From the outset the parliamentary left was thrown into confusion by the on-slaught of Rupert's cavalry. The center, despite heavily out-numbering the attacking Royalists, was severely pressed, only Fairfax's own men holding firm. It is no wonder that one of the Royalist participants in the struggle could comment ruefully, "In probability we might have had the day." But on the right was Cromwell, and on the right the battle was won. It was won, significantly enough, by Cromwell's ad-herence once again to the lesson of Edgehill, the vital lesson of keeping his horse under control so they could mount a second attack. Whereas Rupert's initial charge had been a great success, his men swept on and at the critical point of the battle were two miles away in Naseby busily plundering the parliamentary baggage train. Not so for Cromwell. His initial charge had the same shock power as Rupert's on the other wing, but instead of tearing off in pursuit, he rallied all except one detachment and threw his forces against the exposed flank of the Royalist foot. The combined assault of Cromwell and Fairfax, joined in by Okey, whose dragoons charged from the other side, was too overwhelming, and the Royalist foot was decisively routed. By the time Rupert and his men rejoined the battle, the Royalist cause was beyond saving. The New Model was redrawn into a second line of battle; Rupert may have contemplated a second charge, but at the sight of the New Model, the troops broke and fled toward Leicester.

The aftermath of the battle does not reflect credit on the New Model. It is true that Cromwell's horse apparently retained their discipline, even while indulging the pursuit for plunder that followed victory. The parliamentary foot showed far less discipline and not only plundered the King's baggage but indulged in the wanton killing of the camp followers of the defeated army. For all the fact that the Royalists had themselves behaved in equally barbaric actions only shortly before at Leicester, the enormity of the behavior cannot be excused. It remains one of the few blots on the memory of the Ironsides.

In a very real sense, Naseby settled the outcome of the war, though the fighting was to drag on for some months. It also decided more. Any lingering doubts about the wisdom of "new-modelling" the army were removed. Nor could there be in the immediate future any real uncertainties remaining about the importance of keeping Cromwell in the army. Moreover, a number of the King's papers were seized with his baggage. By revealing the degree to which he was willing to make concessions to the Irish Catholics in return for their military aid, the papers cast serious doubt on the extent to which the King could be trusted, a factor of some considerable importance in the seemingly interminable negotiations with him for a settlement that were to occupy the years ahead. The contents of the papers were widely spread; they were read in the House of Commons and in the Common Hall of the City and were finally printed.

Cromwell saw in the victory the unmistakable intervention of God once again setting a seal of approval on the parliamentary and, indeed, the Independent cause. This "happy victory," as he was to call it, was "none other than the hand of God." But Cromwell was also aware that aspects of the struggle continued. He thought not only of the military mopping up that was to occupy him for the next twelve months. He also thought of the important question he had raised on a number of occasions, the protection of the religious beliefs of his army and the need to find some sort of state solution that could accommodate them. At the end of his report on the battle to the Speaker of the House of Commons, he indicated his concerns clearly. "Honest men served you faithfully in this action. Sir, they are trusty; I beseech you in the name of God not to discourage them. I wish this action may beget thankfulness and humility in all that are concerned in it. He that ventures his life for the liberty of his country, I wish he trust God for the liberty of his conscience, and you for the liberty he fights for." It was an ominous sign of the tension between Presbyterians and Independents that Parliament chose to excise these words from the text when they had Cromwell's report prepared for circulation. The post-Naseby days did not see a coming together of the nation, but a growth in suspicion between those labeled Presbyterian and those labeled Independent. Cromwell might sing the praises of his men and seek guarantees for them; others saw them as hotheaded sectaries who merited close watching.

The remainder of the war lacked the dramatic decisiveness of Naseby, as pocket after pocket of Royalist resistance was methodically reduced. As the war drew to a close, Cromwell seems to have become increasingly conscious of the need of healing the breaches in the nation, the need to pull the nation together as conclusively in the search for peace as its army had come together in the quest for victory. At times he appeared to see in the disciplined coordination and cooperation of the army a prototype of what the state might achieve. Leicester fell four days after the battle of Naseby; the King fled to Wales while Fairfax made for the West Country to engage Goring. At Langport, Fairfax and Cromwell engaged Goring in battle and defeated him. The battle is of interest in several regards. In the first place, it was one of the very few encounters in the English Civil War in which field artillery played a significant role. In the second place, it affords graphic testimony of the disciplined courage of Cromwell's troops. It is sometimes alleged that the battle success of the New Model is in part illusory because of its care to avoid battle under any conditions other than those which virtually guaranteed it victory. Langport gives the lie to these suggestions, for the critical aspect of the battle involved a cavalry charge up a narrow pass toward positions in which Goring's men were very strongly entrenched. The New Model cavalry carried it off, in Cromwell's words, "with the greatest gallantry imaginable" and "brake them at sword's point." In the end it was an overwhelming parliamentary victory and the fall of Bridgewater to Parliament followed close upon it. "To see this," Cromwell reflected, "is it not to see the face of God!"

In the course of the West Country campaign, Cromwell had to engage one force unlike anything he had yet faced. These were the so-called Clubmen, a rural movement of associations formed to keep armies out of their territory, to put an end to free quarter, and to stop the plunder of their cattle. No doubt some of them had less admirable motives and were merely using the general breakdown of law and order to profit by a fit of plundering themselves. From Parliament's side, they were strongly suspected as a possible

Royalist third force. In reality many of them simply reflected the war-weariness and essential desire for neutrality of many of the country people. Cromwell found that he had to put an end to their activities; the manner in which he did so reveals his awareness that they were not actually a military threat and his determination to act as gently as possible in the hopes of healing the wounds of the nation. At times, it was possible to disperse them peaceably. "I assured them," he wrote to Fairfax, "that it was your great care, not to suffer them in the least to be plundered, and that they should defend themselves from violence, and bring to your army such as did them any wrong, where they should be punished with all severity; upon this, very quietly and peaceably, they marched away to their houses, being very well satisfied and contented." Despite the fact that Cromwell tried consistently, as John Vicars put it, "to appease them without shedding of blood," it was not always possible to do so. At Hambledon Hill near Shaftesbury, the Clubmen refused to disperse and Cromwell was forced to attack. But he only did so after repeated efforts to achieve a peaceful solution, and in dealing with them afterward, he was very restrained. They were, to his mind, "poor silly creatures," against whom it was inappropriate to unleash the full force of his troops.

The major military target in the West was the important port of Bristol. Initially held for the Parliament, it had fallen to Prince Rupert and was one of the key Royalist possessions. The success of Montrose in Scotland on behalf of the King increased the necessity of taking Bristol. In late August, Fairfax and Cromwell assured the citizens of the city that their persons and property would be protected if the city surrendered, and on 10 December, the attack on Bristol began. The actual assault took only a short time. Rupert was accused of surrendering the city without a sufficient fight, as the parliamentary commander had been before him, but it seems clear that his position was untenable, with plague raging within the city and the populace quite turned against him. He did gain honorable terms and managed to march away to Oxford with his forces substantially preserved. Again, Cromwell saw it as a stroke of God that such a major city had surrendered in so short a time. And again in reporting to Parliament, Cromwell took the opportunity to plead for freedom of conscience, by pointing out how those of different opinions cooperated in the army even if they could not seem to at Westminster. "Presbyterians and Independents, all had here the same spirit of faith and prayer; the same pretence and answer; they agree here, know no names of difference; pity it should be otherwise anywhere. All that believe have the real unity which is most glorious because inward and spiritual. . . . As for being united in forms, commonly called uniformity, every Christian will for peace sake study and do as far as conscience will permit. And from brethren, in things of the mind we look for no compulsion, but that of light and reason." Parliament responded as before by omitting from the officially circulated version of the letter Cromwell's comments on religion.

From Bristol, Cromwell moved on to conduct three quick and successful sieges. Devizes fell without loss. Winchester took a week, but it too surrendered after a breach was made in the defenses. "You see," Cromwell reported, "God is not weary in doing you good. . . . His favour to you is as visible, when He comes by His Power upon the hearts of your enemies, making them quit places of strength to you, as when He gives courage to your soldiers to attempt hard things." Cromwell, it should be noted, continued to enforce the strictest discipline on his men; one was put to death for violating the articles of surrender by plundering. The third of the sieges was potentially the most difficult. Basing House, which had been fortified for the King by the Marquess of Winchester, was strongly fortified and had already withstood a number of attacks. The assault on Basing House on 14 October did not last long, but it was a bloody affair, since the Marquess refused to ask for quarter. About three hundred of the garrison (roughly a quarter) were killed and an equal number taken prisoner. Among the dead were six Catholic priests and a woman. Cromwell appears to have relaxed somewhat his usually strict discipline in allowing his soldiers to ransack the house. In the end, the house went up in flames, perhaps the result of an accident. In the circumstances, Cromwell ordered that the house was to be totally slighted. It was not simply a vicious act but was dictated in major part by strategic considerations; with the house already in part destroyed by fire, it made far more sense to garrison Newbury than it did to hold on to Basing House.

Cromwell continued to aid Fairfax with the reduction of the West Country throughout the fall and was back in the field in January, 1646, after a very short spell in winter quarters. The Royalist forces they were fighting were dispirited, for the military situation from their point of view had clearly become hopeless. Clarendon had to confess that these remnants of the once proud Royalist side were a "dissolute, undisciplined, wicked, beaten army." In two months, the campaign for the West was over. Cromwell's chief military action was the surprise of Lord Wentworth's brigade at Bovey Tracy on 9 January; despite the fact that Wentworth and most of his men escaped in the darkness and confusion, four hundred horses were captured and the brigade was wholly scattered. There is a revealing glimpse of Cromwell at Totnes addressing those who now flocked to the parliamentary side, stressing not revenge but pacification and rebuilding: "We are come to set you, if possible, at liberty from your taskmasters, and by settling peace, bring plenty to you again." Cromwell remained with Fairfax until Exeter fell and then went to Parliament to report on conditions in the West. The House had already shown itself appreciative of his work before it duly voted him thanks on 23 April for his "great and faithful services." In December of the previous year, the House had proposed, as part of possible peace negotiations with the King, that Cromwell be granted £2500 a year and be made a baron. That suggestion came to naught, but at the end of January, the House of Commons ordered that lands in Worcester belonging to the Marquess of Worcester be bestowed on Cromwell as a reward and the House of Lords agreed.

Cromwell returned to Fairfax and the army in time for the surrender of the Royalist capital, Oxford. The terms granted at the surrender were lenient and generous, and it is probable that the hand of Cromwell should be seen in this. Again, he was stressing reconciliation, not vengeance. But the political situation added particular point to being generous at this time. Shortly before Fairfax had invested Oxford, the King had escaped in disguise and surrendered himself to the Scottish army at Newark. Given the duplicitous nature of the King and the growing breach between the Scots and the New Model Army, it was a highly dangerous situation and there was great fear that the King, having made an accommodation with the Scots, would use them to curb the sectaries of the New Model. The Scot Robert Baillie suspected that the easy terms were simply part of a strategy to win the people to the New Model in anticipation of further strife with the Scots. "The scurvy, base propositions which Cromwell has given to the malignants of Oxford," he wrote, "have offended many more than his former capitulation of Exeter; all seeing the evident design of these conscientious men to grant the greatest possible conditions to the worst men, that they may be expedited for their northern warfare."

The surrender of Oxford on 24 June 1646 marks the end of the first Civil War. Isolated fortresses continued to hold out; Raglan Castle survived until 19 August and Harlech till March, 1647. But the major fighting was done. It would be a gross exaggeration to assert that Cromwell won the war, but it is impossible to conceive of it being won without him. His spirit and determination had been critical. His willingness to attack those on the parliamentary side who would not prosecute the war fully played a major role in the reshaping of the parliamentary army into a national military force. And the discipline and morale of his own troop provided both an example to and a nucleus of the New Model. His own direct military contribution had been as a cavalry commander. In particular, his ability to keep his troops under command and to regroup them for a second charge provided the essential military differential in several key actions. It was a point fully appreciated by his enemies. Clarendon summed it up succinctly: "Though the King's troops prevailed in the charge and routed those they charged, they never rallied themselves again in order, nor could be brought to make a second charge again the same day . . . whereas Cromwell's troops, if they prevailed, or thought they were beaten and presently routed, rallied again and stood in good order till they received new orders." It was, Clarendon added, something which happened only under Cromwell's leadership; it "had never been notorious under Essex or Waller." Nor should Cromwell's concern with the material side of warfare be slighted. From the very first, he had attempted to ensure that his men were provided with good horses and that the men themselves were well equipped, sensibly provided, and well paid. The appreciation of the logistical sinews of war had as much to do with the success of the New Model as any other factor, and here Cromwell set an early and important model.

After the capitulation of Oxford, Cromwell returned to London to reassume his duties in Parliament. He took a house in Drury Lane, and to it he moved his family from Ely. During the war years, his family had changed in size. His son Oliver, as has been noted, died in the service of the parliamentary army. Two of his daughters married. The long courtship of Bridget by Henry Ireton, who was emerging as Cromwell's most trusted colleague, was crowned by their marriage on 15 June 1646 at Cromwell's headquarters for the siege of Oxford. Elizabeth, Cromwell's favorite daughter, had married half a year earlier, on 13 January,

John Claypole, a Northamptonshire squire; Cromwell was already engaged on the final western campaign and had not been present at the ceremony. In returning to London, Cromwell was well aware he was facing a very tricky political situation. War had ended, but peace terms still had to be negotiated. And there was considerable doubt about what those terms should be. During his visit to Parliament in April, Cromwell had been at pains to stress the importance of cooperation between the army and the Parliament in framing the terms. On 24 April he had received from Ireton a letter indicating that the King might treat privately with the army. Cromwell went out of his way to denounce Ireton in the House for communicating the letter to him privately, a denunciation that carried further point because it was delivered on the very day that the marriage contract with Bridget was signed. He then proceeded to read the letter to the House, to stress that the army would not engage in dealing without the knowledge of Parliament. In June, the situation with respect to a settlement was no clearer; indeed, with the King in the possession of the Scottish army it had become infinitely more complicated. The Royalist Lord Astley, on being captured by parliamentary forces in 1646, is reported to have told his captors, "Gentlemen, you may now sit down and play, for you have done all your work, if you fall not out among yourselves." It was a wry comment, but an accurate one.

❧

FIVE

Parliament vs. the Army

THE PERIOD which stretches from the capitulation of Oxford to the trial of the King in January 1649 is of critical importance in attempting to assess the character and motives of Cromwell. At no other point in his career are his motives more difficult to fathom, his true feelings harder to discern. Equally, at no point was he so consistently attacked from every side. From this period emerges the Cromwell of popular tradition — the devious hypocrite who, having won the war for and with his men, betrayed them as they sought to convert military victory into social, political, and economic justice for themselves and their families, and the bloody, ambitious hypocrite who plotted the downfall of his King by Machiavellian practices that eventually left him as the chief of all. Neither view, the one stemming from left-wing propaganda, the other from the right, does justice to the tortured and tortuous path that Cromwell followed in those difficult months. To be sure, these were months in which Cromwell switched positions on more than one occasion; each time he did so had a decisive impact on the course of the revolution and his own personal fortunes. It is all too easy to ascribe to him some master plan whereby he maneuvered all the elements of the political scene in such a way that his own personal elevation was the only outcome. Yet close examination suggests that this cannot have been the case. His own mood of doubt, disillusion, even confusion was clearly genuine and not a skillful facade displayed to confuse his opponents. Indeed, throughout all of the shifts and changes of these years, Cromwell can be seen to have a consistent aim, the achievement of a settlement to the war that would preserve a maximum degree of unity among the previously contending forces. It must be remembered that, for all the radicalism of his position on religious toleration, Cromwell was inherently a political conservative. He was not inclined to abstract, philosophical discussions of politics; rather he was concerned with practicalities. The war had not been fought, in his mind, to overthrow monarchy, but rather to reform it. Thus there was nothing inconsistent in seeking to negotiate some sort of settlement with the King; he was not now, nor was he ever, a theoretical republican. It was the character of the man who was King rather than the nature of the office which led Cromwell along the road which led eventually to the King's death and the creation of a republic.

Instinctively, too, Cromwell was a parliamentarian. He saw Parliament as the agency which had halted a dangerous trend in royal government, as the authority for which he fought during the weary years of war. Yet commonsense observation told him that Parliament was guided frequently by petty, personal interests, that it contained many who distrusted the army and despised the religious opinions which Cromwell shared with many of his men. It was easy enough for him to conjecture that there were those in the Parliament who would willingly, for various forms of personal guarantees, sell out much of what had been gained since the assembling of that body in 1640. Such considerations led Cromwell to the belief that the army was, in some ways, more representative of the nation than the Parliament was and hence entitled to some say in the final outcome. Cromwell desperately wanted Parliament to do right; it was only when he was convinced that it was in the control of men whose motives were suspect that he was willing to concede force should be used against it. Once he had made that agonizing decision, he acted, characteristically, with speed and vigor.

The charge which has stuck most closely to Cromwell is that he was, in all this complicated maneuvering, a hypocrite. The Cromwell who had raised a godly fighting force where promotion came by merit rather than birth, the general who had protected those of diverse opinions in his army, the commander who had said he hoped to see the end of the nobility, became in the end simply one of the Grandees, indeed the grandest of the lot. He who had defended John Lilburne on more than one occasion turned against him, when Lilburne and his followers began to draw the social and political conclusions that flowed from their actions. In like manner, his enemies charged, he had betrayed both Parliament and King to satisfy his own overweening ambition. "You shall scarce speak to Cromwell about anything, but he will lay his hand upon his breast, elevate his eyes, and call God to record; he will weep, howl, and repent even while he doth smite you under the fifth rib," bewailed a left-wing tract of 1649. A tract of the following year, accusing him of devouring "Kings, Crowns and Powers," made the same point: "He was an Hypocrite born, lived all his life hitherto a knave. . . . He can die his intentions into more colours than the chameleon . . . [and will] justify his pretended innocence to your face, yet hug himself in his deep plots to ruin you." It is perhaps closest to the truth to assert that Cromwell came dangerously near hypocrisy in his conviction of divine leadership. Just as he had seen in his battles the hand of God at work, so he threw the label of divine leadership over his political acts. But the critical point is that he honestly believed this. He did not use divine providence as a screen to deceive others; that would indeed have been hypocrisy. He sought divine guidance to lead himself and, though he may have been deceived, it was a deception practiced with all honesty and upon himself. In examining the record of these years, these are points to be borne in mind.

When he moved to London following the capitulation of Oxford, Cromwell found himself in quite different circumstances than he had known in recent years. From being a military hero, he changed into the status of a more humble civilian. Though he continued to bear the honorary title of lieutenant general, his commission had technically expired in July. He continued to draw some payments from the New Model Army, but these probably were simply to cover up the fact that the income promised him by Parliament was not immediately forthcoming. There are a number of hints in surviving records that the adjustment to the relative obscurity of civilian life came hard to Cromwell. A mood of depression seems to have gripped him. It was expressed as early as August, 1646, in a letter to Fairfax: "Things are not well in Scotland. Would they were in England! We are full of faction and worse." From the end of January until the middle of April, he did not even attend to business in the House of Commons. The outward reason was that he was gravely ill from "an impostume in the head." According to his own testimony, he came near to death; "I received in myself the sentence of death, that I might learn to trust in him that raiseth from the dead, and have no confidence in the flesh." But there is a hint that the illness was at least in part the physical result of Cromwell's depressed mental state. Certainly he seemed to despair of the development of events in England. To Fairfax he noted, "It's a blessed thing to die daily, for what is there in this world to be accounted of." It is hardly, one might note, the expression of an ambitious schemer plotting to take all into his own hands. Once again, he seems to have had thoughts of leaving the country, this time in the service of the Elector Palatine, the Protestant nephew of King Charles. It was a cause that had inherent appeal to Cromwell, for it came at a time when there were efforts being made to exclude the Calvinists from the peace settlement being worked out to end the Thirty Years' War. Perhaps most revealing of all with respect to Cromwell's sense of despondency was a conversation with Edmund Ludlow which appears to have occurred about this time. His comments were a mixture of bitterness and regret — regret that what had started as a unified effort had descended into an unseemly squabble among the victors, bitterness that the loyal service given to Parliament by many during the war years now apparently counted for little in the internecine strife between Presbyterian and Independent. "If thy father were alive, he would let some of them hear what they deserve . . . that it was a miserable thing to serve Parliament, to whom let a man be never so faithful, if one pragmatical fellow amongst them rise up and asperse him, he shall never wipe it off. Whereas, . . . when one serves under a General, he may do as much service and yet be free from all blame and envy."

The situation was indeed such as would discourage a man of Cromwell's temper. On the one hand, the national political situation remained chaotic. On the other, the army which hitherto had been a source of unity was cracking badly as disaffection over a multitude of issues from back pay to political grievances spread. The war, in one sense, had settled nothing; the fighting came to an end without anything approaching a peace settlement having been worked out. The very issues over which the conflict had begun, especially the complex web of relationships between King and Parliament, remained as unsolved as they had been when the King rejected the 19 Propositions and raised his standard at Nottingham. The first postwar attempt at a settlement, the Newcastle Propositions, so-called because Charles was held there by the Scots when they were presented to him, contained little that would appeal to anyone save the Scots and the Presbyterians. The explicit curbing of the King's power, including giving Parliament control of the army for twenty years, was more than the King would accept; the religious provisions, heavy in Presbyterian emphasis, were a threat to the Independents. The King adopted the stance he was to employ throughout all the negotiations — namely, keeping his options open — he responded in very general terms, neither saying yes nor saying no. He had begun a long and devious game of stalling for time, confident in the process that he could break the allies asunder and find support for his own cause, leading to a full restitution of his powers. In retrospect, it is clear that the King never had any genuine intention of making lasting compromises and that he was more than willing to mislead and prevaricate when it met his purposes. Before criticizing too sharply the contortions of those like Cromwell who attempted to treat with him, it is well to recall the spirit in which the King approached such dealings. Because he could not be trusted himself, he was, in the last analysis, a man with whom it was impossible to treat honestly.

In December, the political tangle was somewhat clarified when an agreement was reached with the Scots. After being paid off, their army withdrew across the border, and the King was handed over to Parliament. With a final settlement still being sought, it was agreed he should continue in custody, now at Holdenby Hall in Northamptonshire. With Parliament dominated by the Presbyterians and the King in the control of Parliament, the makings of a Presbyterian settlement of the country were present. What stood in the way was the army. The situation was further complicated by conditions in Ireland. There the position of the King's Lord Lieutenant, Ormond, had become increasingly frustrating and dangerous. While the Civil War had raged in England, the Irish rebellion of 1641 had broadened out into a confused struggle involving no less than five armies. Ormond led the King's official forces; his policy all along had been to secure a peace and cooperation with the Catholic rebels so that he could aid the King in England. The Catholic forces had two armies in the field, that of the Irish Catholic Confederates, led by the Gaelic hero Owen Roe O'Neill, which at least paid lip service to loyalty to the King, and that of the papal legate, Cardinal Rinuccini, which was less openly faithful to the King and more interested in the triumph of Catholicism than in any other single aim. Parliament, too, had its official army there under Sir Charles Coote; its main concern was to prevent Irish aid for the King. Finally, there was a Scottish force under Robert Monro, whose intervention in Ireland stemmed from sympathy with the Presbyterian Scottish planters of Ulster. In 1646, Ormond had managed to conclude a peace with the confederate Irish, only to have it upset by the opposition of Rinuccini. By the end of the year, Ormond judged his position to be untenable; he felt he had only the choice between submitting to either the Irish rebels or the English, and in the thought that the latter would at least preserve Ireland as part of the realm of England, he appealed to the English Parliament for aid in February, 1647.

If the Presbyterian leadership of the House of Commons was watching for God's providences, surely this seemed a sign, for it presented them with the opportunity to deal with the major problem in their way, the army. In theory the army should have been disbanded in October, 1646. In February, 1647, a scheme of disbandment was voted. It represented the intention of scrapping the New Model Army, and with it its dangerous Independent sympathies. While Fairfax was to be retained as general, all the rest of the general officers were to be dismissed and in future, no officer was to be employed who was not in conformity with Presbyterianism. Only 4,000 of the New Model horse were to be retained in England; the rest of the horse and the infantry were to be assigned to the Irish service. Following Ormond's appeal, the

House further voted on 6 March that 12,600 men, to be drawn from the New Model, were to be sent to Ireland and commissioners were sent to the army to encourage enlistment for the Irish service.

These developments took place in an atmosphere of suspicion and fear. In December, Cromwell had written to Fairfax that Royalist sympathy was gaining in London and that there was considerable hostility toward the army and the Independents. "We have had a very long petition from the City: how it strikes at the army and what other aims it has you will see by the contents of it; as also what the prevailing temper is at this present and what is to be expected from men." By March, Cromwell was reporting that the situation was even more grave; "There want not in all places men who have so much malice against the army as besots them. . . . Never were the spirits of men more embittered than now." Despite such feelings, there remained the possibility that had Parliament proceeded with fairness and moderation toward the army, they might have avoided a major political crisis. They did not; pushed on by the hope of curbing once and for all the Independent power base in the army and inspired by Presbyterian loathing of the opinions of the sectaries, Parliament steered a course leading to a military revolt that radically altered the nature of the English Revolution.

That the army had grievances was plain enough. The pay of the foot soldiers was eighteen weeks in arrears and that of the horse forty-three weeks. Not surprisingly, there were strong demands from the army that arrears be taken care of before there was serious talk either of disbanding or of reenlistment for the Irish service. Questions about future pay also needed to be settled, as did the question of a guaranteed indemnity for actions undertaken in the course of prior service. On 21 March, when commissioners from Parliament met with army officers to discuss disbandment at Saffron Walden, where a number of troops had been concentrated for the process of disbandment and reorganization, they were presented with a petition over precisely these points. The reaction of the House to the petition was violent and showed an almost total lack of concern by that body for what were genuine grievances on the part of the army that had served it well. The petition was suppressed, and the fiery Presbyterian Denzil Holles pushed through a resolution which declared any who continued to petition in such fashion to be enemies of the state and disturbers of the public peace. Nor was the army any happier with the proposed leadership of the Irish expedition. The House elected Skippon as field marshal and Sir Edward Massey as lieutenant general of horse. When these arrangements were presented to the army officers at Saffron Walden on 15 April, their answer was "Fairfax and Cromwell and we all go," and the following day the cavalry officers and a number of the infantry officers penned an appeal to Parliament in the same vein. Two further developments within the army caused additional alarm in Westminster. One was the spread among the soldiery of the ideas of the Levellers, a politically radical group which advocated a far broader general participation in politics than England had yet known. Originally a civilian group, the Levellers found willing listeners among the soldiers of the New Model, for they championed the soldiers' grievances and at the same time talked of a political settlement that would apparently give a voice to the common man. While it may be doubted how many in the army fully understood or were committed to the political program of the Levellers, the support of their grievances made them for the moment ready adherents. The second development was the election of representatives — Agents or Agitators — by the regiments to bring pressure on Parliament and to present the case of the army. In April, the horse regiments took this action and in May, the foot regiments followed their example.

The position of Cromwell in this unfolding crisis was a

tricky one and the proper interpretation of his actions is crucial to understanding the man. As the crisis deepened, he was to find himself under attack from both sides. The Presbyterians in Parliament became convinced that Cromwell was playing a hypocritical, double game, assuring them on the one hand that the army would disband, and then behind their backs stirring the army up to revolt. On the other hand, because Cromwell was clearly concerned about the breakdown of discipline in the army and continued to try to find ways of working with Parliament, he came under severe attack by the radicals as well. To compound the difficulty, Cromwell faced the crisis in a weakened condition, being just in the process of recovery from his long illness of the winter.

Neither view is fair to Cromwell. He was not so devious nor so Machiavellian as his detractors thought. He was genuinely caught in the middle and only moved clearly to one side, that of the army, when it seemed the only course left open. He sympathized with the grievances of the soldiers; at the same time he feared what might be the consequences of a Presbyterian-dominated settlement. Yet he was equally concerned, as a political conservative, about the entry of the soldiers into politics and worried lest their struggle with Parliament should topple all recognized authority and produce a state of anarchy.

The situation was not one which lent itself to conciliation and negotiation. The army was too united to be bought off cheaply; the initial parliamentary offer of six weeks' arrears of pay to those who disbanded without going to Ireland came far too late to be of use as a bargaining counter. But the Presbyterian leadership of Parliament itself was too determined to be able to make effective compromises. In May, Cromwell was sent with three other commissioners to Saffron Walden with further concessions, two weeks' additional arrears and a promise of indemnity. His behavior reveals that he was still at that time honestly seeking to preserve unity between the army and Parliament. He made every effort to bring the officers and men into obedience with Parliament: "Truly, gentlemen, it will be very fit for you to have a very great care in making the best use you can both of the votes and of the interest that any of you have in your regiments, to work in them a good opinion of that authority that is both over us and them. If that authority falls to nothing, nothing can follow but confusion." He returned to the House to report to them that the army was "under a deep sense of some sufferings" and the soldiers "much unsettled." Under the influence of that report it seemed for a brief moment as if concessions might be made, and it was agreed that ordinances should be prepared to meet the main demands. But the possibility of conciliation was a total illusion; behind the scenes the Presbyterians had decided to force their way through and had actually hatched plans for bringing in the Scots to create a settlement. On 25 May they proposed a total reversal of the policy of conciliation; the army was to be disbanded at once by a series of separate gatherings so no united resistance could occur and none of the grievances raised by the soldiers through the Agitators was to be addressed.

Fairfax's regiment was to be the first disbanded on 1 June, but by that date the army was in general revolt. Urged on by the Agitators, who told them that "the good of all the kingdom and its preservation is in your hands," the army refused the orders to disband. Instead, Fairfax's council of war ordered a general rendezvous of the army for 3 June; it simply recognized rather than directed the way things were going. "I am forced," Fairfax confessed, "to yield something out of order to keep the army from disorder or worse inconveniences."

With the breach between Parliament and the army an open political fact, the position of the King assumed the greatest importance. The Independent leadership were well aware of the danger that the Presbyterians might seize the King and return him to the Scots, at whose hands he could return to settle the kingdom in alliance with the Scots, the Presbyterians, and English Royalists. It was vital to the Independents' position that they take action to prevent this happening. Discussions revolving around this issue took place at Cromwell's house and at the Star Tavern in Coleman Street. The exact nature of the discussions is not known. What is known is that Cornet Joyce, apparently acting under orders from London, secured the magazine in Oxford on 1 June and on the next day secured the person of the King at Holdenby House. Then, after a frantic appeal for further instructions, Joyce appears to have panicked and decided to move the King closer to the site of the army rendezvous. The seizure of the King by the army was the final action needed to force Cromwell's hand. It is not certain to what extent he was in on the planning of this event; certainly he knew about it, for Joyce had met with him the night before he left for Oxford. But Joyce's decision to carry the King away from Holdenby appears to have been his own, despite his later attempts to pin responsibility on Cromwell. In any case, Cromwell left London in the early morning of 4 June and made for the site of the army rendezvous; the Presbyterians had planned to arrest him the next day when he arrived at the House of Commons.

For all his attempt throughout the spring to negotiate an understanding, Cromwell had now decisively thrown in his lot with the army. This should not be taken to mean he had sympathy with some of the more extreme claims being made by the Agitators and by the Levellers. On the contrary, it seems evident that he threw his lot in with the army in part through a hope to restore order and discipline and to prevent the radicalism of the Levellers from spreading. He was desperately concerned to preserve the unity of the army, especially in the face of the Presbyterian threat. The army had threatened to act without him. Sir Gilbert Pickering, writing nine years later, claimed that Cromwell joined forces with the army only after "the third letter came to you from them, wherein they peremptorily told you that if you would not forthwith, nay presently, come and head them, they would go their own way without you." Once Cromwell had sided with the army, the preservation of its unity became for him a political necessity. Sir John Berkeley sensed the realities of the situation accurately when he noted, "After Cromwell quitted the Parliament, his chief dependence was on the army, which he endeavoured by all means to keep in unity, and if he could not bring it to his sense, he, rather than suffer any division with it, went over himself and carried his friends with him into that way which the army did choose." If there were any constant in the political history of the rest of the revolution, this was it.

The mood of those assembled at the general rendezvous of the army was a combination of the heady enthusiasm out of which revolutions are made and concern by those like Cromwell who sought to restore command and discipline to a potentially anarchic body. The grievances of the soldiers were rehearsed and all present at the rendezvous bound themselves by a solemn engagement not to disband or divide until their rights were secured. The most revolutionary step was the creation of a Council of the Army, which included not only the general officers, but two commissioned officers and two privates from each regiment. It was a risky experiment from the standpoint of Cromwell, but one necessary to give visible form to army unity. Cromwell himself was quick to work for the reestablishment of order through more traditional channels than this representative assembly. Within the council of war, Cromwell was supreme and that body, rather than the Council of the Army, controlled military affairs; within a month, it had successfully bypassed the Council of the Army as the source of real direction. It was an action which again exposed Cromwell to bitter criticism from the Levellers. Lilburne lamented in July, "You have robbed, by your unjust subtlety and shifting tricks, the honest and gallant agitators of all their power and authority, and solely placed it in a thing called a Council of War."

Imbued with its new sense of power and purpose, the army began a cautious advance toward London. Far too late, a terrified Parliament offered conciliation. It promised full payment of arrears and canceled Holles's March resolution calling the petitioners enemies of the state. Such gestures had little impact on any army firmly convinced that those most consistently standing in the way of a just and peaceful settlement were the Presbyterian members of Parliament. To be sure, the army could be cautiously polite to the commissioners from Parliament who came down to meet with them. But they showed no signs of apology for what they had undertaken, and the commissioners left with cries of "Justice, Justice" ringing in their ears. On 10 June, from Royston, the army sent a letter to the City of London. The letter was signed by all the chief officers, but the hand of Cromwell (notably in the insistence that there was no violent result intended and in the stress on toleration) is clearly evident.

From St. Albans on 14 June the army's declaration gave a clearer sense of the political dimension of their demands. It stressed that arbitrary power lay at the root of all political evils and pointedly suggested that such power could be exercised by a Parliament as well as by a single ruler. Hence the present Parliament should be terminated and plans laid for a more truly representative assembly.

As the army turned away from London and fell back to Reading, the army leaders began the process of negotiation with the King they had seized. There is every indication that Cromwell approached the negotiations with sincerity, vigor and a genuine desire to achieve a permanent settlement. It was an impossible task, and it brought criticism and suspicion on him from every side. The Presbyterians feared a settlement made without their influence and possibly at their expense; the army radicals feared that Cromwell was selling them out for personal gain. Above all, it was impossible to negotiate in an open and direct manner with the King, who saw in all these developments only the opportunity to restore himself. Ireton in vexation exclaimed at an early point in the negotiations, "Sir, you have an intention to be an arbitrator between the Parliament and us, and we mean to be it between your Majesty and the Parliament." Despite the obvious difficulties, the initial phase of negotiations went, on the surface, surprisingly well, so well in fact that St. John felt compelled to tell Cromwell he was doing "the King's business" too quickly. Cromwell honestly believed in what he was doing. In July he apparently commented that it was "not only a most wicked, but a very difficult if not an impossible design for a few men, not of the greatest quality, to introduce a popular government against the King and his party, against the Presbyterians, against the nobility and gentry, against the laws established, both civil and ecclesiastical, and against the whole genius of the nation, that had been accustomed for so many years to a monarchical government." The sentiment rings true. Cromwell saw the restoration of the King as a necessary condition for the preservation of order and the protection of property. The King, properly restored, was the appropriate counter to the rumblings of social radicalism coming from among his own troops. "No man," he noted, "could enjoy their lives and estates quietly without the King had his rights." Had the King been a man of more integrity and honesty than was Charles, Cromwell's hopes might have led to a useful settlement. But Charles was seeking aid anywhere he could find it; both he and the Presbyterians were in contact with the Scots — and, for all the honesty of Cromwell's attempted negotiations, they were doomed to failure, even in this period when they seemed to progress most satisfactorily.

The continuance of these exterior threats was very much in the foreground during debates at a general council of war held in Reading on 16 July. There was considerable pressure from within the army for taking decisive action, specifically marching on London to reduce Parliament to their own way of thinking. In the discussion that ensued, Cromwell and Ireton argued for a different sort of course. Cromwell spoke strongly against the use of force; he was deeply troubled by the long-term political implications of the army acting against the House. "Whatsoever we get by a treaty," he said, "it will be firm and durable, it will be conveyed over to posterity. We shall avoid the great objection that lies against us that we have got things of the Parliament by force, and we know what it is to have that stain lie upon us." Parliament, he urged, should be used rather than attacked. Their party was gaining strength in that assembly daily; if it were properly reformed and purged (by getting rid of Holles and the other prominent Presbyterian leaders), Parliament would work for them and the common good. "I do not know that force is to be used except we cannot get what is for the good of the kingdom without it." Again, Cromwell stressed the importance of unity, the concern for which had brought him conclusively to the army's side in the first place. "You may be in the right and I in the wrong, but if we be divided I doubt we shall both be in the wrong." Cool heads prevailed and the march on London was temporarily set aside.

For his part, Ireton had seized the opportunity to move the discussion from the immediate tactic of taking London to a broader consideration of proposals on which a settlement might be based. The upshot was the so-called Heads of the Proposals, a remarkable document constructed at speed and under pressure. The Heads of the Proposals were fated never to receive a fair hearing. Before the King responded to them, the volatile political scene had erupted again. On the one hand, the King was encouraged by what he heard from Scotland with respect to aid from that quarter. On the other hand, London became the scene of political violence. On 21 July, crowds in London pledged to maintain the covenant and demanded that the King be restored on his own terms. Both Houses of Parliament denounced the engagement but on 26 July, a rowdy mob of apprentices and discharged soldiers literally besieged the two Houses, and forced them to restore control of the London militia to a Presbyterian-dominated committee. Two days later the King, encouraged by these developments, turned the army proposals down flat. The overt confidence with which he spurned these proposals alarmed even his own advisers, and from that moment, Cromwell's dedication to treating with the King began to be less noticeable.

In any case, the tumult in London forced Cromwell's attention in another direction. After the stormy mob scenes of 26 July, Parliament adjourned until 30 July. In the interval, the speakers of both Houses and many of the Independent members fled to the army for protection. On 6 August, on the invitation of the borough of Southwark, which provided a modicum of legality for the action, Cromwell and the army led them back in triumph to London to the cry that they were securing a free Parliament. It was a fatal decision, but in some senses it was the logical outcome of Cromwell's siding with the army in June. Now, for all that Cromwell hoped that traditional leadership would continue to operate in the army, the military had clearly elevated itself above the Parliament; the possibility of a civil constitutional settlement, which, given the attitudes of the parties concerned, was never very high, had all but vanished. The ascendancy of the army was reflected in declining attendance at Parliament. By the end of August only 7 peers were attending and the House of Commons rarely numbered above 150. Cromwell was still loath to admit that it was now the army which was dominant and that politics had passed into more forceful hands; in September he was much involved in having Major White expelled from the Army Council for declaring that there was no "visible authority in the kingdom but the power and force of the sword." But

Cromwell had himself been much provoked by the actions of the Presbyterians in Parliament. He commented darkly to Ludlow that "these men will never leave till the Army pulls them out by the ears." The heavily biased *Memoirs* of Denzil Holles are not often to be trusted wholly, but in them there is a sense of the political reality that had settled on England in the late summer of 1647: "The Army now did all, the Parliament was but a cypher, only cried Amen to what the Councils of War had determined. They make themselves an absolute Third Estate, have commissioners residing with them from the Parliament, agents from his Majesty and abuse both sufficiently; as solemnly treated with as if [they were] no subjects, but a body subordinate to neither, vested with an independent authority, claiming only from God and their sword."

Cromwell was, by now, in an extremely awkward position. He felt the necessity to continue the unpromising negotiations with the King, who had now been moved to Hampton Court. At the beginning of September, he got the King to agree to accept the Heads of the Proposals, probably by threatening a reversion on the part of Parliament to the more restrictive terms of the earlier negotiations at Newcastle. The more he persisted in the negotiations, the louder the denunciations from the left, both in the army and outside it, became. Cromwell continued to think that the reestablishment of the monarchy was the surest way to prevent anarchy, but he received little cooperation in his efforts. The King continued to be duplicitous and the danger that he would reach a settlement with the Scots before he did with the English who held him grew steadily. Parliament continued to be impractical and held out for terms on which no settlement could be achieved. While stalemate was achieved at the top, social and political revolution threatened to spread in the army.

The army had interposed its own settlement by entering London, and it was essential for it to maintain unity in the face of all sorts of possible enemies: the King, the Presbyterians, and the Scots. But with the Leveller demands in the army becoming daily more aggressive, this was difficult to do. The publication in October of *The Case of the Army Truly Stated,* which was drawn up under the influence of newly elected Agitators, showed the rift between rankers and Grandees with startling clarity. Alongside the predictable professional grievances, there were broad and radical constitutional demands, including suggestions that the suffrage be greatly extended, that there be biennial Parliaments and that obnoxious taxes of various kinds such as the excise and tithes be abolished. It declared bluntly that "all power is originally and essentially in the whole body of the people." On 20 October, two days after *The Case of the Army* was officially received by Fairfax, Cromwell spoke strongly in the House in favor of monarchy and of a speedy reestablishment of Charles, but the middle ground he was attempting to hold was rapidly slipping away from him. By October, 1647, Levellers had presented to the army commanders a virtual constitutional platform containing this program, the *Agreement of the People.* At the end of October, a general council was held in Putney Church to discuss these demands and to see if it were possible to reconcile the views of the Grandees with those of the Levellers. These discussions, recorded by William Clarke, were one of the dramatic points of the Interregnum and in them it was readily apparent that the dislocation of the Civil War had brought forth a political consciousness and a radical program in the ranks of the army differing markedly from the aims of the men whose actions in 1641–1642 had started the actual fighting. Ireton spoke for Cromwell and the rest of the Grandees when he resisted Leveller arguments for an extension of political rights by stating that no one without "a permanent fixed interest" in the kingdom had a right to partake in the affairs of the nation. The Levellers spoke out boldly, talking of the natural rights of man and of his birthright. But care should be taken to be precise about what the Levellers were advocating at Putney. Many have stated that they were arguing purely and simply for manhood suffrage. But their basic demand, though radical in the eyes of Cromwell and the Grandees, was more restricted; instead of quadrupling the vote, the Leveller demands would have doubled it. Yet even in this program, Cromwell and the officers could see dangers. They exaggerated their case against the Levellers at Putney, as, for example, Ireton did when he charged that the doctrine of natural rights would lead to anarchic communism. But they exaggerated from a real fear. Cromwell may have been in favor of a process that approached democratic promotion in his regiment. He was confident there that he was dealing with an assembly of godly men. But there were sharp limits in his mind to the extent to which democratic principles could be applied in the nation at large, where godly mingled with the ungodly. Though the army radicals themselves stopped far short both of the democracy and of the communism with which they were charged, Cromwell and the Grandees thought they had crossed the narrow dividing line between order and anarchy.

How is one to characterize the role of Cromwell at Putney? Certainly he was in the very center of it, for the meeting was held under his presidency. Then too he had to face a direct personal attack on his efforts so far to seek a settlement for the nation. His "credit and reputation had been much blasted," as he was told directly by one of the Leveller spokesmen, the Agitator Sexby. Cromwell's position in the debate appears consistent with the course he had been following in the previous months, the conservative seeking settlement, agreement, and unity. While doubting the premises on which the Levellers based their arguments, he was wary in dismissing them. "Truly, this paper does contain in it very great alterations of the very government of the kingdom, alterations from that government that it hath been under, I believe I may say almost since it was a nation . . .

and what the consequences of such an alteration as this would be, if there were nothing else to be considered, wise men and godly men ought to consider." Characteristically, he sought God's guidance; when a prayer meeting was called for to start the second day of discussions, Cromwell abjured the Levellers, "I pray God judge between you and us when we do meet, whether we come with engaged spirits to uphold our own resolutions and opinions or whether we shall lay down ourselves to be ruled by Him and that which He shall communicate." While Ireton carried the main brunt of the attack, Cromwell took opportunities to intervene in a calming manner. Throughout the discussions Cromwell displayed one consistent attitude that marked a good deal of his approach to politics. He was essentially a practical man, a man of action. Theoretical schemes had little appeal to him. "It is not enough for us to propose good things"; what they should be concerned with were proposals that would work. He was himself, he admitted, not "wedded and glued to forms of government" which were "but a mortal thing . . . dross and dung in comparison of Christ." He pleaded for consistency with the army's engagements to date and appealed for unity. "Let us be doing, but let us be united in our doing."

For all the arguments advanced by Cromwell and Ireton, the tide in the Army Council was moving against them. On 4 and 5 November, votes in the council passed against their opposition proposing to extend the suffrage to all except servants and beggars and calling for a general rendezvous of the army where it was hoped things would be "settled." In the days that followed, Cromwell won two small but important victories. He got agreement that the Agitators should go back to their regiments until the rendezvous was held, and that there should be separate rendezvous on three different days instead of one mass meeting. The Council of Officers continued to meet, but even there discussion was awkward for Cromwell. In that council on 11 November, Major

Thomas Harrison delivered a violent tirade against the King, calling him "a man of blood" and asking for his prosecution. Cromwell appears to have attempted to calm the discussion, although in the course of it he cautiously admitted that such a judgment might be made "if it be an absolute and indisputable duty for us to do it."

On that same day an event occurred which transformed the political situation; the King escaped from Hampton Court and, while the army did not know where he had gone when they held their rendezvous, he had in fact gone to the Isle of Wight, which was under the command of Cromwell's cousin Robert Hammond. The flight of the King ultimately played so completely into Cromwell's hands that there is inevitable suspicion he had something to do with it. A certain amount of circumstantial evidence would support this conspiracy theory. Clarendon described Cromwell's announcement to the House of Commons that the King was prisoner in the Isle of Wight as being delivered "with so unusual a gaiety that all men concluded that the King was where he wished he should be." It is known that Cromwell had made a visit to the Isle of Wight between 4 and 12 September; no reason has ever been produced for that visit and it is tempting to speculate that it had some connection with the flight of the King. Then, too, Cromwell wrote a letter to his cousin Edward Whalley, who commanded the guard at Hampton Court, intimating that there was a plot to assassinate the King. Since Whalley promptly showed the letter to the King, it has been conjectured that it was a deliberate device to scare the King into bolting. Finally, the escape was planned and carried out with the collaboration of the two men Cromwell and Ireton had been using as intermediaries in the negotiations with the King, Berkeley and Ashburnham. It is possible, given these facts, that Cromwell did encourage the flight of the King. But it is equally clear that he did not control all the details, for both Berkeley and Ashburnham later testified that the details were worked out one at a time in open discussion with the King. If Cromwell had sketched out the broad outlines of the flight, he could count it an extraordinary providence of God (or an equally extraordinary stroke of luck) that everything had fallen in place as it did.

The escape of the King did have a positive impact from Cromwell's point of view on the potentially dangerous rendezvous of the army. When the first of these was held near Ware, Cromwell was able to use the escape as reinforcement for his argument for the necessity of army unity. Two regiments appeared at the rendezvous against orders. After a brief struggle, they were suppressed and one of the leaders, a private named William Arnold, was shot as an example to the others. All the regiments then accepted a remonstrance prepared by Fairfax which promised redress of grievances, called for the dissolution of Parliament and in a very ambiguously worded statement for franchise reform, and criticized the Agitators for causing division in the army. The other two rendezvous passed without incident.

The question of what stance to take toward the King was now of paramount importance. By 26 November, Cromwell had turned as decisively against the King as he had been for him in the negotiations of the summer. Two factors had influenced him. One was the continuing need to maintain unity in the army. Though Cromwell had gained a tactical advantage over the army radicals, he had to accommodate their views, and they warned him that "though they were certainly to perish in the attempt, they would leave nothing unessayed to bring the army to their sense; and if all failed they would make a division in the army and join with any that would assist in the destruction of their opposers." To the practical Cromwell, that left one course open: "If we cannot bring the army to our sense, we must go to theirs." The second factor was equally compelling: by the end of November, Cromwell had finally become convinced of the perfidy and double-dealing of the King. Whether or not the so-called "saddle letter," a letter from the King to the Queen discovered hidden in a saddle and relating how "he thought he should close with the Scots sooner than the others," was what caused Cromwell to desert negotiations with the King is relatively unimportant. The significant fact is that he spoke out strongly against the King in the Army Council on 25 November and carried that attitude into Parliament. In fact, by mid-December the King had reached a secret agreement with the Scots to intervene on his behalf. Even before he rejected Parliament's terms for negotiating (the Four Bills) on 28 December, the mood of the army was one of united opposition to him. At a meeting of the Army Council at Windsor on 21 December, that spirit of united opposition was the most discernible note. The outward show of cordiality between Cromwell and the Levellers was striking and Rainsborough, one of their principal spokesmen at Putney, was nominated for the post of vice-admiral. The attitude toward the King was bitter; it was suggested that he be brought to trial "as a criminal person."

In the House, Cromwell was in the forefront of the battle to secure the passage of the Vote of No Addresses, an agreement that no further discussions should be had with the King. In that debate, Cromwell made his new attitude toward the King abundantly clear; Charles, he stated without qualification, was "so great a dissembler and so false a man that he was not to be trusted." Yet Cromwell does not seem at this point to have repudiated the concept of monarchy. In the House he stated, "Truly, we declared our intentions for monarchy, and they still are so, unless necessity force an alteration." Despite his delivery of what was described as "a severe invective against monarchical government" in the House in February, Cromwell was far from convinced of the suitability of the republican solution being proposed by some. He told Ludlow that he conceded "the desirableness of what was posed but not the feasibleness of it." As late as the end of April, a Royalist sympathizer could report that what Cromwell favored was the deposition of the King in favor of the young Duke of Gloucester. In truth, Cromwell was probably vague about what he did want as he proceeded step by step through the crisis. Ludlow described a dinner party held by Cromwell at this time and went out of his way to comment how evasive Cromwell and his colleagues were about what they wanted; as Ludlow described them, they "kept themselves in the clouds, and would not declare their judgments, either for a monarchical, aristocratical or demo-cratical government, maintaining that any of them might be good in themselves, or for us, according as providence should direct us." The meeting ended in confusion with Cromwell throwing a pillow at Ludlow and Ludlow retaliat-ing as Cromwell raced down the stairs. It might be another case of one of Oliver's bouts of near manic hilarity; probably it only reflects the nervous tension of all those present.

As winter turned into spring with no settlement reached, the situation from the standpoint of the army became in-creasingly worrying. A bad harvest and high prices spawned disorder; a reaction in favor of the King seemed to set in. On 27 March, his Accession Day, there were a number of demonstrations in his favor. In April, the City apprentices rioted and dashed through the streets shouting "Now for King Charles," only to be put down by the cavalry led by Cromwell and Ireton. From north of the border, there was definite news of a Scottish army, while from various counties came calls for a personal treaty with the King and the dis-bandment of the army. In the House itself, many wavered and began to regret the decision to break off negotiations. The Vote of No Addresses was temporarily suspended and actual disbandment proceeded. The Army Council was meet-ing at Windsor when news reached them that their fears had been realized. Helped by the English Royalists, the Scots had seized Berwick and Carlisle. In Wales, a Royalist uprising had occurred in conjunction with the actions of disbanded parliamentary soldiers. The nation was embroiled in war once again. The council had no hesitancy in resolving to subdue the country once again. They added, significantly, that once victory was achieved, the King must be called to account as the author of the troubles.

❦

SIX

The Second Civil War and the Creation of the Republic

AT THE OUTBREAK of the second Civil War, Cromwell was dispatched to South Wales. He returned to the battlefield with several firmly held preconceptions. One was the necessity of taking forceful action to restore technical peace and the possibility of achieving a permanent settlement. The present danger would reunite the godly forces, and he was at pains, in addressing his troops at Gloucester on 8 May, to remind them of their cause and the joint effort they had formerly expended on it. He recalled to their memory how "he had oftentimes ventured his life with them and they with him, against the common enemy of this kingdom . . . and therefore desired them to arm themselves with the same resolution as formerly and so go on with the same courage, faithfulness and fidelity, as sundry times they had done, and upon several desperate attempts and engagements." For his own part, Cromwell pledged "to live and die with them." But it was not solely in a spirit of determination that Cromwell departed for Wales; he was likewise moved by a deep sense of the iniquity of the outbreak. To him, the second Civil War involved something of the nature of a sin, particularly on the part of those insurgents who had earlier been supporters of the Parliament. God had shown his hand in the victories of the army; to turn against them now was to turn openly against God's own dispensation. Finally, Cromwell faced the war with the full realization that Charles I was indeed beyond trust. He may not yet have fully come to the advanced army position that the King was "a man of blood" who should be executed, but he had no doubt that the ultimate responsibility for embroiling the nation once more in civil strife lay on the King.

Even before Cromwell reached Wales, the rebellion there had been effectively checked by the battle of St. Fagans (8 May). Cromwell's military role in Wales became, then, essentially that of mopping up. Only Pembroke Castle, to which the remnants of the Royalist army had withdrawn, offered any real resistance. The terms granted by Cromwell are revealing with respect to his attitude toward the enemy in this second war. To most, his attitude was a generous one; already anticipating the policy he tried to pursue toward former Royalists at a later date, he forbade plundering in the town and tried to show mercy. As Henry Fletcher put it, his aim was "not to be too prodigal of precious blood; knowing that victory to be cheapest which is won without blows." Cromwell did, however, draw a significant distinction between those who had always been Royalists and those who had deserted the parliamentary cause in order to take part in the rising. The latter, he felt, deserved exemplary punishment. They were, in his opinion, doubly iniquitous "because they have sinned against so much light and against so many evidences of divine providence going along with and prospering a righteous cause, in the management of which they themselves had a share." This feeling for vengeance was no passing fancy; in November Cromwell was furious to learn that one of the colonels captured at Pembroke had been allowed to make composition for his punishment and protested that "he apostatized from your cause and quarrel. . . . And how near you were brought to ruin thereby, all men that know anything can tell."

The rising in Wales had been relatively feeble. Elsewhere the situation at times looked more precarious. There was a major rising in Kent in May. Like the Welsh revolt, it was somewhat premature, but it did threaten London. The Kentish rising was made the more serious because the fleet in the Downs also revolted and declared for the King, but Fairfax was able to deal with the threat effectively. At the beginning of June he took Maidstone and shortly thereafter the remaining Royalist rebels were bottled up in Colchester. Here, under Sir Charles Lucas, they did put up a spirited defense and held out until the end of August, but their threat had been broken.

What potentially was a more serious threat was intervention from Scotland. At the beginning of July, shortly before Cromwell secured the surrender of Pembroke Castle, the Scottish army, under the command of the Duke of Hamilton, crossed the border. What might have been a serious threat turned out to be a paper tiger. Hamilton did not have the united support of his own country, where clan rivalries and religious wranglings constantly thwarted united action. The Scottish Presbyterians were badly split between those who would not insist on the King taking the Covenant (the Engagers) and those who would. Veteran campaigners like Leven and Leslie stood aside, along with other opponents of the Scottish regime. The army itself was not half so much the fighting force as the army with which the Scots had entered England in 1644; it was half-trained and contained many raw recruits, the seasoned veterans of the Earl of Leven joining their commander in standing aloof. The army was poorly provisioned, low on ammunition, and badly disciplined. Much depended on cooperation with the English Presbyterians and here Hamilton's task was made even more difficult because English Presbyterians did not fully trust him or his army; their doubts were intensified because of persistent rumors that the Scottish soldiers were to be given English land as a reward for taking part in the campaign. Many of the English Presbyterians likewise distrusted the King, at least on religious grounds, feeling that he ultimately preferred papacy to reformed religion. Finally, the Scottish command structure was noticeably weak. Hamilton's military career had little to recommend it and he was no more a statesman than he was a commander. His second in command, the Earl of Callander, was, at best, a second-rate leader, while his rigid and autocratic temperament was far from what was called for in his position. Perhaps the invasion would have had more force if the King himself had escaped to lead it, but he did not. The limited parliamentary forces in the North under Lambert were able to contain the invaders, though they could not stop Hamilton from joining up his forces with those raised by the English Royalists Langdale and Musgrave.

However, by the time Hamilton had linked up with the native rebels, Cromwell had finished his mopping up in South Wales and was free to act against them. Cromwell's army, it must be admitted, was not in top condition. Their pay was badly in arrears and their equipment in sorry repair. But their discipline remained firm and this stands in great contrast to the Scots. Cromwell's forces, moving from South Wales, covered 260 miles in 27 days and refrained from plundering the countryside in the course of the march. While they were doing so, Hamilton's forces were making a more leisurely advance through Lancashire and had achieved a notorious reputation for plundering and undisciplined conduct. On 12 August, the armies of Cromwell and Lambert joined forces and the following day, Cromwell took the first of two critical decisions affecting the campaign; although the properly cautious move would have been to fall back southward to protect London, he decided to cross from Yorkshire into Lancashire and engage the Scots directly. On the night of 15 August, he took the second key decision.

Having marched into Lancashire, he still had two choices; he could cross to the southern bank of the Ribble and seek to intercept Hamilton somewhere to the south or he could keep to the north bank and engage Hamilton somewhere near Preston. He chose the second course with two main points in mind. First, he was determined to prosecute the war quickly and vigorously; "It was thought," he commented, "that to engage the enemy to fight was our business." Second, he had decided that it was strategically wise to cut off the Scots from their homeland; by attacking from the north, he would drive the enemy south away from potential support and the road back to Scotland. The end result would then be a conclusive one: annihilation of the Scottish army rather than merely its withdrawal back to its native land.

The ensuing battle of Preston, which developed into a running action stretching over several days, is the most difficult of Cromwell's major victories to assess. It turned out to be rather more in the nature of an extended massacre than a real battle. For once, Cromwell faced an almost wholly unworthy foe and the stupidities and blunders of the Scottish army have to be taken into account in estimating the skill with which Cromwell attained victory. The Royalist intelligence proved to be wholly inadequate; as Cromwell and his forces moved rapidly to engage the Scots, the Royalists apparently had no idea at all how near the parliamentary army was nor how great was the danger they were in. Callander's tactical advice throughout the engagement was consistent in its wrongheadedness, and in action Hamilton revealed yet again that his competency, whatever it was, did not lie in soldiering. On the other side of the equation stands the fact that Cromwell's two critical decisions — to cross the Pennines and, having done so, to attack from the north — represented a brave gamble that brought about a decisive battle. And decisive it certainly was, even if Cromwell had been aided by a goodly measure of luck and by incompetence among his opponents. Hamilton's invasion force was shattered and Hamilton himself was captured at Uttoxeter in Staffordshire, while in the South the news of the victory was a critical factor in the decision of Colchester to surrender at last to Fairfax.

As Cromwell and his men turned to move north, there was only one discordant note, but it was an ominous one. The reaction of Parliament to the sweeping victory was hardly consonant with the mood of the army. They showed little open enthusiasm for the result and, on the contrary, proceeded to repeal the Vote of No Addresses and prepared to reopen negotiations with the very man who the army was convinced was responsible for the war. It was an attitude which provoked Cromwell to an outburst of bitterness in a letter of early September to Lord Wharton. "I beseech the Lord make us sensible of this great mercy here, which surely was much more than . . . the House expresseth. . . . Oh, His mercy to the whole society of saints, despised, jeered saints! Let them mock on. Would we were all saints. The best of us are (God knows) poor weak saints, yet saints; if not sheep, yet lambs, and must be fed. We have daily bread and shall have it, in despite of all enemies."

The crushing defeat at Preston had swift political repercussions in Scotland. While Cromwell moved north to Alnwick and summoned Berwick in words that spoke of God's dispensations to his own army and threatened "a second appeal to God, putting ourselves upon him," the forces that Hamilton represented in Scotland (the moderate Engagers) were overthrown. A new government was formed under the influence of Archibald Campbell, the First Marquess of Argyll, an implacable foe of Hamilton. In Ayrshire there were armed risings against the Engagers. To the new men in Scotland, it made greater sense to effect an understanding with Cromwell, who after all had destroyed the army of the Engagers, than to fight a further war with him. Despite the gulf between their strict Presbyterianism and Cromwell's own religious views, they approached Cromwell, and he in reply stressed that common ground did exist, so long as they desisted from attempts to aid the King. "We think," he wrote on 18 September, "one especial end of Providence in permitting the enemies of God and goodness in both kingdoms to rise to that height and exercise such tyranny over His people, was to show the necessity of unity amongst those of both nations. . . . The late glorious dispensation, in giving so happy success against your and our enemies in our victories, may be the foundation of union of the people of God in love and amity."

On 21 September, Cromwell, at the invitation of the new powers in the nation, crossed the border into Scotland. He had high hopes of achieving satisfactory agreement. As he wrote to Fairfax on 2 October, "I hope there is a very good understanding between the honest party of Scotland and us here." On 4 October, he began a three-day visit to Edinburgh, an occasion marked by much outward celebration. His chief aim was to secure immediate guarantees against military intervention on behalf of the King. His position was simple and direct: "Give assurance in the name of the Kingdom of Scotland that you will not admit or suffer any that have been active in or consenting to the . . . engagement against England . . . to be employed in any public place or trust whatsoever. . . . This is the least security I can demand." It was a demand that fitted in well with the desires of Argyll and his followers and by 6 October agreement had been reached on this and on the disbandment of the troops under Monro. In the circumstances, Cromwell must also have had further discussions with Argyll about the future politics of the two nations. What precisely those discussions were cannot be reconstructed; as one contemporary noted, "Whatsoever passed between them cannot be infallibly known." In any case, Cromwell could not have been too certain himself about the future course of events in England. He had been in the field since the outbreak of the second Civil War, cut off from the day-to-day discussions in Parliament. He knew, of course, that the political scene in London was fraught with controversy and contention. The Presbyterian leaders of the House, like Holles, were pushing on negotiations with the King. The King himself doubtless continued his own plotting. The Levellers pushed for their solution, while Sir Henry Vane the Younger continued to press the merits of the army's Heads of the Proposals. All the evidence suggests that Cromwell had not yet made up his mind. It is possible he discussed with Argyll the idea of a settlement in England without the King, but the accusation that he secretly made with the Scottish leader a compact for "the keeping of the King always in prison and so governing without him in both kingdoms" seems most unlikely. Everything about Cromwell's conduct and thoughts in the following weeks indicates that he was far from such a definite decision at this time. He was genuinely in "a waiting posture," waiting, that is, for the providence of the Lord to reveal to him where to turn.

The following weeks were indeed critical ones for the revolution, but they were weeks in which Cromwell was removed from the main focus of events. By 20 October he was back at Durham preparing to finish the military settlement of the North of England. A pocket of Royalist resistance remained at Pontefract in Yorkshire. There, at the request of the York committee, Cromwell and his troops settled down to a leisurely siege. While Cromwell was thus occupied in the North, the political struggle in London reached a crucial turning point.

Cromwell was not alone in being embittered by the second Civil War nor was he the only one worried and upset by the fact that a leading part had been taken by ex-parliamentary soldiers like Colonel Poyer. Many shared his concern that the Royalists and particularly the King, whose intriguing with the Scots had been crucial to the outbreak, had not accepted the lesson of defeat at the end of the first war. The army leadership had cause for wider concerns as well. On the left wing there was renewed Leveller activity calling for deposition of the King, and just as it happened in 1647, left-wing pressure caused the Presbyterians to hasten toward accommodation with their monarch. With key army representation in the House of Commons weakened during the campaign of the second Civil War, Denzil Holles had once again assumed a leading role and pushed anew the old peace policy. With the trickery and deceit of the King so obviously a cause of the fighting then in the process of drawing to a close, this renewal of negotiations with him (the Treaty of Newport) was too much for opinion in the army to take quietly. Parliament looked less and less to be a friend, more and more a part of the political establishment that would have to be altered if a satisfactory settlement were to be found. Increasingly there came calls that the Long Parliament dissolve itself; in addition, more radical demands began to emerge that the army should expel Parliament. And the cry that justice be done on the King and his advisers grew more and more vociferous.

One of the great worries of the army, as Ludlow put it, was "how to secure themselves and the common cause against those counsels that were being carried on in opposition to them under the pretext of making peace with the King." It was to this end that the army drew up a declaration at St. Albans in November, 1648, "showing that the grounds of their first engagement was to bring delinquents to justice, that the King was guilty of the bloodshed in the first and second wars, and that therefore they could not trust him with the government." The Remonstrance of the Army, in its original form, was almost certainly the work of Cromwell's son-in-law Henry Ireton. It appears that in the beginning of November he felt that the time had come to put his draft before the representatives of the army. It is possible that, in a move for army unity, he even urged Fairfax to summon once again the full Council of the Army, though there is no direct proof of this; instead Fairfax summoned a Council of Officers, which met at St. Albans on 7 November.

It was not until three days later that Ireton's draft was laid before the council. Here, because of its drastic and outspoken language, it stirred up considerable opposition. In what appears to have been a direct response to the hostile initial reception of Ireton's draft by the council, a petition from three regiments was presented to Fairfax when the council met on 11 November. Fairfax, who was conservative and inclined to monarchy, stood firm, however, and this seriously compromised Ireton and his followers, for they could not proceed in direct opposition to their own general. A series of conferences ensued which attempted to work out a compromise between the views of Fairfax and those of the soldiers, who insisted that the first thing that should be done was "to cut off the King's head and force and thoroughly purge if not dissolve the Parliament."

On the fifteenth, while Ireton worked with the army Levellers to complete the Remonstrance along the lines of a compromise between the Heads of the Proposals and the Agreement of the People, the Council of Officers made its final overtures to King Charles. On the following day, Charles rejected their offer. By now, however, the King's policy of backhanded balancing and deceitful playing off of one party against another would no longer suffice. On 18 November, the Council of Officers adopted the Remonstrance with only two dissenting votes. On 20 November, it was presented to the House of Commons by Colonel Ewer and some other officers acting on behalf of the whole army. The House, needless to say, was hostile to such military interference, but, even given its negative attitude, its handling of the Remonstrance was far from skillful. It postponed consideration of it for a week, and, when that date came, adjourned the debate until 1 December. It appeared likely that discussion was to be adjourned indefinitely. By the nature of its actions, the House was only succeeding in persuading the army that it would take more forceful action to press its views.

There were at least three possibilities for army action. Parliament could be dissolved forcibly by the army, though most did not favor the use of naked force by the military. Parliament could be purged in some way to eliminate those members who were hostile to the army and too willing to reach an accommodation with the King. Or possibly the army could simply sit tight and hope to convert Parliament to their views when the army officers like Cromwell returned to their seats.

On 5 December a meeting was held at Whitehall at which both officers and members of the House of Commons were present. At the meeting, Ireton and the radical Harrison urged that Parliament be dissolved according to the wishes of the army. They argued that if it were only purged, "it would be but a mock parliament and a mock power." In the end, the meeting adopted a more noncommittal resolution that Parliament had forfeited its trust and that "it was the duty of the army to endeavour to put a stop to such proceedings." A committee was appointed, containing three army officers and three members of Parliament; together they were to decide on a course of action that would put the revolution into effect.

The actions of Parliament at this point were such as to impel the army to drastic steps. The King had been removed by the army from the Isle of Wight to Hurst Castle for safer keeping and on 4 December, Parliament had solemnly voted that this action, which they referred to as insolent, had been done without their consent. Two days earlier they had, despite all, voted to continue negotiations with the King and on 5 December, they decided that the answers of the King to their tentatives were "a ground for the Houses to proceed upon for the settlement of the peace of the kingdom."

On the morning of 6 December without any direct authorization from Fairfax, the army made its most overt interference in the political life of the nation. The approaches to the House were occupied by soldiers and Colonel Pride, with the aid of Lord Grey of Groby, turned aside those members who the army had decided must be purged. The first action of the members who had been permitted to take their places was to send the sergeant at arms to liberate the excluded members, who not only had been denied access to the House but had also been imprisoned in a nearby inn. It is possible that this was done merely for the sake of appearance and that the members of Parliament who had been allowed to sit were content with the action. But there are some indications that a number of the members, perhaps even approaching a majority, acted thus in resentment to army interference in the affairs of the House, however much some of them might have approved of the army's ultimate intentions. An appeal was made to Fairfax for the discharge of the members, but only two of them were liberated. On that same evening Oliver Cromwell arrived in London. He announced, according to Ludlow, that he had not "been acquainted with this design; yet, since it was done, he was glad of it, and would endeavour to maintain it."

What, in fact, had Cromwell been doing in the weeks that had seen this critical intervention develop? Ostensibly, he had been occupied in the North with the siege of Pontefract Castle. Yet he was clearly aware of the shape which discussions were taking. The weeks had been anguished ones for him, as he painfully felt his way toward his own course of action. Some clues exist to chart the evolution of his thinking. Initially, he seems to have been reluctant to accept the position of the army radicals. When Lilburne visited him in the North, he did not find him very sympathetic. Yet at the same time, Cromwell continued to show his persistent concern for army unity; it was partially at his initiative that the discussions were held between the Levellers and the officers on the contents of the Remonstrance. In the first of two revealing letters to his cousin Robert Hammond, written on 6 November, Cromwell reveals himself as a man who had not yet made up his mind on a number of the key issues. Very noticeably, he made no mention of the possibility of putting the King on trial, nor did he specifically reject the Treaty of Newport, then in progress. At the same time, the letter revealed that he was less hostile to the Levellers than Lilburne might have supposed; "how easy to take offence at things called Levellers, and run into an extremity on the other hand, meddling with an accursed thing." Above all, he wrote of the desire for unity, defending his recent discussions with the Scottish Presbyterians on that ground: "I profess to thee I desire from my heart, I have prayed for it, I have waited for the day to see union and right understanding between the godly people (Scots, English, Jews, Gentiles, Presbyterians, Independents, Anabaptists and all)."

By 20 November, Cromwell appears to have moved closer to a resolution on the side of the army demands. As he wrote to Fairfax on that day, "I find a very great sense in the officers of the regiments of the sufferings and the ruin of this poor kingdom and in them all a very great zeal to have impartial justice done upon offenders; and I must confess, I do in all, from my heart, concur with them; and I verily think and am persuaded they are things which God puts into our hearts." His second letter to Hammond on 25 November, is a remarkable document, a sort of a summary of his mental debate with himself, and it reveals that by then he had reached some tentative decisions in favor of the army cause. "We in this Northern Army were in a waiting posture, desiring to see what the Lord would lead us to," he commented to Hammond. Now providence pointed toward action along the lines suggested by the army. "There are cases in which it is lawful to resist," he noted, and if one took the safety of the people to be the supreme law, then the Treaty of Newport was suspect; it would frustrate "the whole fruit of this war . . . and all [would be] most like to turn to what it was, and worse." Above all, he reminded Hammond, as he no doubt had reminded himself, the interventions of the

Lord pointed the way for them. "My dear friend, let us look into providences; surely they mean somewhat. They hang so together; have been so constant, so clear and unclouded. Malice, swoln malice, against God's people, now called Saints, to root out their name; and yet they, by providence, having arms and therein blessed with defence and more."

For all that Cromwell may have reached some sort of decision by this time, he still lingered in the North. Sometime on or shortly before 25 November, he had seen the Remonstrance of the Army and had written to Fairfax, "We have read your declaration here and see in it nothing but what is honest and becoming Christians and honest men to say and offer." He promised to join Fairfax speedily, in fact being expected at Windsor as early as 2 December. Yet he did not arrive until after Pride's Purge was completed on 6 December. It can only have been deliberate. And for that deliberate stalling, one explanation seems most plausible: Cromwell was hoping against hope that Parliament would see the way to purging itself. Cromwell had a deep, lasting, and basic respect for the institution of Parliament. He was very troubled that force was necessary against it. He did not take part in that act of force directly, though surely he knew the directions things were tending; he only accepted it as an accomplished fact when it had happened.

The decision to purge Parliament had only one logical outcome, the trial of the King. In understanding Cromwell's attitude and role in the following weeks, it is important to remember that his initial concern, unlike some of the more radical members of the army, was trial, not necessarily execution. And he was as concerned that others guilty of offenses be brought to the bar as he was that the King be. His son-in-law Ireton had resolved on the King's death earlier, but Cromwell was only gradually to see the inevitability and necessity of it. Bishop Burnet recalled that Ireton "was the person that drove it on, for Cromwell was all the while in some suspense about it." It appears that Cromwell attempted through intermediaries some further discussions with the King in December. On 21 December, a Royalist agent reported that Cromwell was not at one with the radical fringe of the army on the subject of the King's execution. "I have been assured," he wrote, "that Cromwell is retreating from them, his designs and theirs being incompatible as fire and water, they driving at a pure democracy and himself at an oligarchy." As late as the meeting of the Army Council on 25 December, Cromwell still had doubts about the execution. He told those assembled that "there was no policy in taking away his life." But the following day in the House of Commons, Cromwell utterly and finally rejected the King. "When it was first moved in the House of Commons to proceed capitally against the King, Cromwell stood up and told them, that if any man moved this upon design, he should think him the greatest traitor in the world, but since providence and necessity had cast them upon it, he should pray God to bless their councils." Providence and necessity. What had brought Cromwell to this sudden revelation is unclear, perhaps the failure of his approaches to the King. What is clear is that the decision taken, Cromwell bent himself to the task with characteristic single-mindedness and purpose. A special high court of justice to try the King was created by parliamentary acts on 6 January 1649, and when Algernon Sidney protested against the validity of the court, Cromwell's brusque reply was "I tell you we will cut off his head with the crown on it." For all that, Cromwell does appear to have been deeply concerned that there should be a show of legality. To Bradshaw, who was chosen president of the court, the radical Henry Marten, and others, Cromwell pointedly commented, "I desire ye to let us resolve here what answers we shall give the King when he comes before us, for the first question that he will ask us will be by what authority and commission do we try him." The answer that Marten offered was as revolutionary as it was appropriate: "In the name of the Commons and Parliament assembled and all the good people of England."

The trial of the King was more a showpiece than an actual trial, but it was a showpiece that ultimately failed. For all of the attempts to give to the proceedings the trappings of legality, no pretense could disguise the fact that it was a revolutionary act and that only one verdict was possible. Many stayed away from the trial, though some 88 persons nominated to the court did put in an appearance at at least one session. The cautious and moderate Fairfax was among those who stayed away; his wife was not, and when the charge was read against the King, she called out, "It's a lie . . . Oliver Cromwell is a traitor" and had to be hustled from the court. There were other difficulties of a more serious nature to be faced in the course of the trial. On Saturday, 27 January, when Charles was brought to the court to hear the sentence declared, he appealed to be allowed to speak before the Lords and Commons. John Downes, a Member of Parliament for Arundel, attempted to make a speech in favor of what he considered a reasonable request. He was stopped by Cromwell, and when the court withdrew into the Court of Wards to hear Downes present his case, Cromwell turned on him "with a great deal of storm" and swept aside his arguments in favor of the King, dismissing Charles as "the most hard-hearted man that lives upon the earth." As the trial moved toward its inevitable outcome, there appears to have been some difficulty in persuading members of the court to sign the warrant for the execution. Cromwell himself had no qualms; he signed the warrant third after the president of the court, Bradshaw, and Lord Grey of Groby. But others apparently had second thoughts; Clarendon relates how Cromwell and others held Richard Ingoldsby down and forced him to sign. How much faith one should put in such stories of compulsion is hard to tell. After the monarchy was restored in 1660 it obviously was a matter of self-interest to claim that compulsion had been employed. Richard Ingoldsby's signature on the warrant does not betray signs of force, for all that Clarendon and Ingoldsby himself said. But there can be little doubt that Cromwell, in a determined mood, was capable of exercising all sorts of pressure on the waverers. And clearly he was in a determined mood. The accounts suggest he was, in fact, swept along by that frantic sort of exhilaration that took hold of him on more than one occasion before a battle. It was reported that he laughed, smiled, and jeered in the Court of Wards during the confrontation with Downes, while Colonel Ewer related the bizarre story of how Cromwell and Henry Marten had inked each other's faces with their pens like schoolboys after they had signed the warrant. Cromwell's further determination was shown by his rejection of an appeal carried to him by one of his own relatives, Colonel John Cromwell. Presented with the case for saving the King, Oliver's reply was simply that "times were altered, and Providence seemed to dispose things otherwise, that he had prayed and fasted for the King but that no return that way was yet made to him."

Of the King, it must be said that he acted out these final days of his life with a dignity befitting his office. He refused to recognize the competence of his judges and hence refused to plead to the charges. In the accounts of the trial, which were widely circulated, his case had a compelling logic to it, and it became a key ingredient to the myth of the martyr king. The trial which was designed to expose his iniquities to the world at large ironically did more to enhance his reputation than many of the acts of his life. On 30 January, the King went to his death. Historical tradition has long had it that Cromwell came on that night to view the body of the King at Whitehall and that, gazing at the corpse of his former monarch, he sadly commented, "Cruel necessity!" The story rests on a feeble foundation, and does not seem an adequate summary of Cromwell's reaction. Necessity it was, but Cromwell was firmly convinced that providence had brought it to that point. No one could dispute that the execution of the King was a violent act, that it marked a point in the revolution from which no retreat was really possible for its actors, and that it had been carried out, in the last analysis, by a small group of desperate men. Though they claimed to act throughout, in Marten's phrase, "in the name of the Commons and Parliament assembled and all the good people of England," it was truer that they acted in the name of the army and a purged Parliament. But some things must be said in their favor. They were not the first English subjects to dispose of their King and they were at least open in their actions; it was not "done in a corner" but in the view of the world. And given the nature and behavior of the King, it was an action necessary to the preservation of the revolution. By the tortuous diplomacy of the last years of his life, all Charles really created was an unanswerable case for the necessity of his own removal. There is little evidence of remorse on any of the regicides' parts. Even Cromwell, who had honestly sought ways to preserve the King, came in the end to realize the necessity of it all. By the following year he could describe the execution of the King as "the great fruit of the war . . . , the execution of exemplary justice upon the prime leader of all this quarrel." He came to view the manner in which the trial and execution had been conducted as "a way which Christians in after times will mention with honor and tyrants look at with fear." The vast majority of the regicides, in company with Harrison, who had been among the first to call for judgment on "the man of blood," felt that in destroying their King they were obeying a higher mandate than human political convention. "I followed not my own judgment; I did what I did as out of conscience to the Lord," Harrison noted. Cromwell would have concurred wholeheartedly.

The execution of the King began the first of the experiments in government which England was to experience in the next eleven years. In one sense, the particular form which the government took — rule by the Rump — was only an expedient. The Rump itself was a tight little oligarchy, not a representative body in any real sense of the word, and most people probably expected that it would soon put an end to itself in accordance with the persistent demands of both army and civilians. In fact, it was to preserve itself until 1653 and was dissolved at that point only as a result of renewed interference by Cromwell and the army. In a more general sense, though, the new government was seen as a permanent new departure in form. England had destroyed its King in the name of the people. A week later, a further part of the political establishment was attacked by a resolution that the House of Lords was both useless and dangerous. It was not, however, until 19 March 1649 that an act was passed eliminating it. It must be admitted that this was not, by then, a great loss; only a tiny handful of peers continued to attend and of these only two were actively concerned with politics and both of them were quickly elected members of the House of Commons. On 17 March, the monarchy itself was formally abolished and in May the realm of England was by act of Parliament converted into a republic.

The settlement was in many ways cautious rather than radical. This is shown, for example, by the slowness with which the monarchy was abolished and the republic proclaimed. It was also shown by a declaration of the judiciary which maintained that the "fundamental laws" of the country would be protected. The caution of the settlement enabled a number of conservatives to take the oath to the new government without unduly taxing their consciences, but at the same time it was bound to disappoint the doctrinaires, who genuinely desired to make all things new. Neither a republican like Ludlow nor a Leveller like Lilburne could be wholly content with the way things were emerging. In addition, there remained a considerable amount of latent royalism in England. If the people had been unwilling to raise an effort to save their King as he went to the scaffold, many still felt an attachment to royalty and monarchical forms; already there were signs of a veritable cult of the martyr king. In short, the rule of the Rump Parliament rested on a very narrow basis. The new great seal of the republic spoke of "the first year of freedom by God's blessing restored." It was not just Royalists who doubted the appropriateness of those words; from the radical side John Lilburne would soon be writing pamphlets about England's new chains discovered.

Cromwell viewed the changes in government in a pragmatic, not a theoretical, way. Never one to theorize about ideal or utopian states, he sought unity and stability in the state and justified what had been done on thoroughly practical grounds. He appears to have had reservations about the abolition of the House of Lords; his enemies, like Ludlow, attributed such opposition to his own ambition, seeing him as one who curried favor among the peers in order to enhance his own position. Such motivation seems unlikely. Cromwell was later to consider a second House sensible both as an advisory body and as a check on the actions of the House of Commons. It is not unlikely that his views tended in this direction already. When he came to justify the abolition of both the House of Lords and the monarchy, he did so on the grounds that they were acting against the people rather than forwarding their interests. The House of Lords, he noted, was "at that time very forward to give up the people's rights, and obstruct what might save them, and always apt enough to join with kingly interest against the people's liberties." Looking back on the events in 1653, he recalled that "the King's head was not taken off because he was king, nor the lords laid aside because Lords . . . but because they did not perform their trust." His was not the attitude of a doctrinaire republican.

Cromwell played a key role in the new Council of State, which had been granted wide executive powers by act of Parliament; he even acted as its first chairman, though he surrendered that position a month later to John Bradshaw. Likewise, he took an active part in a new High Court of Justice which heard the cases of some of the followers of the King — Hamilton, Lord Capel, the Earl of Holland, Lord Norwich, and Sir John Owen. All were found guilty and three executed; Goring and Owen were reprieved, but it is indicative of Cromwell's attitude toward those whom he viewed as responsible for the second Civil War that he voted for the death penalty. In the first weeks of the new regime, Cromwell appears to have been both optimistic and free from any doubts about the process which had brought it into being. Whitelocke recorded having had dinner on 24 February with Cromwell and Ireton and noted that both men were "extremely well pleased" with the way things had developed. Cromwell conversed at length about the "wonderful observations of God's providence." The renewal by Cromwell of negotiations for the marriage of his son Richard to Dorothy Mayor, broken off in the political confusion of the end of the year, also suggests Cromwell's feeling that normal routines were being restored. But the confident sense that normal times existed could only have lasted for a very short period. From every side danger threatened the republic. The execution of the King had caused a swift reaction throughout Europe, and the Commonwealth was virtually in diplomatic exile. The King's son had been proclaimed Charles II in Scotland as soon as his father was dead. In Ireland, Ormond concluded a treaty with the Irish Catholics in January and Charles II had been invited there to head the Royalist cause. The danger from Ireland was very real, but to raise a force to strike it down created for the Parliament the problems of 1647 all over again. Many of the same army grievances remained — arrears of pay, reluctance to disband, disinclination to volunteer for service in Ireland. And the Levellers, far from content with the new regime, provided a ready focus for such discontentment. It was no wonder that when the Council of Officers discussed the proposed

Irish expedition on 23 March, Cromwell was at pains to warn them not only of the external dangers but particularly of the internal one: "There is more cause of danger from disunion among ourselves than by anything from our enemies." Before Ireland could be faced, the problem of dissidents within the now triumphant army had to be faced.

SEVEN

Ireland and Scotland

IN SOME RESPECTS the political situation in 1649 resembled that of 1647. The situation in Ireland demanded solution; the problem of raising an army to bring about that solution threatened the regime. But there was one key difference between the two years. In 1647, the army discontents assumed particular importance because a number of the officers, Cromwell included, threw in their lot with the rank and file; in 1649, those same army officers were, for all practical purposes, the government and there was hence never any possibility of their backing the left-wing demands in the army. A further difference from 1647 was that there now could be no serious dispute about who should command the Irish expedition. Despite the fact that he was under violent attack from both the left and right, Cromwell was the un-disputed candidate for the position. The position was not a wholly comfortable one for Cromwell. Suspicion of his motives since the trial and execution of the King ran high; both Levellers and Royalists hinted darkly that he aimed at the crown himself, and the press on more than one occasion referred to him openly as "King Oliver." Cromwell also must have been aware that a campaign in Ireland would give his various opponents the chance to unite against him in his absence, while the fact that Ireland had been the graveyard of a steady succession of English reputations could not have been far from his mind.

When he was formally asked by the Army Council on 23 March to take on the generalship, he made his position clear in a cautious statement. He had no doubt about the seriousness of the Irish situation; particularly he drew attention to the upsetting prospect of the English government being overturned on behalf of the King by the intervention of a foreign power. And of such foreign threats, that from the Catholic Irish was to him the most distasteful. "I had rather be overrun with a Cavalierish interest, than a Scotch interest: I had rather be overrun with a Scotch interest, than an Irish interest; and I think of all this is most dangerous. . . . All the world knows their barbarism." Even those who honestly sought the restoration of the monarchy in the person of Charles II could not desire it in such a way. He indicated that if it were the will of God that he should go, certainly he would. On a more practical basis, Cromwell indicated clearly that any expedition which went to Ireland would have to be prepared fully and carefully. Adequacy of supply and pay were, he knew, preconditions of success and he was not prepared to go unless they were taken care of.

Cromwell repeatedly sought the Lord in these trying days. It was perhaps a sign of his uncertainty as to how to proceed. The hostile Presbyterian Clement Walker has preserved a picture of Cromwell in precisely this posture, and for all the bias of the account, it retains credibility. According to Walker, Cromwell was one among a number who were moved on the Sunday after Easter to prayer and sermonizing. "At last the spirit of the Lord called up Oliver Cromwell, who standing a good while with lifted up eyes, as it were in a trance, and his neck a little inclining to one side, as if he had expected Mahomet's Dove to descend and murmur in his ear; and sending forth abundantly the groans of the Spirit, spent an hour in prayer and an hour and a half in a sermon. In his prayer he desired God to take off from him the Government of this mighty people of England, as being too heavy for his shoulders to bear." To Walker, this prayer was "an audacious, ambitious, and hypocritical imitation of Moses," but there is every indication that its sentiments were genuine. Cromwell was to profess repeatedly that he did not seek personal power and glory, that he desired nothing more than a return to his life as a country gentleman. He may have sensed in his heart that it was not, in the conditions of the time, to be, but that does not make the wish any less sincere. The overweening ambition of which he was so often accused does not seem to be a part of his character.

If Cromwell was uncertain about some things, he was resolute about others, notably the danger posed by the Levellers on the left. Only a quarter of a year before, he had written to Hammond that there was no fear of the Levellers. But the growing opposition of this group to the regime when they realized that the aims of the Agreement of the People would not be achieved had made of them enemies to be curbed. Some of the key Leveller leaders, including John Lilburne and Richard Overton, were arrested and brought before the council, on the grounds that the Leveller tract, *England's Chains,* was seditious. Lilburne, listening through the keyhole, heard Cromwell thump the table and exclaim, "I tell you, sir, you have no other way to deal with these men but to break them or they will break you; yea and bring all the guilt of the blood and treasure shed and spent in this kingdom upon your heads and shoulders, and frustrate and make void all that work that, with so many years' industry, toil and pains, you have done, and so render you to all rational men in the world as the most contemptible generation of silly, low-spirited men in the earth to be broken and routed by such a despicable, contemptible generation of men as they are. . . . I tell you again, you are necessitated to break them."

Breaking the Leveller influence in the army was a key part of the preparations for the Irish campaign. The efforts to do so confirmed that Cromwell was correct in his estimate that the Levellers were dangerous enemies. Mutiny broke out in the army, in the first instance led by Robert Lockyer. He was captured and shot, but his funeral was turned into a massive public demonstration of support for the Leveller cause. In May, there were further mutinies in four regiments. The two most serious outbreaks were at Salisbury in Ireton's and Scrope's regiments and at Banbury, where Captain William Thompson led the mutiny in Colonel Reynold's regiment. Cromwell combined conciliation with force in dealing with the threat. He was sympathetic with the soldiers' concern about arrears of pay, even if he had no sympathy for the broader political program contained in the Agreement of the People, a new version of which had recently come from the pen of Lilburne. Fairfax and Cromwell went to the West to cope with the deterioration of control in the army. At Andover, Cromwell won many back to his side with a warm speech in which he assured the soldiers that he would "live and die with them." The main threat of the various risings proved to be relatively easily curbed; the one real danger was Thompson's mutineers, who moved south from Banbury with the intention of joining the Salisbury soldiers. Cromwell apparently first decided to treat with them, sending Major White to them with a message that he and Fairfax "would not follow with force at their heels." He then apparently quickly changed his mind, and by a remarkable march of forty-five miles before midnight, fell on the surprised mutineers at Burford in the middle of the night. A short, confused and futile battle followed, and the mutiny was over. The following day Parliament passed a Treason Act, which gave to that body the powers formerly reserved to the

King in this respect and significantly added to the list of treasonable offenses stirring up mutiny among the troops by a civilian.

The crushing of the Leveller mutiny at Burford was followed by two set pieces, each appropriate in its way. Cromwell and Fairfax went on from Burford to Oxford, where they were splendidly entertained and each awarded an honorory Doctorate of Civil Law. Oxford had been the Royalist capital, and the list of Oxford Royalists is long and distinguished. New men came to predominate there during the revolution, and they too were a noteworthy group. It is appropriate that Oxford, for all its Royalist associations and despite the fact that Archbishop Laud had been its vice-chancellor and one of its most distinguished college presidents, should award such an honor to Cromwell. Cromwell was not a scholar — indeed, he was not a reflective or speculative man — but he did have a deep respect for learning and a keen appreciation of the importance of institutions like Oxford to the nation. In a speech on this occasion, he stressed the importance of learning to the Commonwealth and added that the new masters of the state were determined to encourage it. They were not idle words; he would later give direct and active support to them, both at the university and at the elementary and secondary level. Later, on 7 June, the City of London staged a lavish banquet to celebrate Cromwell's and Fairfax's triumph over the Levellers. It was a gesture of solidarity with the new political dispensation. Inadvertently, it reemphasized the narrow base on which the new settlement rested; the procession from Westminster to the City met with catcalls as well as cheers. But the grace at the banquet suggested what it was all about; it invoked the biblical curse on the man who removed his neighbor's landmark. Whatever else Cromwell, Fairfax and the new government stood for, they embodied in their program one central conservative plank: they stood for the defense of property.

The bulk of Cromwell's time between the suppression of the army mutinies and his actual departure for Ireland was spent in assuring that the expedition would be adequately equipped and financed. Cromwell accepted the command on 30 March; his insistence on proper logistical support delayed his arrival in Dublin until 13 August. It was far from easy to raise the necessary funds; in late June Cromwell, on the authority of Parliament, attempted to raise the sums in the City by guaranteeing them against sums to be raised by the excise. The attempt was not a success. It was only through windfall revenue, from the sale of deans' and chapters' lands and the royal fee-farms, that £30,000 of the estimated £100,000 necessary was raised. Shortly after the beginning of July, Cromwell had his artillery and ammunition shipped to Dublin. It was indicative of the care with which he prepared the campaign that he took so much concern over the artillery; hitherto in the battles he had fought, artillery played, on the whole, an insignificant role. In Ireland, he knew he would be facing a series of sieges, and, characteristically, he determined to assure himself an appropriate upper hand in equipment.

Before Cromwell left London he secured two personal supporters, very different in character, but each important in sustaining his effort. In practical terms, by far the most important convert to the Cromwellian cause was Roger Boyle, Lord Broghill. Broghill was a member of a powerful Anglo-Irish family and a man of diverse genius in his own right. He had originally campaigned for Charles I in Ireland and was in fact on his way to the continent to offer his services to Charles II when Cromwell intercepted him and persuaded him to side with the republic. It was a critical conversion, for Broghill represented precisely the group that needed to be conciliated if the Commonwealth was truly to pacify Ireland. The conversion was also sincere; Broghill became one of the very few men who were truly Cromwell's intimates, with whom he could discuss matters openly, confidentially, and without the trappings of his office standing in the way. Even Cromwell's severest critics acknowledged that he was an almost uncanny judge of men. Dr. George Bate, for example, commented of him that "no man knew more of men; nay, if there was any man in all England that was singular in any act or faculty, he could not be hid from him." Bate also observed that Cromwell "never bestowed a place or office, till first he weighed it exactly in the scales of his own profit, that he might thereby reap considerable advantage to himself." Broghill admirably satisfied both conditions; a man of considerable personal ability, he won as much for Cromwell in Ireland by persuasion as Cromwell was himself to win by the sword. The second important adherent Cromwell drew to his side prior to leaving for Ireland provided support for another side of his character, the side which saw the Irish expedition as a holy crusade. This was the preacher John Owen. They met at Fairfax's house on 19 April, when Owen preached a fiery anti-Catholic sermon; shortly afterward, Cromwell invited him to come on the expedition to Ireland. Owen testified to "the daily spiritual refreshment and support" he gained from Cromwell; there can be little doubt that Cromwell received in turn steady support for his conviction that he was doing God's work in crushing the Catholics in Ireland.

Cromwell departed from London on 11 July and made his way to Bristol and then on to Milford Haven. At the beginning of August, he was still there awaiting the promised funds for the expedition. While he was there, a potentially alarming piece of news broke. In the confused welter of the Irish scene, General Monck had made an understanding with the Gaelic Irish leader Owen Roe O'Neill. In the context it made sense as a device for keeping O'Neill from joining the anti-Commonwealth forces being forged by Ormond. However, Monck was now forced to capitulate to Lord Inchiquin, and the secret agreement became public. It is highly probable that Cromwell had known of and approved the agreement, but in the circumstances of August, it was necessary to disavow any knowledge of it. Monck must take the full blame and, as Cromwell was reported to have written to the Council of State, he "found Monck inclinable to do this." Monck's loyalty in covering up the fact that Cromwell and the Council of State had known of all this in advance preserved the outward appearance of a godly Puritan crusade for Cromwell's expedition. It was a loyalty Cromwell was not to forget and was later to reward.

Just before Cromwell actually sailed for Ireland in mid-August, there came from Dublin news of an extremely encouraging kind. The beleaguered parliamentary forces of Colonel Jones had broken out of Dublin and inflicted a surprising defeat on Ormond's forces at Rathmines. Cromwell could only interpret it as a clear sign from God. "This is an astonishing mercy; so great and seasonable as indeed we are like them that dreamed. What can we say! The Lord fill our souls with thankfulness, that our mouths may be full of His praise — and our lives too." Surely that on which he was embarked had been signaled as a holy crusade.

Cromwell's Irish expedition has remained a blot on his reputation. The campaign was short, sharp, and brutal. The stamp of his mind was well indicated by the speech he made on his arrival in Dublin. "As God had brought him thither in safety, so he doubted not but, by his divine providence, to restore them all to their just liberties and properties; and that all those whose heart's affections were real for the carrying on of the great work against the barbarous and bloodthirsty Irish, and their adherents and confederates, for the propagating of the Gospel of Christ, of the establishing of truth and peace and restoring that bleeding nation to its former happiness and tranquillity, should find favour and protection from the Parliament of England and himself and withal should receive such endowments and gratuities, as should be answerable to their merits." Despite Cromwell's declaration that the soldiers were forbidden to do wrong to "the County People," his message was a clear one.

Several observations need to be made about the circumstances surrounding Cromwell's campaign in Ireland. Such observations may go a long way toward providing an explanation for why he acted in such a violent manner, though explanation, it should be cautioned, is substantially different from justification. A combination of prejudice and hard political realities dictated what he and his troops did; they do not excuse it. In the first place, there was Cromwell's personal attitude. In his views of the Irish he was no better and no worse than the overwhelming majority of his compatriots. The prevailing English view of the Irish stressed their ignorance, crudity, superstition, and barbarity. The powerful myths that had grown up around the 1641 rising had created a dominant desire for revenge, and in seeking that revenge one Irishman was viewed very much as another. Cromwell, too, as has been noted, was convinced he was embarked on a godly crusade against the Catholics. While in England he could extend some form of toleration to Catholics who did not seek to disrupt the regime, the whole nature of recent Irish history seemed to him and to others an unequivocal demonstration of the fact that the profession of Catholicism was, in Ireland, a political act as well as a religious one. There was, for Cromwell, no case for the lenient treatment of Catholicism in Ireland, for the Catholics had already, by repeated acts, demonstrated themselves to be enemies of the godly state. To the Governor of Ross, he wrote: "For that which you mention concerning liberty of conscience, I meddle not with any man's conscience. But if by liberty of conscience you mean a liberty to exercise the mass, I judge it best to use plain dealing, and to let you know, where the Parliament of England have power, that will not be allowed of." In part, he was simply making a statement of fact; the celebration of the mass *was* illegal in

England and wherever the sway of the English Parliament extended. But for the Irish, he was also saying more. Their politics and their religion had become synonymous and where one could not be tolerated, neither could the other. In assessing Cromwell's attitude during the Irish campaign, one must also remember that at this time his conviction that he was acting as the avenging sword of the Lord was conspicuously strong; he was in an almost messianic phase. Whether it was in any way connected with his health is hard to say. At Ross he became very sick and described himself as "crazy" in his health; too much should probably not be made of this, for it was, in all likelihood, the first onslaught of the low malarial fever that was to trouble him later, rather than a psychological condition.

There were solid practical reasons for the nature of his campaign as well. Cromwell was overwhelmingly aware of the fact that the Irish expedition had to be speedy, conclusive, and as cheap as possible. Ireland unsubdued represented a very real, back-door threat to the English republic, and with international opinion decidedly hostile and the continental distractions of the Thirty Years' War ended, it was a back door that needed to be shut both firmly and quickly. Beyond that, the new regime in England, under attack from nearly every side on the domestic front, needed the prestige that came from victory. But that victory would have to be achieved at the least possible cost, since the finances of the republic were clearly precarious (it was already living on hand-to-mouth expedients like the windfall revenue from the sale of deans' and chapters' lands) and it could scarcely in the circumstances risk too much additional burden on the hard-pressed taxpayers. Finally, it must be remembered that Cromwell had his own personal reasons for seeking a quick, decisive solution. In Ireland, he was dangerously cut off from the political maneuvering in London, while Ireland itself had a long standing tradition of ruining the reputation of English adventurers. His own personal position was in constant risk during the Irish campaign, and he must have sensed that some at home who were so anxious for him to lead the expedition secretly hoped that he would become bogged down there.

Cromwell's campaign was conducted both on the field and off it. His prohibition of plundering had been intended in part to lure waverers from Ormond's side and among the Protestant troops at least it appears to have had some success. Likewise his important ally Broghill had as his chief function swinging some of the Protestant landlords to the Cromwellian side, and this policy too had its effect. But it is from the events of the battlefield that Cromwell's Irish campaign is remembered. From Dublin, he advanced north to commence the siege of Drogheda. On 11 September the town was sacked, and a massacre occurred. The garrison, almost to a man, and all priests who were captured were killed. The estimate of those slain ran as high as four thousand, though three thousand is a more likely figure. Cromwell's grim but exulting comment on the slaughter was indicative of his mood: "I am persuaded that this is a righteous judgment of God upon these barbarous wretches, who have imbrued their hands in so much innocent blood." It was a Puritan revenge for 1641. The argument was, on the whole, spurious; there was little, if any, connection between the garrison of Drogheda and the massacres of 1641. In a cooler frame of mind, Cromwell offered two justifications for what he had done. One was purely technical; the rules of war in that time allowed the slaughter of a garrison which refused to surrender when in a hopeless position. The second reason was based on military considerations. Cromwell hoped by this first forceful stroke to terrify the opposition into surrender. "It will tend," he wrote, "to prevent the effusion of blood for the future, which are satisfactory grounds to such actions, which otherwise cannot but work remorse and regret."

The lesson was repeated on 11 October at Wexford. Once again there was a refusal to surrender, and after eight days, the town fell and was sacked. Wexford was a town of unusual importance to Cromwell's forces; not only was it one of the natural landing spots for communication with the continent, but it was also a center for piracy. The reduction of the town was as bloody as what had occurred at Drogheda, yet it happened in a noticeably different manner. At Drogheda, the policy of slaughter had been Cromwell's decision taken in the heat of battle; at Wexford, it appears that his normally well-disciplined troops literally ran amok, and no effort was made to control them. Nearly two thousand troops, priests, and civilians were killed.

The policy of violence had positive short-term military results. Dundalk and Trim, presented with the example of Drogheda, surrendered tamely. From the Royalist side, Ormond commented, "It is not to be imagined how great the terror is that those successes and the power of the rebels have struck into this people. . . . [They] are so stupified, that it is with great difficulty I can persuade them to act anything like men towards their own preservation." The long-term results, in terms of helping to create a lasting hostility to the English, have clearly been less fortunate.

The first campaign swept all before it. Ross surrendered as soon as the walls were breached. Desertions from Ormond's army mounted. In October, Ormond's garrison was expelled from Cork and in November Youghal, Kinsale, and Bandon, along with some smaller centers, came over to the English side. Cromwell campaigned unusually late into the winter with the hope of speedy solution uppermost in his mind. By the beginning of December, when the siege of Waterford was abandoned because of the lateness of the season, the success had been considerable. The coast of Ireland from Londonderry to Cape Clear, with the exception of Waterford, was under Cromwell's control; it was, as Cromwell noted, "a great longitude of land along the shore, yet hath it but little depth into the country." It was a success that had been bought at a high cost. Cromwell reported to

Parliament on 25 November that "A considerable part of your army is fitter for an hospital than the field." Cromwell himself had fallen ill, while Colonel Jones, the victor of Rathmines, had died of sickness.

In the interval between campaigning, Cromwell issued a declaration on 14 January which embodied much of his view of what he was doing. Encouraged by the drift of Protestant settlers to his side and hoping that the ordinary folk of Ireland could be made at least politically subservient to the English regime, he lashed out at the Irish Catholic clergy and those who remained faithful to them. In part he was responding to a convention of the Irish clergy at Clonmacnoise on 4 December which had, in effect, called for a Catholic countercrusade against the English. Cromwell's version of Irish history contained more than a few fanciful elements, but it was probably typical of English feelings. "You say your union is against a common enemy; and to this if you will be talking of union, I will give you some wormwood to bite on, by which it will appear God is not with you. . . . You broke this union! You, unprovoked, put the English to the most unheard-of and most barbarous massacre (without respect of sex or age) that ever the sun beheld. And at a time when Ireland was in perfect peace, and when, through the example of the English industry, through commerce and traffic, that which was in the natives' hands was better to them than if all Ireland had been in their possession and not an Englishman in it. . . . Is God, will God be with you? I am confident he will not."

Cromwell went on to stress that the English invasion stemmed from a desire to avenge the evils that had been done and to spread the benefits of England's godly way of life, rather than from an intention to appropriate Irish lands. "We are come to ask an account of the innocent blood that hath been shed. . . . We come to break the power of a company of lawless rebels. . . . We come (by the assistance of God) to hold forth and maintain the lustre and glory of English liberty in a nation where we have an undoubted right to do it." Irishmen have long had occasion to view Cromwell's declaration as hypocritical. This is hardly surprising in view of the fact that virtually from the outbreak of 1641, money had been raised in England for the subjection of Ireland on the guarantees of Irish land. And the subsequent Cromwellian settlement of Ireland, with its policy of transplantation and expropriation, tended to confirm that the "lustre and glory of English liberty" was not necessarily the most obvious consequence of becoming, in effect, an English colony.

At the end of January, Cromwell was in the field once again. The first phase of his campaign had concentrated on the coastal cities; the second phase involved the reduction of the inland fortresses in Munster that still held out. In this stage of the campaign, Cromwell displayed considerably more charity and mercy than he had shown at Drogheda and Wexford. Fortresses which surrendered were generally treated in relatively generous fashion. At Cahir and Fethard, for example, the clergy were spared, and the former also secured a guarantee against the plunder of the estates and properties of its inhabitants for the future, a guarantee that Cromwell specifically honored five years later when he was Protector. Kilkenny held out longer and did not seek terms until after a second assault had begun, but Cromwell agreed to protect the city from plunder by the soldiers in return for a payment of £2,000 "as a gratuity to his Excellency's army."

By April, only Clonmel, Waterford, and Limerick remained as major strongholds still unsubdued, and the uneasy alliance that Ormond had pulled together was in the process of rapid disintegration. At Clonmel, Cromwell experienced one of the few setbacks in his military career. There a garrison of 1,500 men under the leadership of Hugh O'Neill, the nephew of Owen Roe O'Neill, offered stern resistance. Working in close cooperation with the mayor and the townspeople, they swore "to defend the town to the utmost of their power" and though they ultimately had to surrender it, they made Cromwell pay dearly for it. O'Neill had cleverly constructed massive fortifications within the town walls, forming lanes which served as a cover for his guns. As the Cromwellian forces surged through the breach in the outer wall, they were trapped by O'Neill's main defenses. Unable to retreat because of the press of men behind them, they were slaughtered when O'Neill opened fire. Some two thousand were killed. A second assault produced little better; though the casualties were fewer, Cromwell's forces again had to retreat. O'Neill could not hold the town indefinitely; there was plague in the town and no realistic hope of relief. Having done his service as long as could be expected, he and his men escaped from the town at night. The mayor then treated for terms, which Cromwell granted generously. His generosity was sorely taxed when he discovered, on entering the town, that O'Neill and his men were gone, but it is to his credit that after a momentary outburst of anger, he scrupulously kept to the terms he had promised. It was a victory that brought with it little of the sweetness of success.

Already before he had attacked Clonmel, Cromwell had been under pressure to return to England. As early as 11 January, there had been intimations that he should return to deal with the rapidly deteriorating Scottish situation, but he had chosen to ignore those in order to proceed with his inland campaign. On 9 April, the Council of State ordered him to return, but it took another letter to him before he finally embarked on 26 May. He left the completion of the conquest of Ireland to his subordinates. Ireton remained as president of Munster and commander-in-chief, reducing Waterford in August and the stubborn center of Limerick in June, 1651. Ireton himself did not live to see the conquest finished. He died of fever in November, 1651, literally worn out by his endeavors. Under his successors, Ludlow and Fleetwood, the process of subjugation was brought to a close, the last city to resist, Galway, surrendering in May, 1652.

Though Cromwell had left before the conquest was complete and though the subsequent settlement had been dictated in many of its outlines before he came to power, both conquest and settlement have inevitably been identified in the Irish mind with Cromwell. As the man who stalked that sorry land with Bible in one hand and sword in the other, Cromwell has become an Irish folk ogre. Some of the reputation is clearly justified. The brutality of Drogheda and Wexford may have been dictated by the fact that war is always ugly, particularly so when ideological passions run high. But the "effusion of blood" still appals, and Cromwell's reputation is lessened thereby. Added to this are the evidences of Cromwell's hatred of the Irish Catholic clergy; again, the attitude is explicable in terms of contemporary English prejudice and in terms of the political implications of Catholicism in Ireland, but it is an attitude that remains open to criticism. In assessing Cromwell's role in Ireland, one aspect is all too frequently forgotten, and that is that he did have a vision of what Ireland could be. Cromwell's assertions that he came, in part, on a civilizing mission have been all too frequently dismissed as the rankest hypocrisy, yet there is more than a hint he was thoroughly conscientious when he made them. Not that his vision would have been ultimately acceptable to the Irish; it was wholly within the framework of the paternalistic colonialist. But before Cromwell is dismissed only as a bloody and bigoted conqueror, his words to John Sadler should be recalled. He was writing to Sadler in December, 1649, attempting to persuade him to accept the office of Chief Justice of Munster. "We have a great opportunity to set up, until the Parliament shall otherwise determine, a way of doing justice amongst these poor people, which, for the uprightness and cheapness of it, may exceedingly gain upon them, who have been accustomed to as much injustice, tyranny, and oppression from their landlords, the great men, and those that should have done them right as, I believe, any people in that which we call Christendom." And to Ludlow, Cromwell commented that Ireland was "capable of being governed by such laws as should be found most agreeable to justice, which may be so impartially administered as to be a good precedent even to England itself; where when they once perceive property preserved at an easy and cheap rate in Ireland they will never permit themselves to be so cheated and abused as now they are." Irish historical tradition notwithstanding, there was more to Cromwell than the Puritan fanatic.

Cromwell's return to London provided only a brief respite between campaigns. The understanding he had reached with Argyll was shattered by the trial and execution of the King and, with Ireland now subdued, Scotland had become the great hope for the restoration of the monarchy. That war with England was delayed as long as it was resulted solely from the fact that Charles II found considerable difficulty in effecting an actual agreement with the Scots. Though he was proclaimed the day after the news of the former King's execution reached Edinburgh, it was a proclamation with conditions; he would be placed on the throne after he gave "satisfaction to the Kingdom in those things that concern the security of religion, the union betwixt the Kingdoms, and the good and peace of their Kingdom according to the national covenant and the solemn league and covenant." Thus satisfaction depended on his coming to terms with the Presbyterians. Charles did try to work a Scottish solution without them, but the purely Royalist expedition under Montrose foundered. The only alternative left to him was to sacrifice Montrose and come to terms with the Presbyterians. Montrose was executed in May; on 10 June, Charles sailed for Scotland and took the Covenant just before he landed. It was a painful move for Charles; harassed by the Presbyterians both publicly and privately, he was willing to stick it out only because he saw Scotland as the possible stepping-stone to England. His own feelings about the Presbyterianism to which he was being forced remained cool; Presbyterianism, he remarked, was no religion for a gentleman. And he was facing Presbyterianism in an advanced form; under the terms of the Act of Classes passed the year before, no public office or army post could be held by a person who was not a wholehearted supporter of the Covenant. It was a factor of some importance in his ultimate defeat; intolerance forced a number of able men from the army at a time when he could have used them.

In England, the major problem to be faced was the command of the English expedition. Fairfax remained the commander-in-chief, but he indicated a firm intention not to command any force that would invade Scotland. Cromwell's detractors have argued that Oliver deliberately forced out his commander so that he might take all into his own hands. There is no evidence, only rumor, to support this assertion, and clear evidence that, on the contrary, Cromwell tried hard and sincerely to persuade Fairfax to accept the command. Colonel Hutchinson noted how Cromwell, in his presence, had spent the better part of the night trying to convince Fairfax. Cromwell, too, had misgivings about fighting the Scots; to his mind, there was something disturbingly wrong when two godly nations came to blows, and his whole conduct of the campaign shows that this fact troubled him deeply. But he viewed the situation realistically; the war would occur, and it would be better for England to be on the offensive. As he argued to Fairfax, "that there will be war between us, I fear is unavoidable. Your Excellency will soon determine whether it be better to have this war in the bowels of another country or of our own, and that it will be in one of them I think without scruple." Fairfax's only reply was that probabilities were not sufficient conditions to make war on a neighbor; and he stood by his intention to resign.

It was thus as General of the Forces of the Commonwealth

of England that Cromwell departed from London on 28 June, after the shortest of breaks from active campaigning. Not all his preparations had gone as smoothly as he would have liked. He intended to appoint George Monck, who had served well in Ulster, to a colonelcy in one of the regiments, but the troops rejected him, since their memory of him was as one who had fought on the Royalist side at Nantwich in 1644. Cromwell did not have such scruples; when he found a good man, he was determined to employ him, but a new regiment formed of men from Newcastle and Berwick had to be formed for Monck, while Lambert took over the command originally intended for him.

Cromwell's approach to the Scottish campaign was wholly different from the attitude in which he had faced Ireland. There he had a mission and he fought what he considered a holy war. Against fellow Protestants he could not have the same feeling and he was reluctant to force the issue to arms if it could be settled in words. He later commented that "since we came in Scotland, it hath been our desire and longing to have avoided blood in this business." In his first declaration to the Scots he sought at length to explain the English position and to express his warm feelings for the godly among the Scots. Only at the end did he indicate that if it came to war, he would not be found wanting. "To the truth of this let the God of Heaven . . . judge of us when we come to meet our enemies in the field, if through the perverseness of any in authority with you, God shall please us to order the decision of this controversy by the sword." Even his private correspondence reveals his uneasiness about the situation in which he found himself. Writing to Richard Mayor, he exclaimed with evident anguish, "I need pity. I know what I feel. Great place and business in the world is not worth the looking after; I should have no comfort . . . but that my hope is in the Lord's presence. I have not sought these things; truly I have been called unto them by the Lord." The explanation for the difference between his attitudes toward Scotland and Ireland was to be found in one simple fact; as he himself put it, "God hath a people here fearing his name, though deceived." It was not a sentiment he could have expressed about Ireland.

Cromwell's concern that his army should not plunder was clearly connected with the same attitude, yet it had military logic behind it as well. It was important to Cromwell that the country people not be turned wholly against him; if the Scots under Leslie chose to fight essentially a guerrilla war, such a situation would be difficult in the extreme. Cromwell was at pains to remind the Scots of the discipline of his forces on their previous incursion. "What injury or wrong did we then do, either to the persons, houses, or goods of any? Whose ox have we taken?"

The initial stages of the campaign were immensely frustrating to the English. Despite the numerical superiority of his forces, Leslie had a keen sense of their inadequacies. They were badly trained and the religious purges had removed many of the most hardened veterans. Leslie thus decided on a strategy that would evade a major confrontation. He counted on sickness and lack of supply to defeat his enemy, rather than armed might. Throughout the summer he followed this strategy in masterly fashion; Fleetwood wrote with evident irritation at the end of August about "the impossibility of our forcing them to fight — the passes being so many and so great that as soon as we go on the one side, they go over the other." Cromwell advanced to bombard Edinburgh, but even that would not draw the Scots to the field. Frustrated in his desires and in need of supplies, Cromwell fell back east to the port of Dunbar. Leslie with an army of 23,000 men followed him, and there on 3 September Cromwell fought the most impressive battle of his career. Cromwell's position on the day before the battle appeared desperate. The English army, stricken by sickness and worn out by campaigning, had only about 11,000 men capable of fighting. The massive Scottish army had drawn itself up in a position of great natural strength on Doon Hill overlooking the English camp. Cromwell clearly recognized the danger; in a letter of 2 September, he noted, "I would not make it public, lest danger should accrue thereby." Yet there remains the possibility that Cromwell had deliberately placed himself in this position in order to draw Leslie out to fight. Leslie himself was certainly working on the assumption that Cromwell was preparing to ship his men out; that Cromwell ever contemplated such a course seems unlikely from his temperament and from the position such a defeat would have put him in politically. The fact that he sent for the artillery expert Richard Deane to join him at Dunbar also stands against such an interpretation. And Cromwell's own resolute faith in God's support remained firm. In the same letter in which he admitted the English position was precarious, he still displayed the confidence that stemmed from this unshakeable conviction. "Our spirits are comfortable (praised be the Lord) though our present condition be as it is. And indeed we have much hope in the Lord, of whose mercy we have had large experience."

So long as the Scottish troops remained on Doon Hill, the situation was a standoff. The Scottish guns could not reach the English; the English were clearly in no position to attack. On Monday, just after Cromwell had finished praying for guidance with his officers, it was noticed that the Scots were leaving their commanding position and coming down to the lower ground. To Cromwell, it was yet another clear sign from God: "God is delivering them into our hands; they are coming down to us." The decision to move had not been made by Leslie, but by the Committee of Estates, yet there is reason to believe that Leslie did not disagree with it. With the harvest approaching, he had cause to worry that his forces would shrink as men slipped off home. And in any case, he appears to have underestimated Cromwell's actual strength, believing that he had already shipped half his men and all his great guns.

If Cromwell's victory was made possible by the ill-fated descent of the Scots from Doon Hill, his own acute observation of the disposition of the Scottish forces played a major role in his success. He noted that the Scottish deployment had crowded their right wing of horse on the edge of the sea, leaving them little ground for maneuver. Likewise he noted that there were several openings along their stretched-out line. A daring plan was conceived that involved crossing six cavalry regiments and three and one half foot regiments over the stream and glen that bisected the battlefield. Accomplished at night and totally without the knowledge of the Scots, the maneuver is a striking example of the disciplined control of Cromwell's army. The battle the next morning, at a critical juncture of which Cromwell threw his own regiment into one of the gaps he had noted in the Scottish line, was an utter rout. Whitelocke graphically put it that "the Scots were driven like turkeys by the English soldiers." Three thousand were killed, ten thousand taken prisoner. Before the battle, Cromwell had seemingly been in a tense mood; one report recalled him riding through the regiments on the night of 2 September "biting his lips till the blood ran down his chin without his perceiving it." During the battle, that near-manic excitement which seemed to catch hold of him in such moments was much in evidence: "he did laugh so excessively as if he had been drunk, and his eyes sparkled with spirits." Afterwards, characteristically, he ascribed success to God. Dunbar was, he wrote, "one of the most signal mercies God hath done for England, and His people, this war."

Dunbar did not end Scottish resistance. Leslie escaped to Stirling, there to raise another force, albeit a much smaller one. The King too was still in arms, while others escaped to the West to try to raise resistance there. But if religion had divided and weakened the Scots before Dunbar, it did so doubly afterward. The convinced Presbyterian was as likely to read God's hand into events as Cromwell was, and the message of Dunbar was unmistakable. Many of the stricter Covenanters saw in it the message that they had been unduly lax in the matter of Charles II and the Covenant. The split between those who felt this way (the Remonstrants) and those of milder conviction who still sought alliance with the King (the Resolutioners) increasingly divided Scotland, and provided Cromwell with ample opportunity to win people to his side by propaganda. Cromwell moved on to Edinburgh on 7 September, though the castle there was not to surrender to him until December. Through disputation and discussion, Cromwell sought to persuade the Scots to his way of thinking, arguing that since God had favored the English at Dunbar, he must also favor their looser form of religion. He defended the Independent position vigorously, responding to criticism of lay preaching by the retort "Are you troubled that Christ is preached? Is preaching so exclusively your function? . . . Your pretended fear lest error should step in is like the man who would keep all the wine out of the country lest men should be drunk. It will be found an unjust and unwise jealousy to deny a man the liberty he hath by nature upon a supposition he may abuse it. When he doth abuse it, judge." What Cromwell was trying to do, as Whitelocke put it, was "to win them by fair means rather than to punish them." And his cajoling was remarkably successful; many of the extreme Presbyterians were persuaded to a position of neutrality, some to cooperation.

Not all could be done by persuasion, though much was. In December Lambert was able to defeat the Resolutioners of the Southwest, who remained impervious to Cromwell's overtures. The King was officially crowned on 1 January at Scone, and continued to attract support for his cause, for all Cromwell's work. In February Cromwell determined to attack the main center of Royalist activity, the kingdom of Fife, but now the impact of almost incessant campaigning caught up with him, and he fell seriously ill. Rumor spread that he was actually dead, much to the delight of backers of the

Royalist cause. In May, he was suffering from the torment of a stone as well as from persistent fever. By early June he had recovered, but it had apparently been a near-run thing.

Cromwell's sickness inevitably delayed the Scottish campaign. He was acutely conscious of pushing it on in order to avoid stretching the war into another winter and causing the English Parliament an expenditure it could not afford thereby. Indeed, his attempt to return to campaigning before he was well caused more than one relapse. But in August he had pushed as far north as Perth. He had embarked on a calculated policy to bring the war to a conclusion. By pushing north, he had left the road to England open; it is clear that he did it deliberately to draw out the Royalist forces for a final battle before winter closed in again. He wrote to the Speaker explaining what he had done. "I do apprehend that if he [Leslie] goes for England, being some few days march before us, it will trouble some men's thoughts" but "we have done to the best of our judgments, knowing that if some issue were not put to this business, it would occasion another winter's war, to the ruin of your soldiery."

On 5 August, Leslie crossed the English border. The King was naïvely hopeful of gathering support on his march south, but little actually materialized. The memory of the last invading army from Scotland lingered, and enthusiasm for his cause was noticeably lacking. As other forces gathered to resist the King's advance, Cromwell, by a remarkable march down the East and across the Midlands, blocked the road to London and pushed the Royalist army deeper into the trap. On 22 August, the exhausted Royalist army, numbering only about 16,000, had entered Worcester. By 27 August, Cromwell and Fleetwood were only some fifteen miles away with a vastly superior force. On 3 September, exactly a year after the great victory at Dunbar, Cromwell engaged the King; there is more than a suspicion that he delayed his final attack so that it would coincide with that auspicious anniversary. The battle itself showed Cromwell at his best as a field commander. Admittedly, his forces vastly outnumbered those of his foes, but the conduct of the battle was exemplary, and involved a high degree of coordination, discipline, and skill, particularly in the deployment of two bridges of boats to replace bridges destroyed by the besieged Royalists. Cromwell, in the heat of battle, showed great personal bravery and leadership. One witness recalled that "my Lord General did exceedingly hazard himself, riding up and down in the midst of the fire; riding himself in person to the enemy's foot to offer them quarter, whereto they returned no answer but shot." In the end, an overwhelming victory was achieved. The Royalist forces were wholly defeated and routed; the King himself, after a series of romantic adventures, escaped to the continent, where he was to remain until the Restoration. "The dimensions of this mercy are above my thoughts," Cromwell wrote. "It is, for aught I know, a crowning mercy." For Scotland, it meant the end of independence. Monck finished off the Scottish resistance. Stirling fell on 14 August, the Committee of Estates was seized at Alyth on 28 August, thus eliminating the government. Dundee was taken on 1 September. In May, 1652, Dunottar Castle, the last stronghold still in arms, capitulated.

For Cromwell, it was his last appearance in arms, and a fitting climax to an extraordinary military career that placed him among the greatest commanders of history. He had grown weary in the conflict. From Dunbar he had written his wife, "I grow an old man and feel infirmities of age marvellously stealing upon me." A newsletter commented slightly later in a similar vein, "My lord is not sensible he is grown an old man." But there was to be little rest, even though the fighting was done. The task of "settling and healing" remained. Cromwell had reminded the Speaker of the House of this after Dunbar. "Curb the proud and the insolent, such as would disturb the tranquility of England though under what specious pretences soever; relieve the oppressed, hear the groans of poor prisoners in England; be pleased to reform the abuses of all professions, and if there be any one that makes many poor to make a few rich, that suits not a commonwealth." After Worcester, the Genoese agent reported to his government, "The generalissimo will do what he pleases." As the country turned to the problems of settlement, Cromwell was to discover that, in many ways, this was not to be so.

EIGHT

The End of the Commonwealth

WHAT IT WAS that Cromwell truly wanted in the years immediately after Worcester is not always immediately apparent. His great victory had earned him £4,000 a year from a grateful Parliament and Hampton Court as a residence. His entry into London on 12 September could only be called triumphal, and at least one of his close associates, Hugh Peters, went so far as to suggest to a friend that Cromwell would make himself King. Yet others saw nothing in his behavior to indicate that he was thinking such ambitious thoughts. In October, the Tuscan resident commented that "there cannot be discovered in him any ambition save for the public good," and even Whitelocke, who was soon to become suspicious of Cromwell's intentions, remarked that "he carried himself with great affability and in his discourses about Worcester would seldom mention anything of himself, but mentioned others only, and gave, as was due, the glory of the action to God." In truth, the position of Cromwell in the two years after 1651 contained much that was paradoxical. He was viewed, and rightly so, as the most powerful single person in the country. As Captain General of the

Army, member of Parliament, and member of the Council of State, he stood visibly in a position of authority. Some indication of his prestige is given by the fact that in 1651 and 1652 he was the first choice in reelections to the Council of State. But for all the trappings of power, his position was not unlike what it had been at the end of the first Civil War, for he did not, in fact, control policy and was forced into an uneasy course of trying to balance and mediate between ultimately antagonistic bodies, army radicals and parliamentary conservatives. At the same time, he was uncertain what role he should play; the workings of God's providence were more difficult to discern in the world of politics than they had been on the field of battle. There can be little doubt that Cromwell felt the burden keenly and that it was the compulsion of perceived duty rather than naked ambition that motivated his actions in these critical months. "I am a poor weak creature . . . yet accepted to serve the Lord and His people. Indeed . . . you know not me, my weaknesses, my inordinate passions, my unskillfulness, and every way unfitness to my work. Yet, yet the Lord, who will have mercy on whom he will, does as you see."

Cromwell himself had frequently indicated an agenda of reform, notably of the law and of the church. The central problem was to find some basis of unity from which reform could proceed, and in this respect, the political settlement was central. In essence, the government of the Commonwealth was a provisional one. There had been calls for a dissolution and the election of a new Parliament in the late 1640s. After Worcester, such calls were revived with increasing stridency. Yet the problem was far from simple. If, on the one hand, those of a more progressive character feared that members of the Rump would find ways to perpetuate themselves in office, it was equally true that genuinely free elections on a wider franchise raised the possibility of a house dominated by enemies of the revolution — by Presbyterians, Royalists and neuters. Cromwell took an active part in the discussions of a more permanent political settlement. When the issue of dissolution was debated on 12 September 1651, he was added to the committee to consider an election; for all his efforts, little was achieved, beyond setting a date three years in the future (3 November 1654) for a new Parliament. Cromwell did not confine his efforts to find a political settlement to activity in Parliament. He appears to have spent considerable time in informal discussions, seeking that political program which would achieve the maximum degree of unity possible. Typical of Cromwell's efforts was the meeting of M.P.'s and army officers called at Speaker Lenthall's house in December, 1651. At the meeting, Cromwell argued strongly for the need to come to a settlement of the nation. The nub of the question was what sort of settlement; as Cromwell put it, "Indeed it is my meaning that we should consider whether a republic or a mixed monarchical government will be best to be settled; and if anything monarchical, then in whom that power should be placed." The division of opinion at the meeting reveals the extent of the problem. The lawyers present inclined to some form of monarchical government. Sir Thomas Widdrington, for example, not only argued that a "mixed monarchical" form would be best but suggested that one of the sons of Charles I, the Duke of Gloucester, should be chosen for the role. The army officers were inclined to a more radical solution; Desborough asked pointedly, "Why may not this as well as other nations be governed in the way of a republic?" Cromwell's own position appears to have been somewhere in the middle. Though a firm believer in parliamentary government, he was not, any more than he had been in the late 1640s, a theoretical republican. His pragmatic sense of politics suggested to him the need for a strong executive power in the state, yet even though he was willing to consider the use of Gloucester, he had considerable doubt about the wisdom and feasibility of a return to the Stuart line. He agreed that "a settlement of somewhat with monarchical power in it" would be the most sound solution, but he did not choose to elaborate on the nature of that mixture. At the same time, he agreed with the position of the army that a new Parliament was a political necessity. But as a believer in Parliament, he wanted that change to come from Parliament itself. "I pressed the Parliament as a member to period themselves, once and again and again, and ten, nay twenty times over."

For all the discussions, the political problem remained intractable and the sought-for unity elusive. In 1652, Cromwell expressed the dilemma clearly in a conversation with Whitelocke; the problem, he said, was "how to make good our station, to improve the mercies and successes which God hath given us, and not to be fooled out of them again, nor to be broken in pieces by our own particular jarrings and animosities one against another, but to unite our counsels." Such perceptions were leading Cromwell into uncomfortable patterns of thought. On the one hand, the Parliament he had helped to create by Pride's Purge was not, in his mind, equal to the task facing it. Conservative by nature and unwilling to get on with the business of needed reform, it was at the same time unwilling to put an end to itself and help in the search for alternative settlements. He confessed to Whitelocke, "There is little hopes of a good settlement to be made by them, really there is not. . . . We all forget God, and God will forget us, and give us up to confusion." Indeed, some form of restraint on this particular parliament was becoming, to Cromwell's way of seeing things, increasingly necessary. "Some course must be thought on to curb and restrain them, or we shall be ruined by them." On the other hand, it looked increasingly as if there would have to be, once again, a resort to direct action, and in the absence of consensus, such action might have to be taken by a single powerful person. "What if a man should take upon him to be King?" Cromwell asked Whitelocke. It was not intended to be a rhetorical question, though it does not prove that Cromwell's ambition had led him to dream of a crown. Yet the question had been posed, and that, in itself, is indicative. As always, Cromwell was seeking the hand of God in the events around him. The longer settlement was postponed, the longer Parliament remained stubbornly unreformed, the more it became plausible to consider that God intended a different kind of settlement. To Cromwell, the great victories of the war could not be regarded as meaningless; as uncomfortable as it may have been to his innate political feelings, he had begun to sense a divine plan that would thrust on him a kind of personal power he did not directly seek. Indicative of his changing attitude was his comment to a group of London clergy who, in 1653, were discussing the possible dissolution of the Rump. The prominent divine Edmund Calamy told Cromwell bluntly that the public would not tolerate forceful action in this regard. "There will be nine in ten against you." Cromwell's answer was, "But what if I should disarm the nine, and put the sword into the tenth man's hand; would that not do the business?" That he framed his answer in the form of a question may suggest his mind was not made up on the issue, but the tone of the exchange reveals a growing willingness to consider forcing reform by means as arbitrary as any used by the Stuart kings. The exchange highlights the political dilemma that troubled the rest of Cromwell's political career. Seeking admirable ends by unpalatable means did not rest easily on Cromwell's conscience; the burden that he felt God was placing upon him was a heavy one, and his protestations about it cannot be written off as the cynical utterances of a crafty and ambitious politician. For Cromwell, the only solace in such a situation was the conviction that God's will was working its inexorable way. But justification by personal success, which faith in God's providence could all too easily become, was a dangerous attitude to assume as well.

One aspect of political settlement that seemed abundantly clear to Cromwell was that reconciliation should be reached, as far as possible, with the defeated Royalists. He felt strongly that some form of pardon for the acts done in the prior decade must be passed in order to heal the deep wounds in the country. Yet even here he was unable to persuade a sufficient number of M.P.'s to achieve what he saw as necessary. An act was passed in February, 1652, but it had been so mangled by exceptions and restrictions that it did not serve effectively the aim of reconciliation. Throughout the debates, Cromwell fought the restrictions. It is a comment on the political situation that what he saw as political expediency, others saw as part of a sinister plan to further his own interests. To Ludlow, Cromwell's actions were only undertaken "that so he might fortify himself by the addition of new friends for the carrying on his designs."

Two other major areas of concern — the church and the law — also cried out for reform and in both areas Cromwell was again to feel frustration. Cromwell felt strongly about both matters; as Ludlow recalled, "it was his intention to contribute the utmost of his endeavours to make a thorough reformation of the clergy and law." In making such a statement, he was cognizant of the entrenched interests which would resist reformation of any kind. "The sons of Zeruiah are yet too strong for us, and we cannot mention the reformation of the law but they presently cry out we design to destroy property; whereas the law as it is now constituted serves only to maintain the lawyers and to encourage the rich to oppress the poor."

That there was a considerable need for law reform cannot be doubted. Cromwell's protestations on the subject are only a minute part of a vast torrent of criticism aimed at the legal system and the legal profession. To be fair to the Rump, it must be acknowledged that much time was spent in the discussion of law reform, but such discussion led to very little in the way of concrete action. While it seems clear that Cromwell's concept of reform was more limited than that of a number of critics (he tended, for example, to think more often in terms of reform of procedure than he did in terms of reform of content), he can have felt only disappointment and frustration as a result of this lack of action. And the political circumstances causing that lack of action must have been profoundly disturbing to him. It is probably true that the major factor inhibiting reform through parliamentary action was the number of lawyers in the House who had vested interests to protect, but the situation was further complicated by the general hostility between the army and Parliament, especially in the post-Worcester period. The whole issue of law reform became part and parcel of the struggle between the military and the civil authorities; while army pressure could at times force the House to take specific actions, it also tended to provoke an attitude of determined resistance. Recent research has demonstrated that, despite its sanctioning of the execution of the King, the Rump was not inherently a radical body. Its capacity to perceive sensible measures of reform as radical attacks on the position of the landed classes because they were backed by the army is graphic testimony of that body's incapacity to serve the reforming role that Cromwell hoped for it.

The question of church reform was equally unsettling. To make a complicated story simple, Parliament had abolished the traditional system of episcopacy without replacing it by another form of national church government. In a few areas voluntary associations of clergymen on the Presbyterians' model had emerged, but the Presbyterian system decided on in 1648 was never firmly established. Widely differing opinions about what form a settlement should take divided the country sharply. Argument focused around two issues — the degree of toleration to be allowed and the system for supporting the clergy financially. Both were issues which deeply concerned Cromwell.

In February, 1652, a committee headed by John Owen, once Cromwell's chaplain in Ireland and now through his patronage vice-chancellor of Oxford, presented to Parliament a scheme for the settlement of the church. In the debates on the scheme, Cromwell indicated his position on the two key issues clearly. Owen's scheme called for a national church settlement with limited dissent. Two sets of commissioners were to be set up: Triers, who functioned as a local committee to oversee the fitness of candidates seeking to be admitted as preachers, and Ejectors, itinerant national commissioners who would eject unfit ministers and schoolmasters. On the issue of toleration, Owen proposed that it should extend to all who were not opponents of the essential principles of Christianity; he and his colleagues produced a set of fifteen fundamentals which they took to constitute those essential principles. On the basis of those principles Presbyterians and Independents were comfortably included, but the more radical sects such as the Fifth Monarchists would be placed outside the limits of toleration. To such an attitude, Cromwell took strong exception. He pressed for a wider and more liberal definition of Christianity and a policy of public tolerance. In a blunt and telling statement he indicated how far ahead of the time he was on the issue of religious toleration. "I had rather that Mahometanism were permitted amongst us, than that one of God's children should be persecuted." While it was not a total and general toleration of which Cromwell spoke, it was an advanced position in 1652.

On the issue of tithes, Cromwell was no less ambiguous, though in this case, he inclined to the more conservative position. The agitation over tithes had a considerable aura of irrationality to it, in that many felt an assault on tithes was the first step toward an assault on the institution of private property. For those laymen who held impropriated tithes in their own hands that was a compelling argument. There was also the more practical problem of how the clergy were to be supported if maintenance by tithes was abolished; radical suggestions that the clergy should labor for their own support had little appeal in traditionally minded circles. At the end of April, Cromwell appears to have been among those who voted for the retention of tithes at least until such time as another method of supporting the clergy could be found. The decision caused considerable displeasure among the more radical sectaries, but it is interesting to note that Cromwell did not sign the August, 1652, Declaration of the Army, which contained, among other items, a call for the abolition of tithes.

Though one of Cromwell's reactions to the proposed religious settlement could be called radical in the context of the time and the other conservative, they were linked by a common characteristic, pragmatism. It was, in Cromwell's view, necessary for the state to seek means to allow the citizens to live in peace, so long as they were in turn peaceful in their actions toward the state. It was a necessary part of the healing process, as well as the foundation of a sound commonwealth. Such an attitude argued for minimal interferences with the private consciences of the citizens so long as they were not obstructive to the functioning of the state. In like manner, the association of tithe abolition with the advanced sects and the fear that it might lead to a general dislocation of law and order inclined Cromwell to favor retention of the system for the present. In any case, the clergy needed to be supported, and, in the absence of an alternative scheme which did not seem to him socially disruptive, Cromwell was led to favor retention of tithes as the only practical course.

While there was little hope for genuine reform and settlement in the manner Cromwell contemplated, what slight hope there was was further set back by international developments. In one sense, Cromwell's actions had a profound influence on foreign relations; his victories over the Royalists had made the infant republic a power to be considered. In 1649, England had been an isolated upstart; by 1652, as a result of Cromwell's efforts on land and Blake's at sea, the Commonwealth had indicated that incurring its enmity involved an element of risk. Something approaching a broad settlement had been reached by the Treaty of Westphalia, which ended the Thirty Years' War in 1648, but the two great continental powers France and Spain continued their struggles with each other. Each sought the aid of England, and in 1651, it appeared that Spain had the greater chance of gaining the initiative. It had recognized the Commonwealth in December, 1650, and had allowed Blake's fleet the use of Spanish ports; France, on the other hand, had withheld recognition and sheltered Rupert's fleet. In addition, though Spain was traditionally associated in the English view with the horrors of the Inquisition, there were many in England who could find in 1651 greater reasons to object to France on religious and political grounds. The Huguenots of southern France were under considerable pressure and the revolt of the Fronde was easily interpreted by enthusiastic republicans in England as a struggle by their political brothers in arms against the growing power of a centralizing monarchy. Beyond that, it was in France that the exiled Royalists gathered around their defeated leader Charles.

Many expected Cromwell to emerge as the gallant leader of a Protestant and republican offensive. Certainly this was what Marvell expected of him when he hailed his return from Ireland by conjuring up images that Cromwell would soon be a Caesar to Gaul and a Hannibal to Italy, and one contemporary recalled that Cromwell commented that were he ten years younger "there was not a king in Europe he would not make to tremble." In fact, Cromwell was not, at this time, in a position to control foreign policy, nor, had he been so, were his inclinations entirely in accord with these ambitious schemes. At the most enthusiastic of times, Cromwell was a conservative revolutionary, and he showed little interest, on the whole, for using England's newfound military might as a weapon for spreading republicanism or, for that matter, Protestantism throughout the European world. His approach to foreign policy tended to be hardheaded and practical rather than doctrinaire; in that, it resembled his approach to domestic politics, and it seems clear that Cromwell had a keen sense of the interaction of the two, well before he was in a position to control effectively the workings of either. That is not to say that his idea of foreign policy was entirely single-minded or without contradiction. In theory, at least, his general concern for the Protestant cause could conflict with his practical calculations of what was to England's political and commercial advantages. In practice, a shrewd assessment of what was practical and useful tended to overrule what was ideologically consistent.

As Cromwell viewed the evolution of foreign policy in the period after the formation of the Commonwealth, there was much to dismay him, however much he was pleased by the new stature given England through the demonstration of its military capacity. Although the situation seemed favorable to a Spanish alliance, Cromwell, virtually from the first, inclined toward an understanding with the French. As his policy developed, he would come to have more carefully thought out reasons for this stance, but from the start, he seems to have displayed the traditional English hostility to the Spaniard. In this, if in nothing else, he reflected, however unconsciously, his sense of the Elizabethan heritage. But there were more concrete, less theoretical, concerns on his mind as well. He always responded sympathetically to the plight of oppressed Protestants, and the case of the French Huguenots was no exception, yet he quickly convinced himself that the English capacity for aiding them would be greater through an understanding with the French monarchy (or by using them as a bargaining lever in reaching such an agreement) than it would be through armed intervention on their behalf. Furthermore, in viewing the French situation, Cromwell was quick to revive another Elizabethan aim, the gaining of a foothold on the continent, specifically Dunkirk. In 1652, it looked as if this might come about, for the French were sorely pressed to retain it and might well have preferred to have it in English rather than Spanish hands.

French unwillingness to meet the English terms added to a continued refusal to recognize officially the republic caused such schemes to crumble; in the last analysis it was Blake's attack on a French squadron sent to bring supplies to Dunkirk that made possible the Spanish capture of the fortress in September, 1652. The action taught the intended lesson; in December, France granted formal recognition to the new English state.

Cromwell had disagreement with these aspects of Rump foreign policy, but they were not ultimately unbreachable differences. Rumper policy toward the United Provinces of the Netherlands had the potential to be quite a different matter. Up until October, 1650, relations between the Commonwealth and the United Provinces were strained by the fact that the stadtholder William II, who exercised considerable political influence, had married Mary, the daughter of Charles I. Whatever political affinity might have existed naturally between Dutch and English republicans was thus, to a considerable extent, neutralized. With the rising ascendancy of the republicans in the Netherlands after William's death in that month, better relations became, in theory, possible. Such a joining of interests appealed strongly to Cromwell. The mutuality of religion and government, coupled with the close association of the two nations in the Elizabethan period, argued to his mind for a close partnership. But such was not to be. The 1651 mission of Strickland and St. John to the Hague to seek "a more strict and intimate alliance and union" was a hopeless failure. Hopes for some form of political union were probably no more than an illusion, but, in any case, close workings between the two nations were fundamentally frustrated by their rival economic positions. Coreligionists and fellow republicans that they were, the United Provinces were also England's chief commercial rival, and through their dominant position in the European carrying trade, especially in the Baltic, they posed more than a casual threat.

The Rump's answer to the breakdown in negotiations was the passage of the Navigation Act in 1651, an attempt to bar the Dutch from commerce in the English colonies, to cut into their profitable fishing trade, and to damage their position with respect to the European carrying trade. The emergent economic nationalism which it reflected was not repugnant to Cromwell; he had a keen sense of the importance of England's trade, but the fact that its main thrust was anti-Dutch was disturbing to him. Two strong but potentially contradictory assumptions which he held were now in conflict. On religious grounds, the United Provinces were a desirable, indeed an indicated, ally. On economic grounds, they were, if not enemies, at least rivals. The act was not in itself a *casus belli,* but actions which flowed from the attitudes that led to its passage, notably the English claim to the right of seizing French goods carried in Dutch ships, were. In May, 1652, following an engagement between Blake and the Dutch admiral Tromp, the two nations were at war. It was an anguishing situation for Cromwell on at least two levels. As an exercise in the conduct of foreign relations, it seemed to him lacking in proper direction. As he commented to members of the Dutch congregation in London, "I do not like the war. . . . I will do everything in my power to bring about peace." He matched his words with actions which, however futile, were at least consistent in their direction. At virtually any point when terms were sought, Cromwell was prominently a member of the peace party. Although inevitably he acquiesced in the conduct of the war, he was persistently troubled by the feeling that it was unwise to be at war with one's potential Protestant allies. It was a concern that was to linger with him when he was in a position to direct foreign policy himself.

Cromwell had a second, and even more direct, reason for objecting to the Dutch war. Not only did it give the Rump another excuse for postponing its dissolution, it caused a complete halt to the movement for reform. In addition, the heavy cost of the war placed the government of the Rump under considerable strain. Already in the precarious position and to a considerable extent maintaining its financial viability by the windfall revenue provided by confiscation and sales, the Rump had to abandon the policy of reconciliation which Cromwell had considered so important for the healing of the nation and resort anew to the policy of confiscation in order to provide for the maintenance of the navy. The blatant injustice of the new confiscations both saddened and angered Cromwell. He commented later that "poor men, under this arbitrary power, were driven like flocks of sheep by forty in a morning to the confiscation of goods and estates, without any man being able to give a reason why two of them should forfeit a shilling."

The sense of frustration mounted rapidly, not only among the army radicals but also with Cromwell himself. "I will not say that they were come to an utter inability of working reformation, although I could say that in one thing — the Reformation of the law. . . . It was a thing we had many good words spoken for, but we know now that many months together were not enough to pass over one word called 'incumbrances.' " To Whitelocke, Cromwell was even more pessimistic. "My lord, there is little hope of a good settlement to be made by them, really there is not." In August, 1652, the army officers presented Parliament with a long list of reforms, demanding "speedy and effectual" actions on these; only Cromwell's insistence had kept from the list a demand for an immediate dissolution of Parliament. By October, the officers and some members of Parliament were meeting regularly to seek a solution. Cromwell recalled his desire in those meetings to achieve a parliamentary solution. "I believe . . . we had at least ten or twelve meetings, most humbly begging and beseeching of them that by their own means they would bring forth those good things that had been promised and expected; that so it might appear that they did not do them by any suggestion from the army, but from their own ingenuity: so tender were we to preserve them in the reputation of the people." Doubtless there is an element of self-justification in Cromwell's recollection of his motives, but, on the whole, he does seem to have tried, nearly to the end, to achieve some sort of parliamentary solution that would cover the naked fact of revolution with constitutional decency. His anguish in 1653 is the pendant to his search for settlement in 1648. What he was gradually being forced to see was that a Parliament traditional and free enough to provide the respectability he desired would not undertake the revolutionary task of reform. He had helped to shape the Rump with the twin causes of constitutionality and reform in mind; he now found that concern for the former had made of the Rump a decidedly nonreform-minded body and that he was asking it to do the impossible. The logic of that situation pushed him inexorably toward the solution he was willing to discuss but reluctant to act on, the further application of nonconstitutional force and the projecting of himself from a position of influence to a position of personal power.

The last days of the Rump Parliament are clouded in confusion. Parliament, alarmed by the rising tide of radical criticism, did turn to the discussion of a bill for a new representative. According to the traditional account of events, the Rumpers converted the bill from one for a new representative to a scheme for perpetuating themselves in power through recruiting the House. This became the official story, and the dissolution of the Rump was publicly justified by Cromwell and others on that ground. Yet it seems clear that this is not at all what had happened. In fact, as the events unfolded the protagonists in the struggle changed their positions sharply. The Rump, which had long resisted dissolution and fresh elections appears to have been converted to the idea that it was precisely that course which would now best serve their purposes. The army, which had pushed this course in the past, became increasingly concerned about its ultimate outcome, fearing that new elections would lead to a parliament of neuters who would undo the revolution. Cromwell, at some point in the spring of 1653, changed his mind too and found himself in opposition to the bill for a new representative which he had so long favored.

How had these confusing shifts of position come about? And how was it that Cromwell and the officers were able to pass off a misleading account of the occurrence which confused historians for generations? As far as the Rump itself is concerned, it seems apparent that they always intended at some point there would be fresh elections. Yet they were reluctant to have such elections until such time as the power of the army had been sharply curbed. Only in this way would it have been possible to achieve the civilian constitutional settlement they deeply desired. By January, 1653, however, it had become clear that the Rump would have to dissolve before the power of the army was reduced. Faced with that realization, they abandoned the recruiting schemes, which had indeed been under discussion, and proceeded with a bill for a new Parliament. There is every indication that they knew that in doing so, they were placing the Commonwealth itself in jeopardy. But their commitment to the government created by Pride's Purge was minimal and, as the most thorough modern scholar of the Rump has indicated, what they were plotting in April, 1653, was not the continuation of their own authority but the undoing of Pride's Purge. It is probable that the Rump would not have moved to this position without the heavy pressure exerted on it by the army. But once the pressure became irresistible, they were willing to gloss over their own internal differences and contemplate a major counterrevolutionary move in order to make the settlement their own rather than the army's.

Cromwell's change of heart, which led to the extraordinary scene on 20 April when he dismissed the Parliament, is more difficult to chart. As was frequently the case before he made major decisions, he had withdrawn into a semi-isolated position in the spring of 1653. He was notably absent both from the Council of State and from Parliament itself. His continued search for some middle ground that would combine respect for parliamentary forms with the impulse for reform left him increasingly cut off. Cromwell did not need the entreaties of the radicals to make him disillusioned with the Rump. His concept of reform had always been a moderate one, but even it had been too much for the Rump to accept; to that side of Cromwell which placed godly reformation first, the Rump could only have seemed a disastrous failure. From the other side, his concern for parliamentary forms strained his relations with the army radicals, and just as had been the case in the late 1640s, his concern for the unity of the army became a major factor in his actions.

On Wednesday, 13 April, the bill for a new representative was discussed for the last time in Parliament; it was intended that a final consideration should be given to it a week later, on 20 April. On the night of 19 April, Cromwell summoned a conference of army officers and M.P.'s to his lodgings to discuss what would happen the next day. At this point he was still seeking a compromise of some sort. Army opposition to the proposed bill, under which Parliament would adjourn for six months and then reassemble on 3 November to give way to the new Parliament, was very marked. The army wanted a definitive dissolution; otherwise, they feared the Rump would find means in the interval to secure the election of a House thoroughly opposed to the army's intentions. The Rump, for its part, knew that immediate dissolution would mean whatever Parliament was subsequently assembled would be screened and controlled by the army. Since feelings ran high on both sides, there was little chance of real understanding being reached at the conference, yet Cromwell felt his way toward what he saw as the beginnings of compromise. It was suggested that there be a dissolution and that the government should be left in the hands of a commission of about forty until the elections were held. "We desired," Cromwell recalled, "they would devolve the trust over to persons of honor and integrity that were well known, men well affected to religion and the interest of the nation." If agreement was not reached on this solution, at least an understanding was achieved, in Cromwell's mind, that the proposal would be discussed further before definitive action were taken. "And upon this we had great satisfaction and had hope, if our expedient would receive a loving debate, that the next day we should have some such issue as would have given satisfaction to all."

The next day, 20 April 1653, proved to be far different from Cromwell's hopes. Although Cromwell had, as late as the evening before, still sought a compromise which would reconcile his desire to preserve parliamentary form with his concern for reform, he had, even then, abandoned his desire for immediate elections because he feared an influx of neuters and Presbyterians into Parliament. When he discovered the next morning that the compromise had broken down, and that the House was proceeding with the discussion of the bill, his hand was forced and he had to choose between one or the other.

Cromwell was meeting with army officers in his lodgings on the morning of 20 April when the news reached him. It is quite probable that he believed the Rump had revived the scheme of recruiting the House and was debating that, but he did not need even this erroneous assumption to be appalled at what was going on. The Rump had broken its word and by doing so had finally, to Cromwell's view, revealed its own base nature, its concern to preserve itself. "We could not believe it that such persons would be so unworthy." The suddenness of Cromwell's decision and the ferocity with which he acted can be traced at least in part to a deep personal feeling that he had been betrayed. Cromwell rushed from his lodgings to the House. For a quarter of an hour or so, he sat in his place, listening to the debate, and then as the speaker was about to put the question, he turned to Harrison and whispered, "This is the time I must do it." Apparently, he began his intervention in a relatively controlled manner; Sidney recorded that "at the first and for a good while, he spoke to the commendation of Parliament, for their pains and care of the public good," but as he got to the heart of the message, his manner changed abruptly. Whitelocke wrote of his speaking in "a furious manner," while Ludlow indicated that he kicked the ground, shouted, and acted "with so much passion and discomposure of mind as if he had been distracted." His measured tones gave way to violent attacks, as he indicated various members were corrupt, unjust, drunkards, and whoremasters. "Perhaps you think this is not parliamentary language. I confess it is not, neither are you to expect any such from me," he cried out in his rage. When a member of the House, Peter Wentworth, attempted to object, Cromwell's answer was blunt. "You are no Parliament, I say you are no Parliament. I will put an end to your setting." He then cried out to Harrison, "Call them in," and Harrison summoned in Lieutenant Colonel Worsley, the commander of Cromwell's regiment of foot, with five or six files of musketeers. The final acts were quickly done. The Speaker was pulled from his chair and led away; spying the Speaker's mace, the symbol of his authority, Cromwell wryly asked, "What shall we do with this bauble?" and turning to the soldiers said, "Here take it away." Grasping the bill for the new representative himself, Cromwell turned on the astonished members left in the House. "It's you that have forced me to do this, for I have sought the Lord night and day, that he would rather slay me than put me upon the doing of this work." And so saying, he rushed from the House. He had been there only about half an hour, but it had been one of the most bitterly decisive incidents of his life.

On leaving the House, Cromwell hurried to tell the officers who had not been present what had happened. To them, he argued it had been an unpremeditated action. One contemporary recalled Cromwell's telling the officer that "when he went to the house, he intended not to do it; but the spirit was so upon him, that he was overruled by it; and he consulted not with flesh and blood at all." In one sense, this was no doubt true; the accounts of Cromwell's behavior in the House on the morning of 20 April suggest that, in his fury, he moved well beyond rational political calculation. The mood that came over him had the same near manic quality that had appeared at similar moments of stress. In another sense, it was not an accurate statement, for his actions of that morning were the working out of a long, agonizing and bitter conflict within himself. He had reached the point in the revolution to which he had not wanted to come. Constitutional niceties and godly reformation were no longer compatible and he had to choose between the two. The revolutionary settlement could not survive without the army and he needed to preserve its unity. It was in the language of the radicals that he steeled himself to this decisive act, and he carried it through in a moment of extreme passion. But the feeling behind his bitter parting words to the House — "It's you that have forced me to do this" — was genuine. He had not sought to play this role; he convinced himself that circumstances led him to it. The experience of the Rump did not eradicate Cromwell's faith in parliamentary forms; he would summon other assemblies with a high hope they would be able to transcend the limitations he had found in the Rump. In each case he would be disappointed. From 20 April, Cromwell's relationship to the revolution became increasingly ambiguous. As a realist, he knew what the political situation was and what he was called on to do. As an idealist, he was appalled by the means he had to use to achieve ends he thought were not just good, but godly. If Cromwell was to become bitter and disillusioned, the seeds of that attitude were well planted by April, 1653.

The Council of State remained the one other body of any legitimacy other than naked force, but without Parliament, it could not stand. In the afternoon, Cromwell came to the Council Chamber, where some councillors had gathered in defiance of the actions of the morning. To them Cromwell stated, "Gentlemen, if you are met here as private persons, you shall not be disturbed; but if as a Council of State, this is no place for you; and since you can't but know what was done at the House in the morning, so take notice that the Parliament is dissolved." The answer of Serjeant Bradshaw was direct, dignified, and pointed. "Sir, we have heard what you did in the House this morning, and before many hours all England will hear it; but, sir, you are mistaken to think that the Parliament is dissolved; for no powers under heaven can dissolve them but themselves; therefore take you notice of that." The protest was futile; there was a force, the army, that could dissolve Parliament. Cromwell knew it all too well; despite inclinations in the opposite direction, he had accepted the realities of the situation to make possible what he thought was a greater good. Shortly after the remarkable events of 20 April, Dorothy Osborne wrote in words that conjured up the confused world in which the Long Parliament had first assembled: "If Mr. Pym were alive again, I wonder what he would think of these proceedings and whether this would appear as great a breach of the privilege of Parliament as the demanding of the five members." As one of those who supported Pym when the Long Parliament met in 1640, Cromwell would have understood the question all too well. It expressed the tragic irony with which he would henceforth live; to achieve the ends that the godly hoped for, the means of the monarchical enemy had to be used. It was not a reality that made for peace of mind.

NINE

The Rule of the Saints

IF CROMWELL was himself troubled by the action that brought an end to the Rump Parliament, the country reacted differently. Whatever its intentions had been, the Rump had succeeded in making itself so unpopular that its passing was received with general relief. Cromwell later recalled, "There was not so much as the barking of a dog or any general or visible repining at it." The sense of general relief, however, barely disguised the continuing political problem; the deep divisions within the revolution persisted and what the future was to be remained wholly uncertain.

The Rump Parliament had, in the last analysis, been brought down by an uncomfortable alliance between persons whose political aspirations were ultimately inconsistent. Cromwell had taken the decisive action, but he had done so with great reluctance. His dilemma was expressed by the comment that "he was pushed on by two parties to do that, the consideration of the issue whereof made his hair to stand on end." The two parties to which he referred were rival factions within the army, one led by John Lambert, the other by Thomas Harrison. What they had in common was a determination to dispose of the Rump. What divided them was their vision of the future. Lambert favored a solution whereby the army would set up a small Council of State, which would govern the country until it was both sufficiently settled and reformed to elect its own Parliament. Harrison, who had been converted to Fifth Monarchist beliefs after Worcester, sought the institution of the rule of the saints and favored a council of seventy godly men fashioned after the Jewish Sanhedrin. A text close to his heart was "The saints shall take the kingdom and possess it" and he was convinced that the moment had come.

Cromwell had dispensed with the Long Parliament with no clear view as to the nature of a new settlement. The options available to him were, in fact, relatively limited. His initial action was to set up a small, temporary Council of State with a membership of only ten, presided over by Lambert. He then referred the larger question of political settlement to the Council of Officers. But what was the settlement to be? Summoning a new Parliament by free election was out of the question. For all of the joy that greeted the demise of the Rump, the revolutionary party did not have a sufficient popular base to risk such a move. Royalists, Presbyterians, disgruntled Rumpers would have combined to make such an approach extremely dangerous. Only the use of arbitrary force and the abandonment of anything approaching free elections would have sufficed to secure a favorable result, and the process itself would have widened rather than closed the divisions within the nation. The dissolution had greatly enhanced Cromwell's personal prestige, and it is possible to conceive of some form of dictatorial settlement built around him. But such a move was contradictory to his basic political principles, though rumors abounded that Cromwell would make himself king or that he would make an accommodation with the Stuarts, backing their restoration in return for a dukedom and the Lord Deputyship of Ireland.

Such solutions were rumors, no more. The realistic possibilities lay somewhere between the hopes of Lambert and of Harrison. Cromwell's decision was complicated by two factors. In the first place, he had genuine doubts about both schemes. Lambert was keen on a written constitution, but Cromwell had little faith in paper solutions. On the other hand, he was not a Fifth Monarchy man and always felt uncomfortable with Harrison's scheme to do without Parliaments. While he agreed with Harrison that government should be in the hands of godly men, his perception of what godly meant was different from that of Harrison, and, in any case, he felt that the godly should exercise their sway through something like a Parliament. In the second place, Cromwell's maneuverability had been, in some key senses, diminished by the dissolution of the Rump. He had sought army unity by his action, but what it most visibly accomplished was to restore him as the hero of the radical sects. To maintain unity, he had to fulfill some of their expectations.

The small Council of State, established on 29 April, was clearly intended to be an interim government; the following day Cromwell issued a declaration announcing that "persons of approved fidelity and honesty are . . . to be called from the several parts of this Commonwealth to the supreme authority." It was his last public utterance on the new government until writs summoning the members of the Nominated Parliament were issued on 6 June. Between those two dates, lengthy and difficult discussions took place in the Council of Officers over a number of key issues including the size of the assembly, the manner in which its representatives were to be apportioned, and the method of its selection. On the first issue, that of size, the position of Lambert was lost from the very start. It was not just the millenarian group around Harrison that resisted the idea of a small sovereign council; Cromwell himself was anxious to replace the former Parliament with a body as broad and respectable as conditions would allow. Once the decision was reached that the members should represent counties, Harrison's proposed Sanhedrin of seventy was itself too small, and the figure finally agreed upon was one hundred and forty; Cromwell was later to claim that it was he who had proposed the number.

Far more contentious was the issue of how the members were to be selected. Harrison put the matter bluntly in a letter to Colonel John Jones: "Being resolved to have in power men of truth, fearing and loving our Lord, his people and interest, the difficulty is to get such: whether my Lord only should call them, or the Saints should choose them, very much sweetly said both ways." Cromwell and the Council of Officers were deluged with advice as to how to proceed, but the advice varied widely. Some of the Fifth Monarchists argued that the gathered churches should elect a new representative, thus ensuring that it would be an assembly of the godly. A few churches sent in lists of names, but these appear to have been unsolicited. In North Wales, Harrison worked closely with the Welsh Saints to establish the membership, but in the last analysis it was the Council of Officers who appear to have made the selection, and they picked whom they pleased.

Cromwell's role in the process and his attitude toward the projected assembly were obviously of the greatest importance. His actions indicate clearly that he had no intention of establishing a personal dictatorship, despite the power that was now within his reach. A proposal that was considered early in the discussions that officers who accepted nomination to the assembly should resign their commissions appears to be a Cromwellian initiative to stress the fact that a military dictatorship was not being contemplated. Both Harrison and Lambert at the two wings of Army opinion opposed it. Nor did Cromwell dominate the selection process within the Council of Officers. In the summons to members on 6 June, he stated that "divers persons fearing God . . .

are by myself with the advice of my council of officers, nominated"; later Cromwell reminded the officers that members "were nominated by themselves; not an officer of the degree of a captain but named more than he himself did." The latter claim may be somewhat exaggerated, but in general it would appear to be true.

Cromwell's attitude toward the new assembly was, then, relatively straightforward. He saw it from the very beginning as a sovereign governing body; when he declared that its members were to be called "to the supreme authority" he had chosen his words carefully and with no intention of ambiguity. His clear intention to hand over power was indicated by his directive to the Dutch Commissioners that in future letters were not to be addressed to "His Excellency and the Council of State" but rather to "the Council of State." Cromwell did not choose to refer to the assembly as a Parliament; that was a title it assumed itself after it had met, but he certainly saw it as a representative body that would bring about the long-desired godly reformation within something approaching the framework of constitutional form. In short, Cromwell held high hopes for this assembly; if he did not share the details of Harrison's vision of the future, he shared the heady sense that the revolution had reached a high point where long-sought aims would at last be realized. The Rump Parliament, of which he had been in so many ways the architect, had been a grievous disappointment to him and with visible reluctance he had disposed of it. Now an assembly was formed of right-minded men who could rise above faction and party and attend to the needs of the nation.

In such hopes, Cromwell was to be once again grievously disappointed. It took little time to reveal that "party" still existed even in the assembly of the godly and equally little time to reveal that the similarities in rhetoric between Cromwell and the saints was dangerously deceptive.

Had the assembly indeed been nominated by the gathered churches, it might well have had more unity than it did, though it would have proven to be even more difficult to deal with from Cromwell's point of view. But those who came together to form what soon became known as Barebone's Parliament (after one of its members, Praise-God Barebone, a London leather-seller and Baptist lay preacher) were the result of a compromise between the intentions originally associated with Lambert and Harrison. The Parliament was a very diverse body; opinion was so divided in the Council of Officers that selection by that body could have produced little else. A persistent tradition has portrayed the assembly as dominated by impractical religious enthusiasts, fanatical men of lower-class origins who had doctrinaire but unrealistic solutions to offer the nation. In truth, the Parliament, though it contained a larger lower-class membership than would have been the case in a normal Parliament, was not without men of political experience nor was it overwhelmed by a host of visionary religious radicals. Only a handful of the members had sat in Parliament before, but no fewer than 115 of the 140 were justices of the peace and 55 were to serve in one or more subsequent Parliaments. Roughly one-third of the members had attended university and about 40 of those summoned had attended one of the Inns of Court. While there was a solid radical core among the membership, estimated at about 40 to 60 people, it was not in a position to dominate if the other elements held together.

When the assembly met on 4 July, Cromwell greeted them with a long, rambling and passionate speech. He spoke with feeling of the train of events that had brought them into being, of the failure of the Rump Parliament, of the heavy obligations laid upon this new assembly to use their power with justice, to promote the Gospel, and to win the support and confidence of the people. Convince them, he urged, "that as men fearing God have fought them out of their thraldom and bondage under the regal power, so men fearing God do now rule them in the fear of God." As the speech wore on, Cromwell's hopes and enthusiasm were expressed in increasingly ecstatic language, language that echoed the phrases of Harrison and the saints. "Truly you are called by God to rule with Him and for Him." What was occurring was yet another "evident print of providence." "I confess I never looked to see such a day as this," he declared, ". . . when Jesus Christ should be so owned as He is at this day and in this work. Jesus Christ is owned this day by your call." And since God in His mercy had brought things so far, there was room to hope for developments even more beneficial. "Why should we be afraid to say or think that this way may be the door to usher in the things that God has promised, which have been prophesied of, which He has set the hearts of His people to wait for and expect? We know who they are that shall war with the Lamb against His enemies: they shall be a people called and chosen and faithful. . . . Indeed I do think somewhat is at the door: we are at the threshold and therefore it becomes us to lift up our heads and encourage ourselves in the Lord. . . . You are at the edge of the promises and prophecies." For the moment at least, Cromwell had forgotten the disillusion that had swept over him at the end of the Rump Parliament; a new and more glorious opportunity was at hand. In his faith that God would guide and lead the assembly, he came close to the spirit of the millenarians; the problems that had proved to be so intractable in the past would be swept away by the power of God.

Of course, it was not to be. The Parliament was as divided as any before it and by mid-July the rift between moderates and radicals was clearly in the open. The actions of Harrison and Lambert symbolize the political problem. Lambert withdrew from the Council of State the day the Barebone's Parliament met. He does not appear to have taken his seat but instead to have withdrawn first to his house at Wimbledon and then to Yorkshire. He was protesting the very nature of the new assembly and the passing of power from the interim Council of State, over which he presided. Three weeks later Harrison and some of his radical friends withdrew from the assembly, to return only toward the end of its brief existence. His protest was the exact opposite of Lambert's — that the assembly was not controlled by the radicals and that in their confrontations with the moderates they found Cromwell, for all the fervor of his opening speech, inclining more and more to the other side.

It is important to appreciate the nature of the splits in Barebone's Parliament in order to comprehend the position Cromwell now found himself in. The splits that appeared were not permanent, formed parties but loose and shifting alliances for the most part. The nearest thing to a formed group was a core of radical members who took a consistent line on nearly every issue, but since they only numbered about 40, they required a bloc of floating votes on any given issue to command a majority in a full House. And the House did split over specific issues on religious, political, and social grounds, providing the radicals with the needed opportunity. Beyond that the radicals proved to be more consistent in attendance than the moderates. Whenever the moderates appeared in strength, as they did, for example, in November at the time for electing a new Council of State, they could control; during much of the autumn when the attendance was thin, the situation favored the radicals.

The outward and visible struggles between moderates and radicals centered on the issues of law and religion. Virtually all, Cromwell included, agreed that reform of the law was necessary. It was a theme Cromwell had preached since his Scottish campaign and he repeated it in his opening address to Barebone's Parliament. But the program of reform envisaged by the radicals went well beyond what Cromwell meant by the term. Cromwell sought reform of abuses, but he was firm in his belief that the essential structure of the common law should be preserved. One radical proposal would have had the effect of abrogating it completely. This was the scheme to reduce the complex fabric of the common law to a simple code, "into the bigness of a pocket book, as it is proportionable in New England and elsewhere." A committee was formed to bring this about. Similarly, the treatment of the Court of Chancery by Barebone's Parliament caused great anxiety to the moderates. No one denied that the court was a scandal and badly needed reform. Its costs and its delays were legendary; in 1653 it was said to be some 23,000 cases in arrears, some of them of as much as thirty years' standing. The answer of the radicals was to vote for its abolition after a single day's debate. To do so without making any provision for another body to assume its jurisdiction was an act that caused considerable alarm to Cromwell and those who thought like him. And Cromwell was well aware of even more outspoken demands emanating from the radical pulpits of the city. There the demand was for the replacement of the traditional laws of England by a code based on the laws of Moses; it was to be the ultimate step in replacing the capriciousness of men by the law of God.

If the radicals' approach to the law was worrying to Cromwell, their attitude toward religion, especially over the related issues of tithes and the maintenance of the clergy, was even more so. At the very outset a proposal to abolish tithes lost by only a few votes and the matter was referred to a committee. Cromwell and the vast majority of the moderates were prepared to consider alternative forms of support for the parochial clergy, but on the whole they stuck on the point that owners of tithes should be compensated if the system were abolished. The radicals, however, were anxious to move beyond the abolition of tithes to the abolition of any form of state maintenance of the clergy. The gathered churches, they felt, should be responsible for religion and each should maintain its own clergy with its own contributions, independent of the state. It was a position Cromwell could not accept; the survival of the ministry was, in his mind, intimately bound up with the provision of public support. In another area that troubled Cromwell, the radicals achieved success; this was a vote to bring in a bill abolishing lay patronage in the church. Rumors abounded that such steps were to go even further; the endowment of the universities were to be attacked, the established church wholly dismantled. Again, the strivings of the radicals in the House were urged on by the preachers at Blackfriars and elsewhere who denounced the parochial clergy as "priests of Baal" and dismissed the church as an "outwork of Babylon."

The objections of Cromwell and the moderates to such demands were in part religious, but in part they were also social. One aspect of the moderate-radical split in the House was plainly related to social origins. Those men in the Parliament who belonged to the traditional ruling group of the nation, the men of birth and property, were overwhelmingly on the moderate side. Those who formed the new element drawn from positions of lower social status had a tendency to be on the radical side. This is not to say that they were the ignorant and base persons of Royalist propaganda. Many had established themselves during the shifts and confusion of the Civil Wars and were now aldermen or fringe members of county society. But they were, on the whole, men who had risen from relative obscurity on the back of the revolution, and, as such, they were less sensitive to protecting the persistent objectives of the moderates than were Cromwell and his followers. For Cromwell and his associates, tithes and lay patronage were not just matters of religious concern; they were also items of property. Tithes had passed in large numbers into lay hands at the time of Reformation; by 1653 they were an integral part of the value of many lay estates. Likewise, rights of presentation, having passed into lay hands, became a valuable piece of property. To attack either was, to the moderates' point of view, to begin an assault on the concept of private property itself. The attack on the common law could be viewed in the

same way, for much of what was under attack was the land
law, which protected the propertied classes. This, taken
together with the overt attack on the clergy, was sufficient to
give Cromwell pause to doubt the wisdom of entrusting
affairs of the nation to such a body. As he looked back later
on the Parliament, the chief source of his discontent was
that "the ministry and propriety were like to be destroyed."

Cromwell had a further reason to be displeased with the
men of Barebone's Parliament. One of his chief desires in
the field of foreign affairs was to bring the Dutch war to
an end. In the summer of 1653, the situation seemed favorable
to this end. Having suffered a considerable defeat at the
beginning of June, the Dutch were prepared to enter discussions and sent envoys to England. Cromwell had high
hopes for the discussions. He intended that they should not
only lead to the end of the war but should lead to a genuine
union of the two nations. It was a wildly visionary scheme
and Cromwell had given little thought to the practical details
by which it might be worked out, but he continued, despite
the coolness of the Dutch, to hold out hope for it. As late
as a conference with the Dutch in mid-November, he was still
quick to convert discussions of alliance into projects of union,
brushing aside concern over sovereignty as being unimportant, merely "a feather in the hat." But if Cromwell's
vision of a union of the two Protestant powers was an illusion, his concern to bring peace between the two was a
soundly based approach to foreign policy. And once again,
he found his way opposed by the radical Fifth Monarchists,
in and out of the House. Harrison consistently berated
Cromwell for seeking peace with the Dutch, while preachers
of a radical stamp urged a holy war against the wealthy
towns of the Dutch merchants. The Fifth Monarchy version
of foreign policy was something akin to a crusade of destruction to humble the mighty on behalf of the Lord; John
Canne spoke for this attitude when he declared, "Speaking
here I say, as it were from heaven, that it is not prizes, or

the enemy's goods, our hearts or hands should desirously be upon, but to destroy Babylon, stain the glory of Kings and kingdoms, and lay low the high and great mountains of the earth." It was an outlook that left the pragmatic and moderate Cromwell aghast.

By the end of August, 1653, Cromwell was clearly in a depressed and despairing mood. Worried by the implications of the radical initiatives in the House, frustrated in his desire to end the Dutch war, under attack from nearly every side, he was, he commented, "more troubled now with the fool, than with the knave." In a letter to Charles Fleetwood, written on 22 August, he laid bare his feelings — his sense of isolation, his despondency over the inability of various opposed factions to work together for the general good rather than pursuing with rigidity their own particular desires, his temptation to withdraw from the pressures put upon him and return to the simple life of a country gentleman. "Truly I never more needed all helps from my Christian friends than now! Fain would I have my service accepted of the saints (if the Lord will) but it is not so. Being of different judgments, and of each sort most seeking to propagate their own, that spirit of kindness that is to them all, is hardly accepted of any. I hope I can say it, my life has been a willing sacrifice, and I hope for them all. . . . Alas, I am, in my temptation ready to say, Oh, would I had wings like a dove, then would I, etc., but this I fear is my haste. I bless the Lord I have somewhat keeps me alive, some sparks of the light of His countenance, and some sincerity above man's judgment." The desire to have the burden lifted from his shoulders, the wish to return to a simpler life were recurring thoughts with Cromwell, but he never gave in to them. Even as he thought of such a possibility, the opposite conclusion was also much in his mind. He later recalled his own doubts about the wisdom of surrendering his power to this assembly. It had been done as an honest attempt to approach a constitutional settlement; now, in his anguish, he wondered whether what he had done was to evade the responsibility that God had laid upon him and manifested to him through a whole series of providences. "As a principal end in calling that assembly was the settlement of the nation, so a chief end to myself was that I might have opportunity to lay down the power which was in my hands. . . . That was, as to myself, my greatest end. A desire perhaps, and I am afraid, sinful enough, to be quit of the power God had most clearly by His providence put into my hand, before He called me to lay it down and before those honest ends of our fighting were attained and settled."

Cromwell was hardly alone in sensing mounting dissatisfaction with Barebone's Parliament. Many, on political, religious, and social grounds, shared his apprehension, if not his disappointment. Significant elements within the army had additional grounds for grievance; the opposition within Parliament to the monthly assessment for the support of the army raised once again the specter that had so often spurred the army to action, the threat of pay falling seriously in arrears. The suggestion made in Parliament that higher officers should forgo their pay for a year in view of the financial needs of the state fanned the discontent to a higher pitch. Lambert and his followers proposed to revive the scheme of a written constitution with a strengthened executive to counter such developments. They knew that they needed the support of Cromwell if their plans were to succeed, but, for all his dissatisfaction with Parliament, Cromwell was not initially prepared to accept their schemes.

The idea of a written constitution was revived as early as mid-October but it made little headway because of Cromwell's attitude. In particular, Oliver shrunk from the prospect of forcibly interrupting another Parliament. Such action was contrary to his basic political feelings, and he continued to hold out hope that the moderates could prevail in the Parliament and bring it to its senses. The elections for the Council of State on 1 November strengthened his resolve to hold on; the moderates emerged with a clear working majority on the Council; Cromwell himself had been unanimously elected, while Harrison stood thirteenth on the list and received only 58 votes. Encouraged by the results, Cromwell spent much of early November attempting to mediate between the groups led by Lambert and Harrison. Lambert continued to push his cause; in late November, he presided over a meeting of officers in London at which the current situation was discussed and a proposed new constitution was considered. It would appear that Cromwell was informed of these discussions at an early stage, though he did not take a direct part in them. No doubt he had a general sympathy with Lambert's intentions, but he opposed the scheme on two counts. In the first place, he raised again his consistent opposition to the forcible expulsion of Parliament. In the second place, he took strong exception to the fact that the proposed constitution would have made him accept the title of King. Lambert and his colleagues appear to have pressed Cromwell hard, but to no avail. "The gentlemen that undertook to frame this government . . . told me that except I would undertake the government they thought things would hardly come to a composure or settlement, but blood and confusion would break in upon us. I refused it again and again." Documentation of these discussions is extremely sketchy, but it would appear that on or about 1 December, Cromwell gave his final refusal to the proposal as then constituted, and Lambert retreated once again, confused and disappointed, to the country.

If Cromwell hoped that patient waiting would be rewarded by the triumph of the moderates in Parliament, he was badly disappointed. On 2 December, the Committee on Tithes reported with a plan for the reorganization of the church and its ministry. It contained a number of points on which the moderates had long insisted, including the guarantee that the present provision for approved clergy would be maintained by Parliament and an affirmation that tithes were legal property. For six days an intense debate was waged on the first article of the report; when the vote came on Saturday, 10 December, the radicals succeeded in having it rejected by two votes. For the moderates, it seemed to be the death blow to the only religious settlement they could accept and a clear sign that the radical force in the House could not be overcome by debate and argumentation. Throughout the following day, the moderates and the discontented army officers met to plan strategy. Cromwell's reluctance to turning out the Parliament forcibly remained the central factor in the discussion; those close to Cromwell argued that the same end could be achieved if the Parliament would voluntarily surrender its authority to him. What he would not take by force, he could be persuaded to accept by default. Within the course of that day, a sizable part of the membership of the House had been persuaded to this course of action, some no doubt accepting it as an honorable form of political suicide on the assumption that the army would put an end to the sitting one way or another.

The moderates arrived at the House unusually early on 12 December and at once launched into a violent assault on the policies, real, projected, and imagined, of the radicals. Capping their assault, they moved "that the sitting of this Parliament any longer, as it is now constituted, will not be for the good of the Commonwealth, and that therefore it is requisite to deliver up to the Lord General Cromwell the powers which they had received from him." Hardly pausing for a debate and never having taken a vote on the motion, they filed from the House, led by Speaker Rouse, who was himself privy to the design. Fifty or sixty members accompanied him to Whitehall, where they signed a document abdicating their powers and returning them to Cromwell. Within two days, a majority of the members appended their names to the document. Some twenty-seven or so members remained in the House; too small to be a quorum, they set about drawing up a protest against the proceedings. When two colonels and some musketeers arrived, the remaining members protested briefly their right to sit, then bowed to necessity and withdrew. The Barebone's Parliament was ended.

What of Cromwell's role in the proceedings? Propaganda at the time saw the events as further confirmation of his quest for power and argued that he had allowed the radicals to run to excess so that a frightened nation would return full power to him. Cromwell himself protested publicly that he had had no part in the scheme to end Barebone's Parliament. Although he was well aware of moderate and army discontent and knew of Lambert's substitute constitution, he had not forced the decision to abdicate by his own actions. "I can say it in the presence of divers persons here that do know whether I lie . . . ," he related to the ensuing Parliament, "that I did not know one tittle of that resignation, until they all came and brought it, and delivered it into my hands." Without quibbling over the precise meaning of "one tittle," we can safely take the statement to be substantially correct.

Two observations might be made about the collapse of Barebone's Parliament. The first is that its demise should not lead us to assume that the moderates' denunciation of it represents the whole story of the assembly. It was an assembly which betrayed some naïve, fanatic, impractical aspects. But it had passed or projected some serious reform legislation as well. The second observation concerns Cromwell. There can be little doubt that the failure of Barebone's Parliament was, in important respects, a crushing blow to Cromwell. Already severely strained by the actions forced on him by the failure of the Long Parliament, he was deeply depressed by this additional failure. In July, he had greeted it with ecstatic hope; by August he was inclined to see it as a body dominated by fools; by December, he acquiesced in its removal, his hopes that the godly would unite in a common cause of acceptable reformation thoroughly dashed. He came to think of the experiment with a nominated Parliament as being "a story of my own weakness and folly." He never denied the honorable nature of the intention, but he lamented the result it had produced. "It was done in my simplicity. . . . It was thought then that men of our own judgment, who had fought in the wars, and were all of a piece upon that account, why surely these men will hit it, and will do to the purpose, whatever can be desired. . . . And such a company of men were chosen and did proceed into action. And truly this was the naked truth, that the issue was not answerable to the simplicity and honesty of the design." Cromwell had not lost all hope, but henceforth his optimism was restricted. He continued to have faith in parliamentary solutions, but never in the future would he again relinquish power completely to such an assembly. He continued to feel the obligation to serve and to lead, but increasingly he came to view that role as being a referee between factions that no amount of persuasion could bring together.

TEN

Oliver Protector

THE RESIGNATION of Barebone's Parliament restored to Cromwell the seemingly unlimited power he had sought to entrust to others when that assembly convened. "My power," he commented, "again by this resignation was as boundless and unlimited as before, all things being subject to arbitrariness and myself a person having power over the three nations without bound or limit set . . . , all government being dissolved, all civil administration at an end." It should occasion no surprise that Lambert and his colleagues were quick to press on Cromwell once again their scheme of government embodied in a written constitution. The nature of the discussions between Cromwell and the Lambert group over the next three days has not come down to us, but certainly much of that discussion centered on the title to be bestowed on Cromwell by the new constitution and the precise nature of the powers he was to assume. His earlier objections to Lambert's scheme had been the existence of a legal assembly and the title of King. The former problem had resolved itself; the latter was removed by substituting the title Lord Protector for that of King. Cromwell's objections to the title must be taken as sincere; in all probability, he still saw his role as essentially a temporary one. Not ambitious for worldly glory, at least in the way his detractors claimed he was, he over and over again considered a withdrawal from public life, only to be drawn back to it by a sense of duty and a conviction that God had marked him out to produce order and hasten reformation in a world that seemed perpetually unruly without his guiding hand. Bishop Burnet, writing of Cromwell's attitude in those critical December days, laid great stress on his personal reluctance to assume something approaching dictatorial powers and on his final agreement to do so on the grounds of present necessities. Cromwell protested, Burnet recalled, "with many tears that he would rather have taken a shepherd's staff than the protectorship since nothing was more contrary to his genius than a show of greatness, but he saw it was necessary at that time to keep the nation from falling into extreme disorder and from becoming open to the common enemy, and therefore he only stepped in between the living and the dead, as he phrased it, in that interval till God should direct them on what bottom they ought to settle."

After a short period of soul-searching, Cromwell accepted the new constitution, the Instrument of Government, and his new position under it. The Instrument was a curious document which did not so much solve some of the persistent constitutional problems as paper over them. Thus a note of ambiguity with respect to Cromwell's personal position was struck virtually from the beginning. Despite rejecting the title of King, Cromwell assumed some of the trappings of regality by his new office. His title, His Highness the Lord Protector, carried such implications, as did his residence henceforth at Whitehall. But the office itself was specified as being elective, the hereditary aspect of traditional monarchy being carefully avoided. Where the document contained the greatest amount of faith and the least amount of helpful definition was precisely the area that had been at the forefront of so much of the political problem, the relationship between the executive and the legislature. Legislative power was to be shared, for it was to reside "in one person and in Parliament." Executive authority was to be in the Protector's hands, yet it was limited. Though the single house Parliament of four hundred members needed only to be summoned every three years for a sitting of at least five months' duration, the Protector could veto none of its bills unless they were contrary to the constitution. Even in the potentially long intervals between parliamentary meetings, the power of the Protector was not without check, for the constitution provided for a new Council of State, considerably more powerful than that which had been set up in 1649. Despite the apparently extensive powers of the Protector, the council was absolutely central to the governmental process. Both domestic and foreign affairs were to be conducted with the advice and consent of the council; control of the armed forces was shared either with the Parliament when sitting or the council when not. The council, moreover, was not a body chosen and controlled by the Protector. Jealous of its own independence and having the right to elect the next Protector, it had more similarities to the self-perpetuating governing bodies of town corporations than it did to a king's privy council. Appointment to the council was for life, and from the start the framer of the constitution, Lambert, and a group of his close associates formed a key part of the membership. As Cromwell put it, the council became "the trustees of the Commonwealth in the intervals of Parliament" and as such, they had considerable potential for limiting his actions. "I was a child in swaddling clothes. I cannot transgress. By the government I can do nothing but in ordination with the Council."

There were certainly parts of the Instrument of which Cromwell could approve wholeheartedly. Most notable in this respect was the religious settlement it envisaged. Cromwell had long sought a form of religious toleration, limited, to be sure, when measured by modern standards, but wide when compared with the attitudes of his own time. He knew by experience how slight a hold on the nation his views had, how easy it was for sects to ask for liberty when out of power and to deny it to others when in power. "That hath been one of the vanities of our contests," he declared; "Every sect saith, 'Oh give me liberty,' but give it him, and to his power he will not yield it to anybody else." The constitutional settlement of the Instrument, however, appeared to guarantee what Cromwell sought; while there was to be a national church, it was to be a noncoercive one. The Christian religion "as contained in the scriptures" was to be "held forth and recommended as the public profession of these nations" but "to the public profession . . . none shall be compelled by penalties or otherwise, but . . . endeavours be used to win them by sound doctrine and the example of a good conversation." All who professed faith "in God by Jesus Christ though differing in judgment from the doctrine, worship, or discipline publicly held forth" were to be protected in the exercise of their religion so long as they did not disturb the peace or cause civil injury to others. The only exceptions were to be Anglicans and Catholics. Translating such provisions into practice in a country which was not ready to accept them would be no small feat, but with the intention Cromwell had no quibbles.

On 16 December 1653 Cromwell was formally installed as Lord Protector. In its own way, the ceremony underlined the ambiguities of the settlement. Clearly the new constitution was the product of a group of army officers and it was being forced on the nation by the power of the army they served. But Cromwell himself wore on the occasion a plain black coat to emphasize that he accepted his new role not as a general, but as a civilian. And to those who assembled to witness the ceremony, he pledged to rule not as a military dictator but as a constitutional head of state. "I do promise in the presence of God that I will not violate or infringe the matters and things contained therein, but to my power observe the same and cause them to be observed, and shall in all other things, to the best of my understanding, govern these nations according to the laws, statutes, and customs thereof, seeking their peace, and causing justice and law to be equally administered." All of the fine words and all of the good intentions (both of which must be taken to be genuine) could not, however, wholly disguise the fact that an immensely difficult political task was being undertaken, the conversion of a thinly disguised military dictatorship into a constitutional and godly government.

The first Parliament under the Instrument was not to meet until September, 1654. The months between his installation in December and the convening of that body provide a useful insight into the hopes and visions of Cromwell. In conjunction with the council, Cromwell had the power, in the interval, to issue ordinances which would have the force of law "until order shall be taken in Parliament concerning them." Cromwell's extensive use of that power in the ensuing nine months provides telling evidence that the repeated disappointments of the post-Worcester years had not made him a totally disillusioned man, nor a leader with a bitter, limited, and noncreative view of how the problems of the nation could be addressed. The tone of the early protectoral months was both businesslike and respectable. Both the council, with which he had to work closely, and other positions in the government were dominated by men of an essentially moderate or pragmatic stamp, men who would support effective government for the good of the country and who were unlikely to be carried away by the sort of sectarian excess that had marked a part of the membership of Barebone's Parliament. Indicative of the shift that had come over government was the appointment of Edward Montagu as Admiral of the Fleet. The fact that he was the son of Cromwell's old rival Manchester was disregarded; he was representative of the respectable men Cromwell

wanted to wed to the new government and his express instructions to root the radicals out of the navy was reflective
of the sort of stance that government wanted to take. Of all
the new men, the one most valuable to Cromwell was John
Thurloe. He had become secretary to the council in 1652;
under the Protectorate, he was to be virtually Cromwell's
right-hand man, serving not only a critical role with respect
to the council but, equally importantly, creating and super-
vising Cromwell's intelligence service. The latter became a
formidable weapon in the hands of the government; as the
Venetian ambassador Sagredo commented, "There is no
government on earth which divulges its affairs less than England or is more punctually informed of those of the others."
Give the number of potential enemies of the Protectorate, the
the service performed by the intelligence service was in-
valuable, and as its head, the efficient Thurloe could scarcely
have been bettered.

In league with men like Thurloe, Cromwell set out to
bring to fruition the kinds of reforms he had long advocated.
Freed from both the reservations of the Rump and the radical
enthusiasms of Barebone's Parliament, Cromwell oversaw an
impressive array of legislation by ordinance. Some eighty-two
ordinances were enacted in the period, covering a wide range
of governmental concern ranging from the maintenance of
the highways to the reorganization of the treasury. At the
heart of the matter, from Cromwell's point of view, were
the ordinances that dealt with reform of the law, the reorganization of the church, and the reformation of manners.
The fact that Cromwell did not regularly attend the council
should not be construed to mean he was not the main force
behind the reforms. He could not always control what it
did; when he was criticized in December, 1654, for not having
abolished tithes, he took refuge behind that fact; as one contemporary recalled his words, he commented that "for his
part he could not do it for he was but one and his council
allege it not fit to take them away." But if not all powerful,

he was nonetheless the impetus for the reform that found its way into this extensive series of ordinances.

Reform of the law had long concerned Cromwell. The targets he selected for reform, notably the Court of Chancery and the criminal law, were no different from the targets Barebone's Parliament aimed at; what was different was both the manner and the method of the proposed reform. In the first place, Cromwell sought to reform the law with the cooperation of the legal profession, "being resolved to give the learned of the robe the honor of reforming their profession." He may have been unrealistic in his hope for widespread cooperation from a profession many of whom had vested interests in the very complexities he was trying to untangle, but he did have some important support, notably from Matthew Hale, who was made a judge on 25 January 1654. In the second place, Cromwell sought in reforming the law to preserve as much of the traditional, existing system as possible. This was no radical sledgehammer, such as that wielded by Barebone's Parliament, to shake the whole edifice of the law; rather he approached reform in his characteristic stance of pragmatic conservatism. His Chancery Ordinance, published in August, 1654, and confirmed by Parliament in 1656, was indicative of his approach. Where Barebone's Parliament had abolished the court, Cromwell regulated and reduced fees, limited the capacity of lawyers to stretch out a case, assured plaintiffs securities for costs, and ordered that cases should be heard in the order of their being set down. Even such moderate reform raised opposition among some lawyers, but it was the sort of reform that it was possible to put into practice. Cromwell was troubled too by the severity of the criminal law and he sought to make it more "conformable to the just and righteous laws of God." To do so, he argued, required the elimination of some existing laws that were, by those standards, "wicked and abominable." He thought, in particular, of the widespread use of capital punishment for petty crimes. "To hang a man for six pence, thirteen pence, I know not what — to hang for a trifle and pardon murder is in the ministration of the law, through the ill-framing of it. I have known in my experience abominable murders acquitted. And to come and see men lose their lives for petty matters; this is a thing that God will reckon for. And I wish it may not lie upon this nation a day longer than you have an opportunity to give a remedy, and I hope I shall cheerfully join with you in it." Cromwell's hopes for reform of the criminal law were not realized; his first Parliament, engrossed in constitutional issues, had no time for legislative reform of the law, while his second Parliament, to whom these words were addressed, chose not to mitigate the ferocity of the existing law.

If law was important for regulating the relations of men, the ultimate guide, religion, was even more a matter of concern for Cromwell. The Instrument of Government itself answered for him some of the central issues. There was to be a public profession of faith, there was to be toleration of a carefully defined sort, and the clergy was to be maintained, either as at present or by some new method developed by the state. In other words, the general principles of the religious settlement were embodied in the constitution; Cromwell's task was to work out the specific means of accomplishing those principles. On the matter of maintenance, Cromwell had little that was new to add to a discussion that had gone on for years. He may have appreciated some of the argument raised against maintenance by tithes, but he was not willing to undo one system until another had been devised that would assure the same results. "For my part," he stressed, "I should think I were very treacherous if I should take away tithes till I see the legislative power to settle maintenance to them another way." To do so, as had been proposed in Barebone's Parliament, would be "to cut the throats" of the ministers. On the whole, the thrust of Cromwell's efforts in this area was not to construct a new system of maintenance but rather to find ways to augment the low income level prevailing in many parishes under the existing system. Cromwell did have constructive approaches to two key aspects of the church. Following the lead of the scheme propounded by John Owen to the Rump Parliament four years earlier, he took steps to see that entry into the ministry was carefully screened and that methods existed for removing from the existing clergy the ungodly and scandalous. By an ordinance of March, 1654, he established a commission of Triers who would sit permanently in London to check the qualifications of proposed clergymen. In keeping with the general tenor of the settlement, the Triers were not to administer any doctrinal tests to candidates; they were simply to ascertain their fitness to be maintained by the state by certifying that each was "a person for the grace of God in him, his holy and unblamable conversation, as also for his knowledge and utterance, able and fit to preach the Gospel." By an ordinance issued in August, 1654, appointing local commissions in the counties to remove scandalous clergy and schoolteachers, he sought to take care of the other side of the problem. There can be little doubt that Cromwell considered the steps he had taken for the right ordering of the national church to be both important and successful. He was particularly pleased with what he saw as the improved character of the clergy; as he told Parliament in 1658, "You have now a godly ministry; you have a knowing ministry, such a one as, without vanity be it spoken, the world has not." It had been the result of the conscientious work of the Triers and Ejectors, who were not deceived by paper qualifications, but sought in each man evidence of God's grace.

A third area of major concern to Cromwell was the reformation of manners. It was a concern that has led to many erroneous impressions of Cromwell himself. To those who accept a caricature of Puritanism for its reality, concern of this sort of confirms an impression that Cromwell was a dour individual, hostile to the arts, and imbued with a sense that sin always lurked close to enjoyment. In fact, nothing could be further from the truth. What Cromwell was concerned with, in the main, was the disorderly behavior that accompanied some forms of social amusement, not the amusement itself. A case in point was the March ordinance that prohibited cockfighting. In deciding on prohibition, the crucial factor had been his perception that such gatherings "are by experience found to tend many times to the disturbance of the public peace and are commonly accompanied with gaming, drinking, swearing, quarreling and other dissolute practices to the dishonour of God and do often produce the ruin of persons and their families." The man who could take pleasure in watching a hurling match and who had a deep, personal love of music was not an enemy of enjoyment but rather of dissolute and antisocial behavior. It was in a similar spirit that he issued ordinances against dueling and supplementing the act against swearing. His suppression of horseracing was more influenced by the fact that Royalists used such occasions to gather for their plotting than by any desire to remove a small pleasure from people's lives. Cromwell took the matter of reformation of manners seriously. "It is a thing I am confident our liberty and prosperity depends on. . . . Make it a shame to see men to be bold in sin and profaneness, and God will bless you. You will be a blessing to the nation, and by this be more repairers of breaches than by anything in the world. Truly these things do respect the souls of men, and the spirits, which are the men. The mind is the man. If that be kept pure, a man signifies somewhat; if not, I would very fain see what difference there is betwixt him and a beast. He hath only some activity to do some more mischief." This was one cause of Cromwell to which Parliament responded with general enthusiasm: his various ordinances were confirmed and Parliament passed similar acts on its own. There remained the problem of adequate enforcement; if local authorities, for one reason or another, chose not to execute the laws, the hope for a national reformation of manners was doomed, unless pressure could somehow be exerted from the center. Cromwell had begun his political career as an opponent of the centralizing tendencies of the Stuart state; once in a position of power, he came to see that this was another feature of Stuart rule he might have to adopt if he was to accomplish the lofty aims he had in mind.

The first nine months of the Protectorate suggest then that Cromwell, far from being dejected and bitter, had a constructive legislative program in mind. They were also the months in which he began to feel his way toward a form of court behavior that was consistent with his new dignity as Lord Protector. There were inevitable ironies in the situation. The only court model for the revolutionary government was the Stuart court that it had overthrown, and in the desire to give stature to the new state, it was inevitable that Cromwell's household began to take on a number of trappings reminiscent of the court of Charles I. It has been all too easy for the critics of Cromwell to read into the elaboration of court ceremonial, the growth of the household, and the outward ostentation further proof of Cromwell's overweening personal ambition. He had displaced a king in order to become like one himself; what he had criticized as extravagant and useless expenditure in others, he now freely indulged in. The matter was hardly so simple. Cromwell and those around him had a keen appreciation of the symbolic importance of such things. The fact that England was a republic was irrelevant insofar as court behavior was concerned. It was important to convey to other nations a sense that the regime had authority; while the court need not be extravagant or unduly splendid, neither could it be niggardly and lacking in protocol. As a military officer, Cromwell was not unused to emphasizing authority in various symbolic ways. He responded to this requirement of his position with a predictable dignity. He was not a man of extravagant tastes, nor was he one who took much pleasure in ostentation. If he dressed better now than he did when he entered the Long Parliament, he still did not dress luxuriously. If he impressed native and foreigner alike with his official presence, he maintained at the same time a healthy dose of his more modest and humble ways. Even writers hostile to him, like Henry Fletcher, commented on this feature. It could be turned into a form of attack, as it was in the pamphlet *The Court and Kitchin of Elizabeth commonly called Joan Cromwell,* published after the Restoration, where modesty of style was equated with "sordid frugality and thrifty business." In answer to those determined to find fault, there was little Cromwell could do. From former radical allies came criticism that it all seemed too much like that which they had fought against; if, on the other hand, economy was instituted, the Protectoral household was held up to ridicule as the refuge of a misplaced family of backwoods country gentry. On balance, Cromwell carried it off with considerable style.

Reform by ordinance and the establishment of authority were two of Cromwell's chief concerns; both of these and much more in his early actions as Protector were guided by a desire for conciliation, by a continuation of the spirit and political sense which had led him to push strongly at an earlier date for a lenient treatment of ex-Royalists. The critical test, to Cromwell's mind, was neither past action nor current belief but rather a willingness to accept the present regime, if only in the negative sense of not acting against it. The laws against delinquents remained in force, but Cromwell did what he could to mitigate their harshest effects. Anglicans and Catholics remained outside the religious settlement, but again, if their words and actions did not threaten the regime or disturb the peace, Cromwell was inclined to proceed in a merciful and gentle manner.

Cromwell's aim of comprehension and conciliation, extending beyond the sphere of religious belief alone, was a sound and admirable policy. Only if the divided nation came to live with its differences while accepting the regime could a militarily imposed settlement be converted into a constitutional one. But it was an aim doomed to failure. The divisions were too deep, the pragmatic moderation of Cromwell too little shared by the rest of the nation. Some, like the disgruntled republican Ludlow, could only see in these initiatives a selfish desire to build up a personal following. Others could accept no olive branch from Cromwell's hands. By 1654 an organization called the Sealed Knot had been formed to carry on underground Royalist resistance. It drew no great magnates to its support; on the whole, they were willing to make their peace with Cromwell's regime or at least adopt a neutral, waiting posture. But it did draw an enthusiastic, if amateur, group of plotters together whom no amount of conciliation could make loyal to the regime. In May, a plot was uncovered by the vigilant Thurloe to seize Cromwell as he was traveling between Whitehall and Hampton Court. The conspirators were quickly rounded up and the two leaders, Gerard and Vowell, were executed on 10 July after a trial by a hastily reconstituted High Court of Justice. If the exposure of the plot hardened some opinions against the Royalists (and there was some suspicion that Thurloe allowed it to go as far as it did before moving against it, precisely for that purpose), the existence of such a threat equally underlined the precarious thread on which the stability of the regime depended, the life of the Lord Protector.

The first Protectorate Parliament, chosen in July, assembled in September. Cromwell chose his great anniversary day, 3 September, for its initial meeting, though he again chose to symbolize the civilian nature of his rule by appearing in ordinary dress. As it was, the day fell on a Sunday, and in the face of protests over such activity on the Sabbath, the opening ceremonies were confined to a brief meeting and address, and a sermon in Westminster Abbey. The following day Cromwell delivered a major address to the new Parliament. It was an occasion of the greatest significance to him. All his previous hopes for Parliament had come to frustration; now more than ever, he appreciated the need to succeed. Unless his government and Parliament could work together, the hope for a genuinely constitutional settlement would be dashed again. The Swedish chancellor, Oxenstierna, had made the point exactly when he stressed to Whitelocke the importance of Cromwell's gaining "the confirmation of his being Protector by your Parliament which will be his best and greatest strength." There can be little doubt that Cromwell and the framers of the Instrument had hoped that the parliamentary elections of 1654 would return a House favorable to the new settlement. Changes both in the franchise and in the composition of Parliament had come into effect with the Instrument with just such intentions in mind. In one sense, they were successful. The disappearance of the advanced party of Barebone's Parliament was a foregone conclusion; if nothing else, the 1654 elections marked the reassertion of rule by men of property. But this was to prove not at all synonymous with natural supporters of the Protectorate government. Only in the Irish and Scottish seats did the government secure an overwhelming backing. Both of these blocs of representatives were new to an elected Parliament, though representatives of both had been nominated members of Barebone's Parliament. If their presence symbolized the union of the three nations under the rule of the Protector, their membership illustrated the capacity of the army in both countries to assure a favorable set of representatives. There is much truth in the assertion that the Irish and Scottish representatives served for the Protectorate in much the same capacity that ministerial pocket boroughs would serve for eighteenth-century governments. But beyond that, the results were considerably more mixed and less favorable to the government. Ludlow noted how, in England, "they better understood the design that was carrying on, insomuch that many persons of known virtue and integrity were chosen to sit in this assembly." Candidates supported by the government were, in a number of cases, defeated and on the other hand a number of pronounced republicans who would be ideologically opposed to the new constitution were elected, including Bradshaw, Scot and Hesilrige. The picture was further clouded by the fact that in a few areas Royalists had been elected as members. The House that Cromwell faced on 4 September, whatever else it was, was was not stacked in the government's favor and would not prove to be an easily malleable body.

Cromwell's opening speech was long, calculated and powerful. It provides an interesting contrast to the opening speech of Barebone's Parliament. The same confident sense that it was an important occasion that would lead to beneficial results was present in this speech. "Gentlemen, you are met here on the greatest occasion that, I believe, England ever saw, having upon your shoulders the interests of three great nations with the territories belonging to them, and truly, I believe I may say it without any hyperbole, you have upon your shoulders the interest of all the Christian people in the world." But there is no hint in this speech that the Protector would surrender his power to the Parliament, as he had done to the earlier assembly; instead the active role of the Protector himself was assumed throughout, and on occasion stated openly. The great themes of the speech — the chaos from which the nation had suffered, the working of God's providence, the need to reestablish traditional order, the hope for healing and reconciliation — were Cromwell's personal glosses on the recent history and future course of the nation. His positions seem clear enough, though some of them seem to smack of a different spirit from that of his views in the early 1640s. The course of the revolution had strengthened what had always been an essentially conservative attitude toward social order. In the course of war, his sense of social democracy had widened, but in the search for settlement, he had come increasingly to feel that the traditional social distinctions were significant and that violent alteration of them only led to instability. "A nobleman, a gentleman, a yeoman, that is a good interest of the nation and a great one. The magistracy of the nation, was it not almost trampled underfoot, under despite and contempt, by men of Levelling principles?" Others, such as the Fifth Monarchists, who had disturbed traditional order came in for their share of the attack also. England had come to such a pass, Cromwell argued, because it had ignored the dispensation of God. "All the dispensations of God, His terrible ones, He having met us in the way of His judgment in a ten-years civil war, a very sharp one, His merciful dispensations, they did not, they did not work upon us." The result, Cromwell reminded Parliament, had been chaos and arbitrary government. "Was not everything (almost) grown arbitrary? Who knew where or how to have right without some obstruction or other intervening? Indeed we were almost grown arbitrary in everything." Elsewhere in the speech, Cromwell referred feelingly to the time when the nation was "rent and torn in spirit and principle from one end to another . . . family against family, husband against wife, parents against children, and nothing in the hearts and minds of men but 'overturn, overturn, overturn.' " The solution was at hand; it was what Cromwell judged to be "the great end" of the meeting, healing and settling. He stressed the steps taken by the new government since its inception, with particular emphasis on reform of the law, the church settlement, and the accommodations made with various foreign nations. Cromwell's basic constitutionalism was evident in his happy reference to the calling of Parliament itself: "One thing more this government hath done: it hath been instrumental to call a free Parliament, which, blessed be God, we see here this day! I say a free Parliament. And that it may continue so, I hope is in the heart and spirit of every good man in

England. . . . It's that which as I have desired above my life, [so] I shall desire to keep it so, above my life." Cromwell ended the speech on the strong and confident note with which he had started. "It's one of the great ends of calling this Parliament, that this ship of the Commonwealth may be brought into a safe harbor, which, I assure you, it will not well be, without your counsel and advice. You have great works upon your hands. . . . I do therefore persuade you to a sweet, gracious, and holy understanding of one another and of your business."

From the very start, it was evident that it was not to be. The House, as all Cromwell's Parliaments were, was too divided against itself to heed the call to peace and unity. It was willing enough to accept Cromwell as head of state; it actually had very little choice in that. But significant elements of the House made it clear from the first day that they would not accept Lambert's constitution, at least in the manner the officers interpreted it. Despite what Cromwell and others assumed was an explicit understanding to the contrary, the House set out to debate the nature of the constitution and to move toward major alterations of its provisions. At the center of their concern was the crucial, undefined element of the Instrument, the precise relationship of Protector and Parliament.

There is considerable suggestion that Cromwell was prepared to make some compromise on the issue. In his desire to achieve a lasting settlement, he was willing to accept a parliamentary constitution in place of the Instrument, if certain fundamental features contained in the Instrument were preserved. On 12 September, Cromwell summoned Parliament to his presence to make his position clear. He stressed his own personal role under the Instrument and his determination to be faithful to his calling. "I see it will be necessary for me now a little to magnify my office, which I have not been apt to do. I have been of this mind . . . since first I entered upon it that, if God will not bear it up, let it sink. But if a duty be incumbent upon me . . . which in modesty I have hitherto forborne, I am in some measure now necessitated thereunto. . . . I called not myself to this place. . . . If my calling be from God and my testimony from the people, God and the people shall take it from me, else I will not part with it. I should be false to the trust that God hath placed in me and to the interest of the people of these nations if I should." After rehearsing the events that had led to the present dispute, Cromwell came to the heart of the matter. "Some things," he declared, "are fundamentals, about which I shall deal plainly with you. They may not be parted with, but will, I trust, be delivered over to posterity as being the fruits of our blood and travail." The four fundamentals he proceeded to list were not only indicative of his own concerns, but reveal a considerable insight on his part into the elements of a genuine settlement. The first was government by a single person and a Parliament, as laid down in the Instrument. Second, there should be clear safeguards that Parliaments should not make themselves perpetual. Third, liberty of conscience was to be guaranteed, and fourth, control of the militia was to be shared by Protector and Parliament. Other elements might be changed; these four, Cromwell indicated, must be preserved. "I say that the wilful throwing away of this government, such as it is, so owned by God, so approved by men, so testified to — in the fundamentals of it — as is before mentioned, and that in relation to the good of these nations and posterity, I can sooner be willing to be rolled into my grave and buried with infamy than I can give my consent unto."

Cromwell did not ask for an endorsement of his four fundamentals. Instead, he asked that each member sign a declaration that he would not propose or consent to an alteration of the government "as it is settled in a single person and a Parliament." Though signing the declaration was to be a precondition to reentering the House, it was not such a violation of parliamentary privilege as might be supposed; it was only asking of each member that he personally take the same engagement which his constituency had taken for him at the time of his election. By evening about 100 members had signed the document; by 21 September, the number had risen to 190. The most obstinate republicans could not accept the formulation, and withdrew from the House. In the end, about 100 members were actually excluded from the House, while those remaining carried on the constitutional debates and attempted to frame a constitution within the guidelines enunciated by Cromwell.

Cromwell had everything to gain from a parliamentary constitution being substituted for a military one, but though agreement was reached on a number of points, two of the issues singled out by Cromwell as fundamentals proved to be continuing points of dispute. The first was the issue of toleration, to which Cromwell had such a deep personal commitment. When Parliament proposed to draw up a list of damnable heresies as well as twenty articles of faith which all must observe, Cromwell and a number of members of the army had to object. A compromise was eventually reached by which the definition of heresy was to be left to the joint decision of Protector and Parliament. The question of control of the army proved even more troublesome. The Instrument authorized the Protector to maintain a force of thirty thousand men; in 1654, those actually in the force exceeded that total by about twenty-seven thousand. Parliament, anxious to cut governmental expenditure, insisted on a reduction to the specified figure and voted only such money as it felt would cover that number. At the same time, it continued to argue that control of the military of the nation should be in the hands of Parliament, a point on which Cromwell steadfastly refused to budge. The debate was not entirely a matter of principle; however much he disliked rule by the sword, Cromwell was acutely aware of the threats to the government posed by dissatisfied elements in the country. The threat of a Royalist insurrection seemed ever present; in-deed, Cromwell charged, dispute and confusion in the gov-ernment could only encourage it. The dissatisfied radicals likewise posed a threat, even within the army itself; the petition of the three colonels, Alured, Okey, and Saunders, actually drafted by the Leveller John Wildman and pub-lished as a broadsheet in mid-October, recalled the demands of the earlier Agreement of the People and called for "a full and free Parliament . . . [which could] without any imposition upon their judgments and consciences freely consider of those fundamental rights and freedoms of the Commonwealth that are the first subjects of this great con-test."

By the late fall, Cromwell had ample cause for irrita-tion. The constitutional dispute continued in unsatisfactory fashion. On top of that, he had had a near escape in a riding accident; while it may have been gratifying to receive ad-dresses of condolence from the Parliament, the accident had only served to reemphasize his personal importance to the political settlement. The Venetian ambassador noted that disorder and confusion would have resulted from his death; both enemies and friends knew that to be a fair estimate. Added to pressures of this sort was a personal loss that could only have added to Cromwell's sense of depression. His mother died in November. Her health had been failing since 1649 and her advanced age meant that death was not a surprise. But she and Cromwell had been very close, and there can be little doubt but that her passing affected him profoundly. In January, 1655, Cromwell wrote to Lieutenant Colonel Wilkes a letter in which he elaborated on his mood. Disappointment, frustration, a note of bitterness were all present in his comments. "If I looked for anything of help from men, or yet of kindness, it would be from such as fear the Lord, for whom I have been ready to lay down my life, and I hope still am, but I have not a few wounds from them, nor are they indeed, in this sad dispensation they are under (being divided in opinion and too much in affection ready to fall foul upon one another, whilst the enemy to be sure unite to purpose to their common destruction) in a capacity to receive much good or to minister good one to another, through want of communion in love; so that whosoever labours to walk with an even foot between the several interests of the people of God for healing and accommodating their differences is sure to have reproaches and anger from some of all sorts. And truly this is much of my portion at the present, so unwilling are men to be healed and atoned."

The note of bitterness was even more marked in Cromwell's speech to Parliament on 22 January 1655. He had summoned Parliament not to exhort and encourage it, but to reproach and dismiss it. Having decided that the five months' period of sitting could be calculated in lunar as well as calendar months, Cromwell took the first possible opportunity to dismiss legally a body in which he was grievously disappointed. Given a great mission, Parliament had failed. Too absorbed in petty and selfish interests, it had not only failed in the process of healing, but it had encouraged the growth of subversion. "Is there not yet upon the spirits of men a strange itch? Nothing will satisfy them unless they can put their finger upon their brethren's consciences, to pinch them there. . . . What greater hypocrisy than for those who were oppressed by the bishops to become the greatest oppressors themselves, so soon as their yoke was removed?" Elsewhere in the speech, referring to another of his four fundamentals, Cromwell uses the same bitter, scornful tone. "Instead of seasonable providing for the army, you have laboured to overthrow the government and the army is now upon free quarter! And you would never so much as let me hear a tittle from you concerning it. Where is the fault? Has it not been as if you had had a purpose to put this extremity upon us and the nation?" The depth of Cromwell's bitterness was revealed in two powerful and remarkable passages in the speech. The first provides almost a theme for the whole address with its emphasis on unwholesome growths in the potentially fertile land of the Commonwealth: "There be some trees that will not grow under the shadow of other trees. There be some that choose — a man may say so by way of allusion — to thrive under the shadow of other trees. I will tell you what hath thriven, I will not say what you have cherished, under your shadow; that were too hard. Instead of peace and settlement, instead of mercy and truth being brought together, righteousness and peace kissing each other, by reconciling the honest people of these nations, and settling the woeful distempers that are amongst us . . . weeds and nettles, briers and thorns have thriven under your shadow! Dissettlement and division, discontent and dissatisfaction, together with real dangers to the whole, has been more multiplied within these five months of your sitting, than in some years before!" The second passage is even more remarkable. The iniquities and dilatoriness of the Rump Parliament had become a staple of Cromwellian rhetoric. Now on an occasion when his bitter disillusion with that body cannot have been absent from his mind, Cromwell chose to draw a contrast between the two assemblies, a contrast in which the Rump Parliament came off the better. "I will say this to you in behalf of the Long Parliament: that had such an expedient as this government been proposed to them and that they could have seen the cause of God thus provided for and had by debates been enlightened in the grounds by which the difficulties might have been cleared and the reason of the whole enforced . . . as well as they were thought to love their seats, I think in my conscience that they would have proceeded in another manner than you have done and not have exposed things to those difficulties and hazards they now are at." From the mouth of Cromwell it was the ultimate denunciation. It remained only to bid the House disperse; "It is not for the profit of these nations, nor fit for the common and public good, for you to continue here any longer. And therefore

I do declare unto you, that I do dissolve this Parliament."
Another Cromwellian attempt to combine healing, reformation, and constitutional government had ended in frustration.

Cromwell's concern about the threats to the regime were
not fancies of his imagination. The efficient Thurloe kept
the government on top of most subversive activity, but there
can be little doubt that the evident disagreement within the
government encouraged its enemies to think of its overthrow.
Some of the protest, annoying though it may have been to
Cromwell, could be quickly brushed aside; the old soldier
calling himself Theauro John, who tossed a Bible, saddle,
sword, and pistol on a public bonfire, declaring them to be
the new gods of England, was not a serious security threat and
was quietly and quickly packed off to prison. More serious
was the kind of threat posed by the three colonels or the
possibility that Levellers, Royalists, even disgruntled republicans might combine in an unlikely alliance to topple Cromwell and his officers. In Scotland, a conspiracy headed by
Major General Overton was nipped in the bud; in England,
Harrison, who might prove a focal point for the Fifth
Monarchists once again, was arrested, while Wildman, the
Leveller plotter, was seized in the act of dictating "A Declaration of the free and well affected people of England now in
arms against the tyrant Oliver Cromwell." Fortunately for
Cromwell, the skill of his intelligence service was matched
by an almost total inability on the part of the opponents
of the regime to coordinate their efforts or to plan any well
thought out subversive activity. Royalist plotting was be-
deviled by an incredibly amateur, naïve, cloak-and-dagger
approach. When a Royalist rising did occur in the spring
of 1655, it was, on the whole, a pathetic affair. In theory,
there should have been a series of coordinated risings in
March; in fact, only one, that led by Colonel Penruddock
and Sir Joseph Wagstaff, amounted to anything. And even
that effort was relatively feeble. Three or four hundred men
followed the call, proclaimed Charles II, and started a march

toward Cornwall, where they hoped to find further support; the army overtook and routed them in Devon. It is reflective of how slight the threat had been that only thirty-nine of the conspirators were condemned to death, and of that number not more than fifteen actually were executed.

The ease with which Cromwell had put down challenge to the regime, coupled with the apparent inability of the Royalists to convert a potential threat into an actual danger and the effective infiltration of Royalist circles by Thurloe's spy network, makes Cromwell's next move, on the surface at least, difficult to explain. The man who had preached incessantly the necessity of healing suddenly reversed his stand. Admittedly, he reduced the size of the army — some ten to twelve thousand men were disbanded in the summer and autumn of 1655 — but that gesture toward satisfying a recurring demand of Parliament was more than offset by the introduction of military rule on a scale hitherto undreamed of. In the late summer and early fall of 1655, Cromwell undertook a scheme of dividing England and Wales into twelve military districts, each under the direction of an officer given the rank of major general for the purpose. The major general not only had the command of the local militia, but he also had at his disposal a "standing militia of horse" in every county, ready to be called out at a day's notice. The cost of maintaining the forces was to be met by a tax of 10 percent on the income of Royalists, the major generals themselves being responsible for collecting it with the assistance of local commissioners. The scheme for financing the major generals was something in which Cromwell took particular pride; as he told Parliament in the following year, "If there were need to have greater forces to carry on this work, it was a most righteous thing to put the charge upon that party which was the cause of it. And if there be any man that hath a face looking averse to this, I dare pronounce him to be a man against the interest of England."

Cromwell's decision to experiment with the major generals

must be seen in several lights. The system was justified as a security measure, and there is no reason to think this was not a serious justification. Even if Royalist plotting had been singularly ineffective, the Protectorate had more than enough enemies to make internal security one of the government's chief concerns. Closely related to the question of security was the maintenance of adequate armed forces. Given his difficulty with Parliament over this issue, Cromwell had little choice; he could either capitulate to Parliament or he could attempt to secure some form of military establishment by extraparliamentary means. The decimation tax on the Royalists seemed to provide just such an opportunity. The military force would pay for itself, or, more accurately, those whom it was designed to police would pay for it. To move in this direction involved a direct repudiation of the policy Cromwell had employed toward the Royalists, and it must be admitted that his rationalization for the change in policy is self-justifying and not wholly convincing. In his declaration of 31 October, which may be taken as the practical inauguration of the system, Cromwell did refer to the Act of Oblivion, but he argued that the leniency contained therein had been made dependent on future loyalty. The 1655 rising had canceled it out and now it was equitable to impose a tax on the whole of the Royalist party because the rising had involved all Royalists by implication, even though only a few had appeared in arms. It was an argument that convinced only the loyal supporters of the government.

Cromwell's declaration viewed the rule of the major generals purely in a military or police sense; nowhere did it discuss their relations to local government. His subsequent issue of instructions for them made it clear, however, that they were to have wide-ranging powers with respect to their areas and that, in effect, their institution was as much a new scheme of local government as it was a measure of police. This further dimension to the rule of the major generals must be considered central to Cromwell's experiment. Frustrated in a desire to achieve godly reformation in conventional ways, Cromwell sought to impose it by the sword. The major generals were themselves given extensive powers with respect to licensing, religion, and moral regulation, but, even more importantly, they were seen as a goad to spur local government to constructive action.

However well intentioned Cromwell's scheme was, the result was a predictable failure. On the one hand, he laid himself open to criticism for overcentralization. It is probably true that the central government never again ran local government so closely before the nineteenth century. But it was precisely tendencies in this direction that had led the country ruling class (Cromwell included) to resist the policy of "Thorough" in the 1630s. To enforce it now himself could only serve to divide him from the very elements of political society he needed to attract if he were ever to establish a rule other than the rule of the sword. That growing split between Cromwell and the ruling class of the country was further spread by the nature of the major generals themselves; many came from outside the counties they administered, some from social origins beneath the dignity of the country gentry. They seemed from the local perspective a threat to the traditional order that was gradually reasserting itself as the effects of war slipped away. When they put pressure on the justices of the peace or simply usurped the justices' duties, when they began to regulate markets, prohibit horseracing, and enforce the ordinance for ejecting scandalous clergy and schoolmasters, they drove deep wedges between the county community and the protectoral government. Unable in the last analysis to support themselves through the decimation tax, they could not be justified on economic grounds. And finally, they were criticized for splitting the nation at the same time they enhanced the control of the central government; when Ludlow commented that Cromwell "divided England into cantons, over each of which he placed a bashaw with the title of Major-General" he voiced a concern felt by a great many. As a security measure, the major generals may have been a success; in virtually all else they must be counted as one of Cromwell's major miscalculations. Nothing else he did has served to identify him so permanently in the popular mind with the military rule he so often professed he wanted to replace.

If Cromwell's efforts at home must be counted as failures, he had more cause to take pleasure in what he had managed abroad. That is not to say that domestic and foreign policy were unrelated, for Cromwell had a keen sense of the interplay between the two, and he treated foreign relations primarily as a means for strengthening his regime, not as an arena in which ideological considerations trampled down practical considerations. Cromwell never shared in the wilder enthusiasm of the pro–Dutch war group; on the other hand when he extricated England from a war he had never approved of in 1654, he did not let his religious sympathies blind him to the advantages to be had. Though some criticized them as too lenient, the terms were useful to England, especially the secret agreement barring the House of Orange from office in the Netherlands, thus cutting off a potential source of Royalist support. Cromwell was not able to convert peace with the Netherlands into the foundation stone of a European Protestant alliance; he quickly discovered that rivalries among the Protestant powers, particularly in the Baltic area, made such an alliance impossible in the long run. In any case, his approach to foreign policy was pragmatic, not ideological. He had the vision to conceive of national foreign policy on what amounted to a global scale, but that global vision was motivated by concrete, practical concerns like the flow of trade and the balance of power, not by idealistic hopes for a union of Protestant nations.

It is, at times, difficult to get to the roots of Cromwellian foreign policy. The language he used was often that of a more ideological age. He justified his West Indies policy with a religious argument: "God," he said to Lambert, "has not brought us hither where we are but to consider the work we may do in the world, as well as at home." When he despatched Whitelocke to Sweden, he told him to bring back a Protestant alliance. In 1655, he intervened on behalf of the oppressed Protestants of the Vaudois, and expressed his moral indignation in no uncertain terms both to the Duke of Savoy and to Cardinal Mazarin. Yet if these seem the actions of a religious idealist, examination shows another side to each decision. The West Indies policy was a bold experiment in colonial empire; for all the justification given to it in God's name, its aims were commercial, economic and strategic. Whitelocke's instructions deal wholly with politics and economics, for all the publicly expressed desire for a Protestant alliance. And even if Cromwell's indignation over the treatment of the Vaudois was genuine (and there is no reason to doubt this), the incident was also a useful diplomatic tool in dealing with France.

Having made peace with the Dutch, Cromwell moved England steadily towards a pro-French and anti-Spanish stand. There were two keys to the policy. The first was actual alliance with France, patiently and carefully negotiated beginning with a primarily commercial treaty in 1655 and culminating in a close military alliance against Spain that led to the cession of Dunkirk to England. The other was an anti-Spanish policy, most fully expressed in the Western Design, Cromwell's ambitious attempt to grasp control of the West Indies from the Spaniards. In undertaking such a venture, Cromwell was stepping well beyond the Elizabethan heritage he much admired. Elizabeth's sea dogs had raided and plundered; Cromwell sought to grasp political and economic power in the area by seizing land and commencing a policy of active plantation. He admittedly had the short-term hope that the seizure of Spanish treasure might be a way of solving the economic problems he faced at home, but his essential aims were truly imperial in scope. The

Western Design was far from an unqualified success. It failed to gain its initial objective Hispaniola, though the expedition took Jamaica instead. The two commanders quarreled with each other, returned home as soon as they could, and found themselves sent to the Tower by a displeased Protector. The hope of floating the Protectorate on a windfall revenue of Spanish treasure never materialized. The process of colonization was slow. And yet, the expedition cannot be counted a total failure. The bold conception of it was an important legacy and Jamaica itself, though it had not been the primary target, was to prove of great significance in subsequent English colonial development.

In retrospect, what is most striking about Cromwell's foreign policy is the steady securing of the English interest on a global scale. Step by step, he built the English position. Blake's activities in the Mediterranean in 1654 and 1655 curbed piracy, but also curbed French ambitions in that direction. The 1654 alliance with Portugal opened up a potentially vast market to English trade. The French alliance led to a foothold on the continent. Cromwell even thought grandly of expelling the Dutch from New Amsterdam and the French from Canada. The English military establishment, especially its newly significant navy, was everywhere feared and respected. It was a remarkable achievement carried out in an astonishingly short period of time. There are those who would argue that the policy was too grandiose, that it outstripped the resources of the country, but they cannot deny that Cromwell had changed England's position in the world.

Scotland and Ireland provided less cause for satisfaction on Cromwell's part. Both had been drawn directly into the English political system by giving them representation in Parliament; both were administered by people close to Cromwell, Scotland by General Monck and Lord Broghill, Ireland by his son-in-law Fleetwood and then by his son Henry. There the similarity ended. The Cromwellian regime in

Scotland was, on many counts, a success. Despite the continuance of sectarian animosity in the country, the Cromwellian administration brought a measure of modernization, removing outdated feudal jurisdictions and encouraging trade with England. Firm rule brought order and with order came some increase in prosperity. In Ireland, on the other hand, the Cromwellian policy fared less well, though it left a permanent imprint on the land. To some extent, Cromwell's Irish policy was shaped by events before he came to power; the original Adventurers had to be satisfied and then so did the soldiers who had fought the Irish campaigns. Building on this situation, Cromwell sought to solve the "Irish problem" by a bold and sweeping policy; Catholicism was to be rooted out, the native Irish themselves transplanted into Connaught and Clare, and the confiscated lands were to be distributed to satisfy creditors and provide for new and safe settlers. The result of the Cromwellian settlement, as imperfectly carried out as it was, was hardship, suffering, and injustice. The extensive confiscation of land accelerated the change already underway in the Irish landholding class; some six thousand landowners were deprived of their holdings. For the peasantry, it was substantially a case of exchanging old masters for new ones. Catholicism was to be totally abolished, and there were major attempts to clear papists out of all towns. The latter effort was not wholly successful, though there was a considerable clearance; in country districts, the impact was less marked and, despite all the Cromwellian efforts, it did not seem possible to lessen permanently the number of Catholic priests. Cromwell likewise hoped to achieve a safe and Protestant Ireland through education; if the children were brought up as Protestants, he argued, the country in time would be won over. That time was not provided, though it is doubtful that the Cromwellian solution would have worked even with all the time and all the money it needed. Too much of what Cromwell planned as reform in Ireland was policy constructed in England out of a vast ignorance of Irish conditions and often wholly ir-relevant to them. The best that can be said for Cromwell's handling of Ireland was that it produced a period of relative order, especially during the administration of his son Henry. On the negative side were immense human sufferings and injustices. If Cromwell had an enduring contribution to make to Ireland, it was to be felt in the fact that Protestants were left holding the bulk of Irish lands and had gathered into their hands extensive power over trade, local politics, and national government. Cromwell helped in a major way to shape the Protestant ascendancy in Ireland; at the same time the very nature of his policies, coupled with the brutality of his earlier military campaign, helped to shape a national tradition in opposition to that ascendancy, an opposition which was nurtured by hatred of Cromwell himself.

At home, Cromwell found himself facing increasing dif-ficulties. Not the least of his worries was a growing body of legal opposition to the Protectorate, much of it stemming from reservations about the power to legislate by ordinance. Thorpe and Newdigate, two of the judges sent with other commissioners to preside at the trial of northern Royalists in April, 1655, proceeded to question the validity of the treason ordinance under which the trial was being held; in so doing, they also questioned the validity of the Instrument of Government under the provisions of which it had been issued. Cromwell could not let such threats pass unchecked; Thorpe and Newdigate were summoned before the council and dismissed. But the same sort of questioning was also raised before the upper bench at Westminster in the case of merchant George Cony. Cony had refused to pay duty on some imported silk. He was committed, released on legal technicalities and then committed again; his second com-mittal and the fine levied against him were based on two protectoral ordinances. His counsel then proceeded to attack the validity of the ordinances, and hence by implication the Instrument. They were committed to prison, but Cromwell's

worries were not over, for the judge in the case shared some
of the same concerns; he was summoned before the council,
and while the case was adjourned, he resigned under obvious
pressure to be replaced by a supporter of the Instrument. In
the end Cony, seeing his case was hopeless, gained his freedom by paying his fine; according to Ludlow, he thereby
"lost his reputation by withdrawing himself from a cause
wherein the public was so much concerned." That may have
been so, but the case had given Cromwell much to ponder.

Cromwell was also discovering in these months that his
defense of toleration could lead to differences not only with
Parliament, but with the Council of State. Such division was
clear, for example, over Cromwell's desire to gain legal readmission for the Jews, who had officially been expelled from
England in 1290. Cromwell's motives in seeking their readmission were not entirely connected with toleration or even
with some vague hope for the conversion of the Jews. In a
very practical sense, he appreciated the possibilities that the
network of Jewish trading connections had both for the
workings of his intelligence system and for the economic
development of England. Though Cromwell was able to
effect a practical readmission of the Jews, he could not effect
a legal one, for he could not carry the council with him. It
says something for Cromwell's determination in the matter
that he did what he did, but the unwillingness of the council
to follow his lead added yet another item to the growing
agenda of matters of concern. Much the same pattern was
revealed by the reactions of the council and Cromwell to
various sects, especially the Quakers. It was plain that Cromwell was more tolerant than the council as a body was. But
he could not wholly ignore what the council was saying; in
their insistence that the radical sects were disruptive of social
order, they made a point that Cromwell reluctantly acknowledged on occasion. He had hoped, vainly and even
naïvely, that some sort of moderate course could bring the
nation together, could resolve the inevitable tension between

individual conscience and public order. He was wrong. In his own soul, he appears to have resolved the paradoxical situation of believing in the salvation of the elect only and maintaining a tolerance of those he felt were not of the elect; in the soul of the nation, he could effect no such resolution.

If public pressures were not enough, Cromwell was also subject to intense personal pressures in the winter of 1655–1656. His own health was questionable. He suffered from the stone, from gout, from a severe boil on his chest. He worried about the sickness of his daughter Elizabeth, already showing the first signs of fatal cancer. He was concerned about the future careers of his sons Henry and Richard. He appears to have thought of quiet, country careers for both of them, but his own position in the long run made that impossible. In 1655, he wrote to Fleetwood about Henry, "The Lord knows, my desire was for him and his brother to have lived private lives in the country, and Harry knows this very well and how difficultly I was persuaded to give him his commission for this present place." The place in question was replacing Fleetwood in Ireland, and Henry's career there revealed that there was little cause to worry about him. Richard was quite another matter. As the eldest surviving son, he was even more in the foreground than Henry. A pleasant enough person, he lacked the competency and determination of his father and brother, but still Cromwell tried to bring him on. He had already served as a Member of Parliament; in 1655 he was appointed to the Committee of Trade and Navigation. As the issue of the succession began to loom larger and larger, so did his importance; his qualities unfortunately could not grow to match his prominence.

Advancing years and accumulating pressures were taking their toll. Though Cromwell recovered from his various illnesses and survived another coach accident in the spring, the signs were present. The Venetian ambassador in 1655 noted that he was "somewhat pulled" in appearance, that his hand trembled and that there were signs that his health was far from perfect. In terms of his own hopes, the years had taken their toll too. The ecstatic mood with which he had greeted Barebone's Parliament, the more restrained but firm optimism with which he had addressed the first Protectorate Parliament were in the past. The hope that reconciliation could be achieved was fast receding. In the summer of 1656, he summed it up in a conversation with Ludlow. Taxed by Ludlow for not achieving "that which we fought for, that the nation might be governed by its own consent," Cromwell answered, "I am as much for a government by consent as any man, but where shall we find that consent? Amongst the Prelatical, Presbyterian, Independent, Anabaptists or Levelling Parties?" The point was well taken; Ludlow's quick answer that consent was to be found "amongst those of all sorts who had acted with fidelity and affection to the public" was a political fantasy, wholly belied by the political facts that Cromwell had come to know all too well.

ELEVEN

Constable of the Parish

UNDER THE TERMS of the Instrument, Cromwell was not obliged to summon another Parliament until 1657. Despite his failure with the first Protectorate Parliament and his awareness that a consensus necessary to ordered, constructive government did not exist, he summoned a second Parliament in the summer of 1656. He did so for two reasons. Above all, he needed money to finance the now open war with Spain. Any hopes that the war would not only pay for itself but for the government as well were now fully dashed. But he had also been assured by his major generals that they could use their influence to produce the sort of Parliament with which he could work, a Parliament where there was a consensus in favor of the Protector and his program because the various opposition elements would all be eliminated.

The campaign in the autumn of 1656 was the most vigorous electioneering campaign since that of 1640. As Thurloe wrote to Henry Cromwell in mid-August, "The day of election now draws near, and here is the greatest striving to get into Parliament that ever was known." The very vigor of the electioneering reflects the absence of a national consensus. The government, of course, made every effort to secure support, but its campaign was faced by widespread opposition stemming from disparate and incongruous sources. To some, the appeal of royalism beckoned; in others, the call of the Fifth Monarchists aroused strong loyalties. The somewhat amorphous republican opposition was much in evidence, and there were futile attempts to make an alliance during the summer between this group and the Fifth Monarchists. Virtually all they had in common was a desire to overthrow the Protectorate; that was a powerful bond, but not one strong enough to overcome the basic differences occasioned by the republican desire to restore in some form or other the authority of the Long Parliament. The political sentiment that seemed most evident and general in the campaign was hatred of the system of major generals. Their interference in local government had rankled; the justice and legality of the decimation tax was much at issue, and the decimators themselves were easy targets for popular outrage. The central government exerted pressure in specific areas to forestall the election of opposition figures. Ludlow, suspected of being a possible candidate for Wiltshire, was induced to retire to the house of his brother-in-law in Essex; Vane, who clearly did aspire to a seat, was summoned before the council at the end of July and on 4 September, after refusing to give security not to act against the government, he was imprisoned at Carisbrooke.

For all the efforts, the results were no more successful, from Cromwell's viewpoint, than any previous parliamentary election. The continuity of membership with its troublesome predecessor was noticeable. The most notable electoral success of the major generals had been to secure their own seats; the wider influence they had promised was simply not forthcoming. Cromwell did not spare them his feelings. "Impatient were you till a Parliament was called. I gave my vote against it but you [were] confident by your own strength and interest to get men chosen to your heart's desire. How you have failed therein, and how much the country hath been disobliged is well known." It would be wrong to picture the Parliament as composed of a formed opposition to Cromwell. The nature of opposition was as diverse within the House as it was among the electorate. But there was widespread feeling that military dominance should be reduced, and that the structure of government as defined by the Instrument should be altered. Both sentiments presented Cromwell with delicate political problems.

When Parliament assembled, some of the potential opposition was set aside in arbitrary fashion; those who were thought to be clearly unsafe were excluded on the authority of the Council. About 120 elected members were excluded in this fashion, and though Cromwell cannot be identified as the author of this policy, it was, nonetheless, bound to reflect on him. Those who continued to sit were, on the whole, willing to support a government that would produce peace and tranquillity, and their actions showed that many of them were willing to seek that tranquillity under Cromwell. For example, they passed one act which annulled the Stuarts' title to the throne and a second making plots to overthrow the government high treason.

Cromwell's customary opening address on 17 September 1656 provides some telling contrasts with similar speeches in the past. Even by Cromwellian standards, it was a long speech, lasting perhaps as much as three hours. While familiar themes appear and reappear, the text as it has come down from the reporters is repetitive, diffuse, unduly longwinded. It is hard not to see in the speech a reflection of the strain Cromwell had been under, and to sense the extent to which the strain was beginning to tell. For all that, Cromwell's treatment of individual themes was wholly in character. Some of his most memorable comments about the reformation of manners, a continuing political aim, were made in this speech. He displayed his long-standing concern that the search for orthodoxy must be tempered with tolerance and mercy: "When we are brought into the right way, we shall be merciful as well as orthodox." His review of recent events justified the major generals on security grounds and praised the steps that had been taken to improve church and state. The theme of the Spanish war, the cost of which had occasioned the Parliament, was boldly trumpeted, linking it to the existence of plots in England. "Why, truly, your great enemy is the Spaniard. He is. He is a natural enemy. . . . He is naturally so throughout, by reason of that enmity that is in him against whatever is of God. . . . He hath an interest in your bowels; he hath so."

Cromwell made a heartfelt appeal at the end of the speech for consensus and good will, hoping yet again that the spirit of God would enable the spirit of cooperation to flourish. He knew what sort of men he wanted in Parliament — "men of honest hearts, engaged to God, strengthened by providence, enlightened in His words, to know His word . . . that is such a spirit as will carry on this work." If such a spirit existed, if Parliament would not waste time in disputing "unnecessary and unprofitable things," then a great work could at last be accomplished. Cromwell left his listeners in no doubt about his view of his own position: "Know assuredly that if I have interest, I am by the voice of the people the supreme magistrate." But Cromwell, the constitutionalist, still sought to work with Parliament, not against or without it. "It is an union, really it is an union between you and me: and both of us united in faith and love to Jesus Christ and to His peculiar interest in the world, — that must ground this work. And in that, if I have any peculiar interest that's personal to myself, that is not subservient to the public end, it were no extravagant thing for me to curse myself, because I know God will curse me, if I have."

At practically every point, the harmonious working together that Cromwell desired failed to materialize. Almost coincident with the opening of Parliament, Captain Stayner defeated a Spanish squadron off Cadiz and captured treasure worth £600,000. It gave to Cromwell's war with Spain a tangible aura of success, and Parliament did vote to approve the war and supply £400,000 for its expenses. But on other counts, problems arose. They arose in the context of the increasing personal authority of Cromwell himself, as opposed to the authority of Cromwell as general of the army, and this, in itself, was a difficult political problem. Many in Parliament shared with Cromwell the desire for an ordered, essentially conservative or traditional regime. They began to take seriously the idea of converting Cromwell's position into that of king, thus linking his authority firmly to a recognized political office rather than to the army. Cromwell was acutely aware of the fact that, whatever was said about authority, power rested with the army, as it had throughout the revolution. He was thus caught, in a sense, in the middle. With a significant element of Parliament, he shared a desire for ordered government; their method of institutionalizing it would, however, create tension with important elements in the army without whose support his power was threatened. The possibility of such tension was revealed early in the Parliament by a motion to make the office of Protector hereditary; the army element reacted sharply to the proposal and Desborough, though he was Cromwell's brother-in-law, indicated in no uncertain terms the army's opposition to such a move.

Two major topics occupied the interest of Parliament. Both of them were contentious, and both raised serious questions about the interlocking relationships of Cromwell, the army, and Parliament. The first concerned the case of James Nayler, a Quaker leader of uncertain and unstable temperament. As the result of a triumphal entry into Bristol, carried out with deliberate imitation of Christ's entry into Jerusalem, Nayler was arrested and brought to London to be tried for blasphemy. The trial, if such it can be called, provided ample opportunity for the opponents of religious toleration to express their views. If, some argued, what Nayler had done was covered under the religious clauses of the Instrument, then the Instrument should be changed. Members vied with each other in suggesting barbaric and gruesome punishments for the defendant. The trial raised serious political questions, notably, by what right did the current Parliament have the power to proceed in such a fashion. The question was put directly by Cromwell in a letter to Parliament on 25 December: "Although we detest and abhor the giving or occasioning the least countenance to persons of such opinions and practices or who are under the guilt of such crimes as are commonly imputed to the said person, yet we, being entrusted in the present government on behalf of the people of these nations, and not knowing how far such proceedings (wholly without us) may extend in the consequence of it, do desire that the House will let us know the grounds and reasons whereupon they had proceeded." Parliament's position was simple enough, if of dubious constitutionality; they had absorbed into themselves the judicial power formerly possessed by the now-abolished House of Lords. From that position they refused to budge, and the best that Cromwell could do was to seek to provide some alleviation of the sufferings of Nayler; he could not stop the trial nor could he prevent horrendous punishment being inflicted. There can be little doubt that Parliament's proceedings in this case raised doubts again in Cromwell's mind about the long-term prospects of obtaining the sort of society he wanted by working in tandem with Parliament. The stress he had placed on mercy and tolerance in his opening remarks had been almost entirely ignored.

The second key issue was wholly predictable, given the nature of the election campaigns, and that was the question of the survival of the major-general system. While the debate was to be anticipated, the manner in which it was worked out was less so. On the same day that Cromwell wrote to

Parliament about Nayler, Desborough moved in the House a bill to continue the decimation tax and hence the system of major generals. That the bill was in difficulty was immediately apparent; it was only by a small majority that permission was secured to put the bill forward. What worried the army leaders the most was that a number who were part of the Cromwellian circle voted against it. If that sign was not clear enough, confirmation that Cromwell had abandoned the major generals, despite his support in his opening speech, was provided in January. To that point Cromwell had not spoken publicly against the major generals; now he did so by proxy. The first speaker in the debate was his son-in-law Claypole. His statement, Ludlow noted, "was a clear direction to the sycophants of the court, who being fully persuaded that Claypole had delivered the sense, if not the very words of Cromwell in this matter, joined as one man in opposing the major-generals and so their authority was abrogated." By an overwhelming majority, Cromwell's supporters put an emphatic end to an experiment that had been, from the first, misconceived. Despite his support of the experiment, Cromwell can never have been fully at ease with government by force. In his frustration he had once again applied the tactics of the battlefield to politics; as on other occasions, it was a mistake.

While the debates were in progress there was a further development complicating Cromwell's position. Another plot to assassinate him was uncovered. This time the intended assassin was an old soldier with Leveller connections, Miles Sindercombe. He had originally intended to kill Cromwell at the opening of Parliament. That failing because of the size of the crowd, he had next thought of shooting him on his way to Hampton Court or of assaulting him in Hyde Park. Finally, he had conceived the idea of setting fire to Whitehall Chapel, hoping in the ensuing confusion to have the chance to eliminate Cromwell. At this point the plot was exposed and on 19 January Thurloe gave a full account of the proceedings to Parliament, missing no opportunity to stress the danger that Cromwell, and through him the nation, had been in. As the House debated the drafting of a congratulatory address to Cromwell on his escape, John Ashe, a member from Somerset, intervened with a thought that was to have significant implications. "I would have something else added, which, in my opinion, would tend very much to the preservation of himself and us and to the quieting of all the designs of our enemies — that his Highness would be pleased to take upon him the government according to the ancient constitution."

It was far from the first time it had been suggested Cromwell should be king; Lambert and the officers had themselves made the same suggestion in the first draft of the Instrument of Government. But coming in January, 1657, it placed Cromwell in an extremely awkward position. Despite abandoning the major generals, Cromwell remained fully aware that he could not risk offending his potential army followers any more.

Nothing was done with Ashe's proposed resolution, but the thought stuck. In February it was reported that citizens were placing bets that the form of government would change, and Vane wrote bitterly, "I did always believe this Parliament would make him King before they parted." The matter came to a head on 23 February. On that day, Sir Christopher Packe presented a remonstrance to the House expressing the views of those who had resolved to effect a basic change in the constitution by giving Cromwell the office and title of King. Packe described his paper as "somewhat come to his hand tending to the settlement of the nation and of liberty and property"; it rapidly became apparent that the document was not his and that he was acting as the tool of others. Packe himself admitted to the member sitting next to him that he had not read the paper through. Actually behind the proposal were Lord Broghill, the former Royalist and now converted Cromwellian, and a number of the lawyers in the

House. The bill, when read, revealed a proposed new settlement that would make Cromwell king, lead to a settlement of the succession (increasingly a key issue as Cromwell aged), and revive the House of Lords. On the issue of kingship, the parliamentary battle lines were quickly drawn. The lawyers, the civilian members of the council, a high proportion of the members from Ireland, and a significant group of country gentlemen led by Sir Richard Onslow appeared favorable to the kingship. Lambert, who argued it was contrary to the principles for which the army had fought and a violation of oaths they had all taken, the major generals, and most of the officers were clearly opposed.

On 26 February, there was a joint meeting of the officers and the major generals. At it, Lambert urged concerted action to counter the move to make Cromwell king, though he was careful to stress that action should be undertaken moderately and with patience. The following day one hundred officers, including the major generals, met with Cromwell to indicate their displeasure with Packe's Remonstrance and their hope that Cromwell would refuse the offer of the crown. Cromwell's answer nicely delineated the dimensions of the political problem. He stated categorically that he had had nothing to do with the introduction of the Remonstrance; indeed he had only seen it for the first time the day before. Cromwell was at pains to point out that he had no particular liking for the kingship. He noted that he had turned aside similar offers in the past, not missing the chance while saying so to remind the officers that their attitude toward the issue had been quite different in December, 1653. And yet there was, he noted, much in the Remonstrance that was attractive. Clearly the experiment with the major generals had been a failure and a new settlement must be found to replace them. "It is time to come to a settlement and lay aside arbitrary proceedings so unacceptable to the nation." The Remonstrance seemed to him to offer possibilities in that direction. The financial settlement proposed in the document was better than anything provided under the Instrument and in all ways, except for the kingship, it seemed an admirable proposal. Cromwell was particularly taken by the proposed revival of the House of Lords, for he saw such a body as an essential check and balance to the power of the existing House. He made the point forcefully to the officers, referring to the case of Nayler as an example of what could happen with an unchecked power. "By the proceedings of this Parliament, you see they stand in need of a check or balancing power . . . , for the case of James Nayler might happen to be your case. By their judicial power they fall upon life and member, and doth the Instrument enable me to control it?"

The speech appeared to have a marked momentary effect on the army, yet the position remained awkward. Cromwell's assessment that a new settlement was in order was valid, but what would happen if Parliament insisted that the kingship was an integral part of it, and major sectors of the army continued to oppose the kingship on principle? Cromwell could do little except adopt a waiting posture. Debate on the Remonstrance proceeded fairly rapidly. On 2 March, discussion of the kingship was postponed until the rest of the proposal had been considered. This move, undertaken apparently at the instigation of Sir Richard Onslow, made possible what emerged as the Cromwellian strategy — secure the useful parts of the proposal first and face the decision on the kingship only at the very end when all the arguments had been heard and the strength of the opposed sides could be gauged. The question of the proposed House of Lords, which Thurloe thought would be "a very hard and doubtful question" passed unanimously and without a division; the logic of Cromwell's speech to the hundred officers had been compelling, at least on that point. Clause by clause the new draft constitution, now labeled the Humble Petition and Advice, came together. On 25 March, after a bitter debate, the House resolved 123 to 62 to ask Cromwell to accept the office and title of King. The request was presented to him on 31 March at Whitehall, but characteristically he delayed his decision.

Although it was generally assumed that Cromwell would eventually accept, his initial answer was a negative one. On 3 April, he stated "I should be very brutish should I not acknowledge the exceeding high honour and respect you have had for me in this paper. . . . Seeing the way is hedged up so as it is to me, I cannot accept the things offered unless I accept all. I have not been able to find it my duty to God and you to undertake this charge under that title." In the weeks that followed, members of Parliament continued to press Cromwell to change his mind; their argument, reduced to its simplest form, was that the kingship was essential to a constitutional settlement. Thurloe summed up the matter well. "Parliament will not be persuaded that there can be a settlement any other way. The title is not the question, but it is the office which is known to the law and to the people. They know their duty to a king and his to them. Whatever else there is will be wholly new, and upon the next occasion will be changed again. Besides they say the name Protector came in with the sword and will never be the ground for any settlement nor will there be a free Parliament so long as that continues, and as it savours of the sword now, so it will at last bring all things to be military." It was an argument Cromwell could understand; it spoke directly to his desire to rule constitutionally, and it correctly indicated that such rule could only come about if the connection between government and army were redefined.

Cromwell's indecision and wavering appear to have been genuine enough. He was, as he put it, "hugely taken with the thing" and he was sure that "the things provided in the petition do secure the liberties of the people of God so as they never before had them." For five weeks conferences and negotiations continued. Cromwell suggested numerous amendments to the proposed constitution, and they were accepted. By the beginning of May, Cromwell had gained what he wanted, and Parliament had come so far with the proposed constitution that it was unlikely to abandon the product of such efforts. Only the title remained unresolved, and towards the end of the negotiations, the supposition was very strong that Cromwell would take it. Whalley, who had agreed to all the settlement except the title, declared in late April that "rather than I would forego the other good things contained in it, I could well swallow that of the title." It seemed as if the opposition to the kingship were crumbling. But this was far from the case. On the eve of his final decision, at a time when it seems reasonably clear that he had resolved to accept, Cromwell was subjected to heavy and decisive pressure from the army. On the one hand, a petition against the kingship by a number of army officers indicated that feeling on the issue was still strong; on the other, "the three great men" of the army, as Thurloe called them, Fleetwood, Desborough, and Lambert, threatened to lay down their commissions if he accepted. They further indicated that "several other officers of quality that had been engaged all along in this war" would do the same. It was sufficient to cause Cromwell to change his mind. On 8 May, in a final speech, he definitively declined the title. He stressed that the proposed constitution was a good one, but he indicated he remained unconvinced on the issue of the necessity of kingship. "I am persuaded to return this answer to you, that I cannot undertake this government with that title of king. And that is mine answer to this great and weighty business." As he had at so many critical turnings in the past, Cromwell under pressure had sided with the army.

The decision came as a considerable surprise, and Parliament was predictably disappointed. It did not, however, miss the broad hint contained in Cromwell's rejection of the title. On 25 May, the constitution was once again offered to Cromwell with the title of Protector replacing that of King and Cromwell speedily accepted. His government now rested as near to having a constitutional basis as it ever would. He ruled by a parliamentary constitution, not an army settlement. He had gained his much desired second House and the power to appoint its seventy members. He could name his own successor. Parliament, too, had made its gains. The power of the council was reduced, though indirectly this aided Cromwell as well since it diminished the power of Lambert in the government. More important, Parliament now had control over its own elections; the power of arbitrary exclusion by the council could no longer be used to seek a pliant body.

On 26 June 1657, Cromwell was, for the second time, installed as Protector. The ceremony was altogether more grand than his first installation. It was a virtual coronation; all that lacked was the crown and the title. The Speaker, representing Parliament, cloaked him in a robe of purple velvet lined with ermine, being, it was significantly noted, "the habit anciently used at the investiture of princes." Even a golden scepter was placed in his hands. Following the ceremony, Parliament was adjourned and Cromwell, newly installed in his dignity, again ruled along with his council.

During the debate over the kingship Cromwell had had ample opportunity to comment on his role. In a significant statement, he reflected on the motives that had brought him to his current position and the manner in which he felt he should conduct affairs. "I am a man standing in the place I am in, which place I undertook not so much out of the hope of doing any good, as out of a desire to prevent mischief and evil which I did see was imminent in the nation. . . . I am ready to serve not as a king but as a constable. For truly I have, as before God, thought it often that I could not tell what my business was, nor what I was in the place I stood, save comparing myself to a good constable to keep the peace of the parish." The glitter of his second installation and the existence of a parliamentary constitution did not alter the fact that this remained, in many ways, his role.

That is not to say that Cromwell abandoned all positive programs and simply sought to keep the peace. There is evidence that despite repeated disappointment, advancing age, and declining health, he was still actively concerned with a program of reform in the spring and summer of 1657. The ever-recurring theme of law reform was still in the air. Education, which had received special attention from his regime, continued to attract his efforts and in May he granted letters patent for the establishment of a new college at Durham for "the better advancement of learning and religion in those parts." It was a noble scheme, responsive to local needs and desires. Its demise at the Restoration was symbolic of what happened generally to the ambitious Cromwellian schemes for strengthening learning and religion.

Two factors, however, placed distinct limits on Cromwell's capacity to achieve constructive reform and forced him back into the role he had defined as that of constable. One was the precarious nature of government finance. Despite a new financial settlement, the gap between revenue and expenditure remained. It was easy enough to trace the problem to its source, the vast expenditures for the army and navy and the continuation of the Spanish war. In addition the new sums promised under the Humble Petition and Advice did not always come in as expected. And yet the heavy military expenditures remained, to Cromwell's mind, absolutely essential if the peace of the three kingdoms was to be preserved. What, he asked Parliament, stood between them and "utter destruction"; it was, he answered, the army "without doubt that keeps this nation in peace and quietness." The second factor was the continuing lack of unity and consensus. With division rampant, Cromwell saw his chief task as preserving order. "Look on this nation," he told Parliament in January, 1658, "look on it. Consider what are the variety of interests in this nation, if they be worthy the name of interests. If God did not hinder, all would but make up a confusion. We shall find there will be more than one Cain in England, if God did not refrain, and we should have another more bloody civil war than ever we had in England. . . . What is it which possesseth every sect . . . that every sect may be uppermost, that every sort of man may get the power into their hands, and they would use it well. It were a happy thing if the nation would be content with rule."

The limitations became apparent as soon as Parliament reassembled in January. During the summer, Cromwell had selected the members of his new upper House. Of sixty-three people invited to attend, forty-three accepted. It was in no way a representative body; seven members of Cromwell's own family were included, as were no less than seventeen regimental commanders. The process of making the upper House safe had, however, weakened Cromwell's hold on the lower House, from which he plucked a number of his supporters for this new honor. In addition, the leading republicans, excluded at the start of the Parliament, now flooded back to the House, where they formed from the start a sizable and hostile party. Notwithstanding, Cromwell greeted the reassembled Parliament with enthusiasm, hope, and apparent confidence. "If God should bless you in this work and make this meeting happy upon this account, you shall all be called the blessed of the Lord. The generations to come will bless us. You shall be 'the repairers of breaches and the restorers of paths to dwell in.' And if there be any work that mortals can attain to in the world, beyond this, I acknowledge my ignorance [of it]."

The optimism vanished almost at once. The House of Commons was soon at the mercy of the republicans, who assailed the new second House, refusing to recognize it as a House of Lords and insisting it should simply be called the other House. They sought limitations on the Protector's power over the army. They wanted the House of Commons to be recognized as the supreme authority in the nation. To facilitate these ends, they arranged for a petition to be signed by ten thousand Londoners and they contemplated replacing Cromwell with Fairfax as commander-in-chief. To Cromwell, it was an all too familiar and depressing scenario. On 4 February, he summoned both Houses and in a brief speech turned them out. He stressed his legal authority under the constitution and the reluctance with which he had accepted power. "There is not a man living can say I sought it, no not a man nor woman treading upon English ground. . . . I would have been glad to have lived under my woodside, to have kept a flock of sheep." But the need for settlement had pushed him into office, and now Parliament by its factious behavior was again threatening that settlement. "You have not only disjointed yourselves but the whole nation which is in likelihood of running into more confusion in these 15 or 16 days that you have sat than it hath been from the rising of the last session to this day." Cromwell, the avowed parliamentarian, had had enough experience with previous parliaments to see there was no point in prolonging this one. "I think it high time that an end be put to your sitting. And I do dissolve this Parliament. And let God be judge between you and me."

Cromwell did not summon another parliament though he was contemplating doing so at the time of his death. His experience with representative assemblies can hardly be called either happy or successful. It is all too easy to assert that it was simply a matter of management, that had he possessed the skill of Elizabeth (to whom he made increasing reference in his latter days), he could have curbed or channeled the opposition. It is a supposition that is difficult to sustain. Cromwell's reiterated laments about the lack of consensus were not simply self-serving apologies; they were accurate assessments of political fact. The more any Parliament approached what Cromwell wanted of it (that is, the less it was subject to army control and purges), the greater the proportion of the House which was implacably opposed to the regime. The more Cromwell attempted to force a consensus, by one means or another, the more impossible became the essentially illusory quest of converting a military dictatorship into a constitutional regime. By January, 1658, Cromwell understood this well, and it lay at the heart of his frustration, disillusion, and increasing bitterness. He was aware too that his actions had endangered his base of power, even in the army. Even his own regiment, in the persons of the troop commanders, indicated their dislike of the present government and spoke "of the goodness of a commonwealth." They continued to express their personal loyalty to Cromwell but couched it in ambiguous terms of "the old cause" which they did not define. Cromwell's answer was to dismiss them all. Thus his position was secured, but officers of his own had joined the steadily widening list of colleagues he had been forced to shunt aside.

From the perspective of a royalist abroad, Cromwell seemed in a strong position in the winter of 1658. Clarendon noted that "from the dissolution of Cromwell's last Parliament, all things at home and abroad seemed to succeed to his wish, and his power and greatness to be better established than ever it had been." Certainly some things pointed in that direction. The aggressive foreign policy he pursued was achieving tangible results; the victory of the Dunes and the capture of Dunkirk stood as evidence of that. Internal threats from his own army or from Royalist plotters, such as those who in May were accused of plotting to set fire to the City, had been convincingly quashed. Two of his daughters, Frances and Mary, had been married the year previously to husbands who, if they were not grand catches, were nonetheless indicative of an attempted rapprochement with the older governing classes. Frances had married Robert Rich, the grandson of the Earl of Warwick; Mary had chosen Lord Fauconberg and had, at his insistence, been married according to the Anglican rite.

Yet the undeniable political fact was that ordered government depended on Cromwell, and Cromwell was an old

man, wearied by a life of rigorous campaigning and subsequent political stress. Not the least of the stresses that had
taken their toll was his search for God's guidance as to his
personal role. It is difficult for a modern person to appreciate
the internal anguish that preceded Cromwellian decisions.
The confident outbursts — even his final defiant "let God be
judge" to his last Parliament — were not the products of a
buoyant spirit, but of an intense and anguished one.

Cromwell's last summer, 1658, was generally an unhealthy
one, for there was widespread malignant fever. On 6 August,
his favorite daughter, Elizabeth, died of cancer. His own
health declined rapidly afterward. Even though he had been
ill before, it seems reasonably clear that deep personal loss
sapped his remaining strength. He was also aware that
deepening financial crisis would force him to call yet another
Parliament and face the strains that entailed. On 20 August,
Cromwell felt that he had shaken off his sickness enough to
go riding in Hampton Court Park, but the Quaker George
Fox, who met him on that occasion, recalled that he "saw
and felt a waft of death go forth against him, that he looked
like a dead man." Cromwell invited Fox to his house to
discuss the sufferings of the Quakers, but the next day when
Fox arrived, Cromwell was too ill to receive visitors.

Cromwell again made a temporary recovery and removed
from Hampton Court to Whitehall, but there his condition
rapidly worsened. "I shall not die this bout, I am sure on't,"
he declared, but the end was upon him. At some point in
his last days, he nominated his eldest son, Richard, to be his
successor in accordance with the constitution. It is ironic
that having brought the country so far, he bequeathed to
them the leadership of a son who had been a source of deep
personal vexation. With none of the qualities of his father,
Tumble Down Dick presided over the collapse of the government that Cromwell had constructed at such a cost; in
charity to him, it is fair to say that even vigorous leadership
could not have preserved the situation indefinitely.

As he lay dying, Cromwell thought often of God, who had been his guide and source of strength throughout a turbulent career. There is a story that he asked an attending minister whether it was possible to fall from a state of grace and, having been assured on this point, he murmured, "I am safe, for I know that I was once in Grace." As a firm Calvinist, he knew the answer to the question when he asked it, but that makes the asking all the more poignant. It suggests a moment of doubt, a worry that he had misinterpreted God's dispensations, a concern that those distasteful things he had done with the aim of fostering a common good had been mistaken. For all that he knew the orthodox answer, it was a real and a revealing question.

There has come down as well a tradition of his prayers in his last days. Characteristically, he prayed not for himself, but for his people, that they might end divisiveness and find common purpose. It was as fine a statement of his political purpose as he ever uttered. "I may, I will come to Thee for Thy people. Thou hast made me, though very unworthy, a mean instrument to do them some good, and Thee service. And many of them have set too high a value upon me, though others wish and would be glad of my death. But Lord, however thou dost dispose of me, continue and go on to do good for them. Give them consistency of judgment, one heart and mutual love, and go on to deliver them. . . . Teach those who look too much on Thy instruments to depend more upon Thyself. Pardon such as desire to trample upon the dust of a poor worm, for they are Thy people too. And pardon the folly of this short prayer, even for Jesus Christ's sake, and give us a good night, if it be Thy pleasure." "Consistency of judgment, one heart, and mutual love" — it had been what he had sought all along, even when he rashly sought to force it by the sword. Dying he spoke from the depth of his being as a constitutionalist, a believer in the capacity of the people, not as a military dictator.

At four o'clock on Friday, 3 September, Cromwell died. It did not pass unnoticed that he left this world on the anniversary of his days of greatest triumph at Dunbar and Worcester.

Cromwell and the Historians

To say that Cromwell has been as controversial in death as he was during his life is no exaggeration. The fact that the monarchy was restored within two years of his death left little opportunity for a balanced contemporary assessment. His death itself occasioned a predictable flurry of commendatory pieces, but even by 1658 his detractors far outnumbered his supporters. In the years following the Restoration there was little good to be said of him. The titles of such pamphlets as *Cromwell's Bloody Slaughterhouse* and *The English Devil* are indicative of the spirit in which he was viewed. The scurrilous "biography" *Flagellum* by James Heath portrayed him as a veritable devil, a man of overweening ambition, hypocrisy, and evil; it went through six editions in the reign of Charles II and clearly contained the image the public wished to retain.

Cromwell's former allies were as scathing in many instances as his former enemies. The radical left had had little cause to love him and had already formed a picture of Oliver as hypocritical tyrant by the end of the 1640s. Over and over again the dual themes of hypocrisy and ambition surfaced as that which men remembered about Cromwell. The republican Ludlow saw him as the betrayer of the Good Old Cause, the man who "sacrificed the public cause to the idol of his ambition." The preacher Richard Baxter thought he had "a secret bias and eye towards his own exaltation" and recorded that while Cromwell seemed "exceeding openhearted," he nonetheless "thought secrecy a virtue and dissimulation no vice." It was an assessment not far different from that of the Royalist Clarendon, who characterized him as "a brave, bad man," and while recognizing in him "a great spirit, an admirable circumspection and sagacity, and a most magnanimous resolution," thought that Cromwell equally possessed "all the wickednesses against which damnation is denounced and for which hell-fire is prepared."

What is surprising is not the vituperative nature of these early assessments, but rather the speed with which people began to give him a grudging respect. When the Dutch war of Charles II's reign went badly for the English, some, at least, recalled that the hated Cromwell had, if nothing else, made England's name respected abroad. Samuel Pepys expressed the feeling well: "It is strange how everybody do nowadays reflect upon Oliver and commend him, what brave things he did, and made all the neighbour princes fear him, while here a prince, come in with all the love and prayers and good liking of his people . . . hath lost all so soon." Not all would have agreed with the judgment; Slingsby Bethel, writing in 1668, felt that Cromwell's anti-Spanish, pro-French policy had been a mistake and had unwittingly tipped the power balance in Europe in favor of Louis XIV, but it was the view of Pepys that prevailed.

By the end of the seventeenth century some Englishmen were prepared to believe that Cromwell's opinion of the Stuarts was not all that ill-conceived. While on the continent the view of Cromwell as devil incarnate, spread by the highly successful biography of Gregorio Leti, was to continue to hold sway, in England more favorable assessments were being reached. Nathaniel Crouch, thinking every man should form his own opinion, felt it "not unacceptable to his Country men to give a plain and impartial account of matters of fact." The nonconformist Isaac Kimber, writing in the early eighteenth century, set out to correct a historical tradition which he found "exceedingly defective"; though he promised not to lessen the bad nor exaggerate the good, he ended up by writing what amounted to an apologia; blaming Ireton and the Levellers for the execution of the King and rationalizing events at Drogheda on the grounds that they saved bloodshed in the long run. The traditional hostility did not, of course, quit the field easily; the Tory Echard and the Whig Old-mixon were at one in denouncing Cromwell in terms that would have been fully acceptable to Heath.

No rounded portrait of Cromwell was possible until much of the voluminous and scattered documentary material on his period became available to the public. Throughout the eighteenth and nineteenth centuries the process of accumula-tion and publication went on. The monuments to that in-dustrious activity of antiquarian scholars are legion: Mark Noble's *Memoirs of the Protectoral House of Cromwell,* uncritical, to be sure, but not without its uses, Thurloe's correspondence, Milton's state papers, Cromwell's letters themselves. In a sense, this effort culminated in the publica-tion of Carlyle's *Letters and Speeches of Oliver Cromwell* in 1845. While it is no doubt true that Carlyle both claimed and received more credit than he deserved, the work had a monumental impact. That is not to say that it alone changed the picture of Cromwell; Macaulay, for example, had already indicated a more balanced picture of Cromwell in his essay on Hallam's *Constitutional History,* in which he took Hallam to task for comparing Cromwell and Napoleon and added grandly of Cromwell that "no sovereign ever carried to the throne so large a portion of the best qualities of the middling orders, so strong a sympathy with the feel-ings and interests of his people. . . . he had a high, stout, honest English heart." But Carlyle's edition did make it possible for Cromwell to be seen at first hand and through his own words. Carlyle had his own particular view of Cromwell which he sought to solidify in his edition; that was the view of Cromwell as Hero, not a hero above rebuke, but a strong leader such as Carlyle thought his own contemporary England needed.

The dominant nineteenth-century view of Cromwell was not, however, to be the rather simplistic one of Carlyle, but rather that of the great nonconformist historian Samuel Rawson Gardiner. His massive history of England in the early seventeenth century remains indispensable. To be sure, there is now considerable dissent from his view that the events of the 1640s were "the Puritan Revolution," but even those who dissent pay his interpretation the honor of conceding it must be refuted rather than ignored. Though his narrative history did not reach the end of the Protectorate, he sketched in it and in other works a memorable, though not definitive portrait of Cromwell. Taking up Carlyle's idea of Cromwell as hero, he transformed him into the Puritan hero of the Puritan revolution; Cromwell's politics, seen through the eyes of a nineteenth-century nonconformist, took on many of the familiar aspects of nineteenth-century liberalism, including toleration and patient reforming. In a way that had profound meaning for Gardiner, Cromwell's very incongruities became his essential, almost defining, characteristic. Gardiner was supremely aware that the contradictions were there, that Cromwell could hesitate and postpone action one time, act with an impulsive stroke the next. He knew, too, that it was this fact of incongruity that allowed such divergent opinions of Oliver, for nearly all his interpreters (at least nearly all those who were writing more than propaganda) had something in Cromwell's utterances and actions on which to base their views. But just as England had become a great nation through blending contradictory forces, in like manner had Cromwell become a great man. Cromwell was the greatest Englishman of his time because he was the very embodiment of it.

Gardiner's work capped a process by which Cromwell, no longer the ambitious regicide and hypocritical tyrant, was transformed into the representative figure of middle-class ascendancy and middle-class virtue. Even Gladstone declared that while he could not love him, he was "a mighty big fellow." The Earl of Rosebery saw him as fighting the battle of freedom and toleration in a nation not ready to embrace those ideals. Theodore Roosevelt went so far as to assert that the English might have been led to "entire self-government" by Cromwell, had Cromwell only had the sterling qualities of George Washington. John Morley, who had serious reservations about Cromwell's capacity and temperament to form a constitutional government, nonetheless stated that Cromwell was "undoubtedly in earnest" in seeking to restore parliamentary rule and concluded that "his ideals were high, his fidelity to them, while sometimes clouded, was still enduring, his ambition was pure."

It is, of course, quite possible to give a completely different twist to the favorable assessment of Cromwell as the embodiment of middle-class aspirations by simply denying the validity of those aspirations. The increasing interest in the course of the twentieth century in the left-wing movements of the seventeenth century has resulted in a totally new perspective on Cromwell. Cromwell was representative of the middle classes indeed, but the middle classes were themselves the oppressing bourgeoisie. Looked at in this way, Cromwell's liberalism recedes, his conservatism advances. He was the spokesman of a class interest that did not extend to the common people; he was not, as Gardiner would have had it, a typical Englishman, but only typical of a certain class that sought to rule at the expense of others. Though prominent in a civil war that toppled a king, he was not, in reality, a bearer of the revolutionary tradition, for he was as opposed to the radical tradition of the new as he was to the "feudalism" of the old.

In short, there have been as many "Cromwells" as there have been historians to write about him. It is a truism that historians are shaped by their own experiences and surroundings and that they reshape their past in a fashion that makes it somehow intelligible to their present. In the 1930s, for example, the rise of the dictators inevitably influenced historians' views of Cromwell; W. C. Abbott, whose great edition of *The Writings and Speeches of Oliver Cromwell* is indispensable to modern scholars, drew labored parallels with Hitler and Mussolini. If such a view appears absurd from the standpoint of the 1970s, it is worth remembering that portraying Cromwell as a Victorian liberal manqué embodies the same sort of error, and, in the last analysis, the same sort if not the same degree of absurdity. Studies of Cromwell continue to abound, and the views offered in them differ widely. Sir Charles Firth's biography, first published in 1900, is, in the main, well within the Gardiner tradition and it remains the best biography yet written. In more recent years there have been studies that stress Cromwell's religion, like the admirable study of R. S. Paul, *The Lord Protector,* which concentrates on the tension within Cromwell between religious ideals and political necessity. Lady Antonia Fraser has, at great length, set out to "humanize" Cromwell and to reveal that there was a man beneath all the abstract conceptions. Maurice Ashley has given us at least two Cromwells, the conservative dictator when he wrote of him in the 1930s, the constitutional liberal of sorts when he wrote of him in the 1950s. Christopher Hill has provided a more complex Cromwell, a man much of his class but having some qualities transcending it; it is the "boisterous and confident" Cromwell of the 1640s whom he admires, though he has sympathy for the "aging, disillusioned" politician of the 1650s who had ceased to have touch with what Hill sees as the real revolutionary thrust of the age.

The debate over Cromwell will continue, for he remains an enigmatic and elusive person. For all the mass of writing he left behind, there is little that has a genuinely personal touch about it. For a public figure, he was an exceedingly private man. He was, of course, as all men are, the product of his own age, but many of the problems he grappled with have endured, disguised in different forms and bearing different labels. In our own day, we worry much about the possible conflicts between liberty and equality; Cromwell, in pondering about the nine in ten said to be against him and considering arming the tenth, was, in very real ways, facing the same issue. The problem of achieving reform without doing damage to constitutional forms remains as live an issue in the United States in 1977 as it was in England in 1655. Part of the continuing fascination of Cromwell is that he addressed those issues, as they were presented to him in seventeenth-century terms, with both passion and compassion. If Cromwell sensed tragedy in his own career, it was because he never could reconcile the two; over and over, he was impelled to use authority to enforce reform, yet that very pattern removed validity from what he accomplished.

What, then, was Cromwell — Heath's hypocritical tyrant, Clarendon's brave, bad man, Carlyle's Hero, Gardiner's Victorian liberal, Abbott's proto-fascist, Paul's anguished Christian, Hill's paradoxical and ultimately disillusioned representative of his time and class? He was none of these, perhaps because he did things that made him seem a bit of each. In the last analysis we might feel that two of his contemporaries observed in him the qualities that set him apart and sustained him through the agony of civil war, political crisis, and personal searching: Marvell when he wrote, "And knowing not where heaven's choice may light, /Girds yet his sword, and ready stands to fight," Baxter when he noted, "He meant honestly in the main."

Further Reading

The bibliography relating to Oliver Cromwell and the English Revolution is voluminous and only a minute portion of it can be indicated here. I have confined this selective list, on the whole, to works of relatively modern vintage. Original materials and older secondary works can be found in the standard bibliographies. Much of the recent work on the period is in article, rather than book form, but I have, for reasons of space, limited the bibliography to books. Two useful bibliographical guides do exist: W. C. Abbott, *A Bibliography of Oliver Cromwell* (Cambridge, Mass., 1929), and P. H. Hardacre, "Writings on Oliver Cromwell since 1929," in E. C. Furber, ed., *Changing Views on British History* (Cambridge, Mass., 1966). Many readers will be familiar with Carlyle's *Letters and Speeches of Oliver Cromwell* (many editions), a classic in its own right but superseded for serious study by W. C. Abbott, *Writings and Speeches of Oliver Cromwell* (4 vols., Cambridge, Mass., 1937–1947). The latter contains in volume 4 a supplement to his 1929 bibliography.

General Histories of the Period

Those who wish to investigate further the general context of Cromwell's career should consult the great work of S. R. Gardiner,

History of England 1603–1642 (10 vols., London, 1883–1884) ; *The History of the Great Civil War* (4 vols., London, 1893) ; *The History of the Commonwealth and Protectorate* (4 vols., London, 1903). Sir Charles Firth, *The Last Years of the Protectorate* (2 vols., London, 1910), carries the narrative to the death of Cromwell. C. V. Wedgwood, *The King's Peace 1637–1641* (London, 1955) and *The King's War 1641–1647* (London, 1958), are briefer surveys for part of the period. I. Roots, *The Great Rebellion 1642–1660* (London, 1966) is a useful one-volume survey that has the advantage of devoting considerable space to the period of the Commonwealth and Protectorate. It also contains a useful bibliography. C. Hill, *The Century of Revolution 1603–1714* (Edinburgh, 1961), while limited as far as narrative history is concerned, is useful on many aspects of the seventeenth century. P. Zagorin, *The Court and the Country* (New York, 1970), is valuable on the origins of the Civil War; as is L. Stone, *The Causes of the English Revolution 1529–1642* (London, 1972).

Biographies of Cromwell

Biographies of Cromwell are legion and they come in a variety ranging from the brief, interpretive essay to the massively detailed volume. By general consensus, Sir Charles Firth, *Oliver Cromwell* (London, 1900), continues to hold pride of place. But numerous studies since then have added in important ways to our understanding of Cromwell. The most detailed recent life is Lady Antonia Fraser, *Cromwell Our Chief of Men* (London, 1973). C. Hill, *God's Englishman: Oliver Cromwell and the English Revolution* (London, 1970), is not exactly a straight biography but is extremely valuable in placing Cromwell's ideas and actions in the context of the revolutionary movement of the seventeenth century. John Buchan, *Oliver Cromwell* (London, 1934), has been unduly neglected, though it is written with great style. R. S. Paul, *The Lord Protector* (London, 1955), is the best study of Cromwell's religious thought, and a plausible case could be made that it is a serious rival to Firth's work for the title of best existing biography. C. V. Wedgwood, *Oliver Cromwell* (revised edition, London, 1973), is a masterpiece of compression, while the brief study by P. Young, *Cromwell* (London, 1962), is particularly useful on military affairs. M. Ashley has written extensively on Cromwell and the Cromwellian period. His first biography, *Oliver*

Cromwell, the Conservative Dictator (London, 1937), is dated but interesting. His *The Greatness of Oliver Cromwell* (London, 1957) is more valuable, while *Oliver Cromwell and His World* (London, 1972) is splendidly illustrated.

Books on Special Aspects of Cromwell's Life

Studies of the armed forces and Cromwell's role as a soldier exist in profusion. Among the best are Sir Charles Firth, *Cromwell's Army* (reprint, London, 1962), and the detailed work of Sir Charles Firth and Godfrey Davies, *The Regimental History of Cromwell's Army* (2 vols., Oxford, 1940). A. H. Burne and P. Young, *The Great Civil War* (London, 1959), is almost exclusively military history, as is P. Young and R. Holmes, *The English Civil War* (London, 1974). A. Woolrych, *Battles of the English Civil War* (London, 1961), is selective in the engagements it covers but full of interesting detail. M. Ashley, *The English Civil War* (London, 1974), is a concise account with a wealth of illustrations. C. Holmes, *The Eastern Association in the English Civil War* (Cambridge, 1974), replaces all previous work on the subject. P. Young, *Edgehill 1642* (Kineton, 1967), and *Marston Moor 1644* (Kineton, 1970), provide book-length accounts of two major engagements.

On the political life of the period, in addition to the major surveys mentioned earlier, there are a number of useful works, though more remains to be done than one might expect. On the Long Parliament, D. Brunton and D. H. Pennington, *Members of the Long Parliament* (London, 1953), and M. F. Keeler, *The Long Parliament* (Philadelphia, 1954), provide much information on the membership. J. H. Hexter, *The Reign of King Pym* (Cambridge, Mass., 1941), was a pioneering study of the politics of the Long Parliament. J. R. MacCormack, *Revolutionary Politics in the Long Parliament* (Cambridge, Mass., 1973), covers the period from Pym's death to the execution of the King. The two most important recent works on parliamentary history are D. Underdown, *Pride's Purge* (Oxford, 1971), and B. Worden, *The Rump Parliament* (Cambridge, 1974); both cast important light on Cromwell. On the trial of the King, see C. V. Wedgwood, *The Trial of Charles I* (London, 1964). G. E. Aylmer, *The State's Servants: The Civil Service of the English Republic 1649–1660* (London, 1973), is an exhaustive study of Commonwealth and

Protectorate administration. On the subject of law reform, which was of considerable concern to Cromwell, see S. E. Prall, *The Agitation for Law Reform during the Puritan Revolution 1640–1660* (The Hague, 1966), and D. Veall, *The Popular Movement for Law Reform 1640–1660* (Oxford, 1970). The Leveller movement has attracted considerable attention; useful introductions to it include G. E. Aylmer, *The Levellers in the English Revolution* (London, 1975); T. C. Pease, *The Leveller Movement* (Washington, 1916); J. Frank, *The Levellers* (Cambridge, Mass., 1955); H. N. Brailsford, *The Levellers and the English Revolution* (London, 1961); and H. Shaw, *The Levellers* (London, 1968). For a stimulating account of radical politics, see C. Hill, *The World Turned Upside Down* (London, 1972). On the question of voters and voting in early Stuart England see the important and original study by D. Hirst, *The Representative of the People?* (Cambridge, 1975).

For Cromwell and Ireland, the older works R. Dunlop, *Ireland Under the Commonwealth* (2 vols., Manchester, 1913), and J. P. Prendergast, *The Cromwellian Settlement of Ireland* (London, 1865), remain useful. D. M. R. Esson, *The Curse of Cromwell* (Totowa, 1971), and P. B. Ellis, *Hell or Connaught!* (London, 1975), are spirited but not always reliable. Superseding all previous accounts of the English administration of Ireland from 1649 to 1660 is T. C. Barnard, *Cromwellian Ireland* (Oxford, 1975). Cromwell's role in Scotland has been less well served. W. S. Douglas, *Cromwell's Scotch Campaigns* (London, 1899), is useful. The introductions to three volumes of the publications of the Scottish History Society also contain valuable material: Sir Charles Firth, ed., *Scotland and the Commonwealth* (Edinburgh, 1895), and *Scotland and the Protectorate* (Edinburgh, 1899); C. S. Terry, ed., *The Cromwellian Union* (Edinburgh, 1902).

On foreign policy generally there exists no adequate overall summary. G. M. D. Howat, *Stuart and Cromwellian Foreign Policy* (London, 1974), is sketchy. J. R. Jones, *Britain and Europe in the 17th Century* (London, 1966), is suggestive. C. Wilson, *Profit and Power* (London, 1957), is useful on relations with the United Provinces. C. P. Korr, *Cromwell and the New Model Foreign Policy* (Berkeley, 1975), is not as comprehensive as the title sounds, but is instructive about relations with France. J. N. Bowman, *The Protestant Interest in Cromwell's Foreign Relations* (Heidelberg, 1900), should be read in conjunction with the important essay by R. Crabtree, "The Idea of a Protestant Foreign Policy," in I. Roots, ed., *Cromwell, A Profile* (New York, 1973), and the sources cited there. Closely related to foreign policy and also containing important material on internal conditions is M. Ashley, *Financial and Commercial Policy under the Cromwellian Protectorate* (London, 1962).

Religion was central to Cromwell and many of his contemporaries. The best study from the point of view of Cromwell is the Paul biography. Other works that can be consulted with profit on religious aspects of the Cromwellian period include M. Walzer, *The Revolution of the Saints* (Cambridge, Mass., 1965); W. M. Lamont, *Godly Rule* (London, 1969); B. S. Capp, *The Fifth Monarchy Men* (London, 1972); H. Barbour, *The Quakers in Puritan England* (New Haven, 1964); L. Solt, *Saints in Arms* (Oxford, 1959); and the old but still useful W. A. Shaw, *A History of the English Church during the Civil Wars and Under the Commonwealth* (London, 1900).

As is evident from the number of important works of very recent vintage, Cromwell and his period remain the scene of considerable scholarly industry. Five collections of essays deserve mention, not just because each of them has something useful to say with respect to Cromwell, but also because, taken together, they give something of a view of where scholarship is now concentrating: E. W. Ives, ed., *The English Revolution 1600–1660* (London, 1968); R. H. Parry, ed., *The English Civil War and After* (London, 1970); G. E. Aylmer, ed., *The Interregnum* (London, 1972); C. Russell, ed., *The Origins of the English Civil War* (London, 1973); B. Manning, ed., *Politics, Religion, and the English Civil War* (London, 1973).

Index